日本語由来の英語を理解するガイド

HANG with JAPANGLISH

Understanding Wasei-eigo and other Japanese-made English

LAUREN GREEN IMAI

Translations by Tamaki Tiballi

Library of Congress Number: 2025915998

First paperback edition August 2025

ISBN 979-8-9899078-6-1 (Paperback)
ISBN 979-8-9899078-8-5 (Hardcover)
ISBN 979-8-9996509-0-0 (eBook)

Lauren's Language Lessons, LLC
Houston, Texas, USA
www.LaurensLanguageLessons.com

Table of Contents

5 CLOTHING & FASHION
衣服・ファッション........................61

6 DESCRIBING PEOPLE
人物描写..................................83

7 FEELINGS, EMOTIONS, ENCOURAGEMENT
感情表現・励まし........................97

8 FOOD & DRINKS
食べ物・飲み物........................ 107

INTRODUCTION: WHY I WROTE THIS BOOK

One of my earliest students from Japan once told me that Japanese people love Kentucky at Christmas. I was baffled. I didn't know Kentucky was so popular in Japan; many Americans haven't even been there. I wondered why it was so popular. "Have many Japanese people visited there?" I asked, genuinely curious. "Oh yes, many people eat Kentucky every Christmas," my student answered confidently. After more discussion, I learned that Kentucky did not mean the same thing to Japanese people as it did to me. Something had been lost in translation.

During my early years of teaching English to Japanese students, I noticed that students would often say English words that didn't fit the context of our conversation and didn't make sense. "I don't want earrings; I want pierce." I'd feel confused and try to ask clarifying questions to understand their meanings. "You want pierced ears but you don't want to wear earrings? I don't understand." Students would feel frustrated, wondering why I didn't understand the English they were speaking, but in reality, they were speaking Japanglish.

Japanglish is a fascinating version of English spoken in Japan, much like Konglish in Korea, Singlish in Singapore, or Kongish in Hong Kong. It includes many borrowed English words [gairaigo] with similar meanings and sometimes just slightly different pronunciations (*cake* ケーキ). Japanglish words are typically written using Japanese katakana, one of several writing systems in Japan that is predominantly used to write words of foreign origin. As a result, it is often widely assumed that nearly any foreign word written in katakana must be English.

However, Japanglish also includes hundreds of Japanese-made English words [wasei-eigo] with completely different meanings than their English counterparts. Sometimes, there are even words that are neither Japanese nor English and come from an entirely different language (*pierrot* ピエロ). There are many others that are technically English but in practicality don't exist at all (*food fighter* フードファイター, *salaryman* サラリーマン) while others are creative abbreviations of English words that are unrecognizable outside of Japan (*appo* アポ).

In many ways, Japanglish reflects the special history that Japan has shared with the English-speaking world and serves as a fascinating and evolving example of the ever-changing world of language and our ever-growing global connectedness. However, outside of Japanese communities themselves, the Japanese version of English gets lost in translation, and misunderstandings abound.

Virtually every American who has spent significant time in Japan can tell you a story about a language misunderstanding while speaking English with someone who was otherwise fluent. In Japan, business partners will be quick to share their

mail ad and make an ***appo*** at their ***buil***. A friend may invite you to a ***live*** or perhaps a ***nighter*** that's going to be really ***high tension***. Someone might tell you they love to eat ***egg sand*** and ***ice*** at the beach, and you will likely come across ***home doctors*** who prefer to give shots in a patient's ***hip***.

The purpose of this book is to serve as a guide for English speakers who are interested in learning about Japanglish, Japan, the Japanese language, and Japanese culture! The aim of this book is to help avoid some of the confusion and miscommunications that are often encountered when one is unfamiliar with Japanglish. Maybe you are hoping to visit Japan soon; maybe you plan to work or teach in Japan; maybe you work closely with Japanese expat or immigrant communities; maybe you're a businessperson regularly working alongside Japanese companies; maybe you love Japanese culture, manga, anime, J-pop; or maybe you just love learning about other cultures and languages! Whether learning for business or pleasure, this book is for you!

In this book, you will learn many words that have different meanings in Japanglish and in standard English and others that are technically English but only exist in Japan. You will likely find that a few words in this book simply come from British-style English (*purse* パース) and have similar meanings when spoken in the UK and in Japan but have different meanings when spoken in North America. You will also hear some English words that are common in Asia (*washlet* ウォシュレット) but are relatively unknown to the rest of the English-speaking world. You will also hear some personal stories of my own brushes with Japanglish along with a few cultural pointers that I've learned along the way. My hope is that this book will help you better understand your friends, clients, coworkers, favorite celebrities, J-pop, manga, anime, and more!

If you are a native Japanese speaker wishing to speak English more fluently, please check out *When English Isn't English: A Practical Guide to Avoiding Japanglish* 「英語なのに英語じゃない：Japanglish を避けるための実用ガイド」

Special Note 1: Language is constantly changing! Even in the years of writing and putting together this book, new Japanglish words have been adopted; older Japanglish words have become outdated; and some previously obscure words have become mainstream and commonly used even in English circles.

It's also important to keep in mind that English itself is extremely diverse. This book focuses on American English and does its best to include British English. It does not address the differences that may be found between Japanglish and other varieties of English. Differences between American English and British English are well-known, but even within just the United States, there can be regional differences in certain word choices as well as differences based on one's age, generation, socioeconomics, life experiences, subculture, ethnic background, field of work, and much more. For example, people in the UK tend to say "trainers" while people in the South and West of the United States are more likely to say "tennis shoes" while those in the Northeastern United States are more likely to say "sneakers." Similarly, those under the age of 25 are more likely to use the newly abbreviated term "sus" to describe someone or something "suspicious." You may find that depending on your own language background, your usage of included terms may differ slightly.

Since this book is not meant to serve as a complete dictionary, rather a helpful resource, I have included the most common, useful, or relevant information. With those caveats, I have done my best to make this book as extensive as possible, knowing that because of the diversity of English itself and the ever-changing nature of language, it will never be completely possible for this book to be truly all-inclusive.

Special Note 2: It's helpful to keep in mind that some Japanese consonants do not correspond exactly with one English letter. As a result, there can sometimes be slight differences in romanization of terms. Similarly, the Japanese language does not have an L sound equal to that in English, and the Japanese R sound falls somewhere in between that of an English L and R. As a result, most English L sounds will translate into Japanese as something like an R, though not completely equivalent. As an example, the term レバー may be translated to English as "liver" or "lever" and may even sound close to "river" where the actual Japanese pronunciation would be somewhere between those sounds.

Note about QR Codes: Scan the QR code located on each chapter title page to hear audio for Japanese pronunciation of the words included in each chapter! For a continuous playlist of all chapters and words included in this book, scan this QR code →

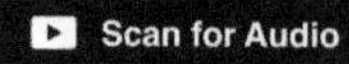

Academics, School, Education

1

学問・学校・教育

Anket (Enquete)

an-kē-to 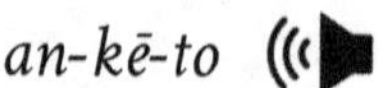

アンケート

Meaning in Japan:

Survey, questionnaire

Example Japanglish Sentence:

街頭アンケート調査の人が私に「もし5分ほどお時間があれば、文化の違いについてのアンケートにご協力いただけると嬉しいです」と声をかけてきた。

The survey researcher said, "If you have an extra five minutes, we'd love your help with our *anket* about cultural differences!"

Translated to English:

The survey researcher said, "If you have an extra five minutes, we'd love your help with our *questionnaire* about cultural differences!"

Broken English

bu-rō-kun in-gu-ris-shu 

ブロークンイングリッシュ

Meaning in Japan:

Casual, informal, everyday English

Example Japanglish Sentence:

私は、ビジネス英語よりもブロークンイングリッシュの方が好きだ。

I like speaking *broken English* more than business English.

Translated to English:

I like speaking *casual/informal English* more than professional business English.

CENTI

sen-chi

センチ

Meaning in Japan:

Centimeter

Example Japanglish Sentence:

小さなサンセベリアが、今は、10センチになった!

My little snake plant is now 10 *centi*!

Translated to English:

My little snake plant is now 10 *centimeters* tall!

CUNNING

kan-nin-gu

カンニング

Meaning in Japan:

Cheating on a test or copying someone else's answers

Example Japanglish Sentence:

ぼくは、先生に「先生、太郎君が、
ぼくの答えをカンニングしてくる」と言った。

I told my teacher, "Sensei, Taro is *cunning my answer*!"

Translated to English:

I told my teacher, "Sensei, Taro is *cheating off of me* / *copying my answer*!"

DEMERIT

de-me-rit-to

デメリット

Meaning in Japan:

Disadvantage, negative point, con

Example Japanglish Sentence:

テキサスに住むデメリットの一つは、公共交通機関が少ないことだ。

One *demerit* of living in Texas is that there aren't many public transportation options.

Translated to English:

One of the *disadvantages* of living in Texas is that there aren't many public transportation options.

INPUT

in-put-to

Meaning in Japan:

This is only used in regards to language learning. *Input* refers to reading, listening, and gaining knowledge through those forms of studying.

Example Japanglish Sentence:

今週末は何もインプットせず、アウトプットばかりだった。
とても空虚な気分なので、またインプットを始めたい。

I didn't *input* anything this weekend for English; I only did *output*.
I feel so empty and need to start doing *input* again.

Translated to English:

I didn't do any English *reading or listening practice* this weekend. I just practiced speaking. I feel so drained and need to start *studying* again.

MAN TO MAN

man-tsū-man

マンツーマン

Meaning in Japan:

One on one, private (like a private lesson)

Example Japanglish Sentence:

私は、マンツーマンで英語を勉強したい。

I'd like to study English *man to man*.

Translated to English:

I'd like to study English *one on one* / *in a private lesson*.

MERIT

me-rit-to

メリット

Meaning in Japan:

Advantage, positive point, pro

Example Japanglish Sentence:

最終決定をする前に、すべての選択肢のメリットとデメリットを考慮することが重要だ。

It's important to consider the *merits* and *demerits* of all the options before making our final decision.

Translated to English:

It's important to consider the *pros* and cons of all the options before making our final decision.

Minus

mai-na-su

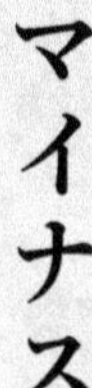

Meaning in Japan:

Disadvantage, negative point, con

Example Japanglish Sentence:

テキサスでの生活には、公共交通の不便さといったマイナス面も存在する。

One *minus* of living in Texas is that there aren't many public transportation options.

Translated to English:

One *disadvantage* of living in Texas is that there aren't many public transportation options.

Native

nei-ti-bu 

ネイティブ

Meaning in Japan:

A native speaker (of a language)

Example Japanglish Sentence:

彼女から英語を習いたい。
ネイティブだからね！

I want to learn English from her. She's a *native*!

Translated to English:

I want to learn English from her.
She's a *native speaker*. *English is her first language*!

ō-bī

OB

オービー

Meaning in Japan:

This is an abbreviation of "Old Boy" and refers to a male alumnus of your school/ college/university who was older and graduated before you

Example Japanglish Sentence:

彼は私の大学のOBだ。ビジネスクラブのメンバーで、私より2年早く卒業した。

He's an *OB* from my university. He was part of our business club and graduated two years before me.

Translated to English:

He's an *alumnus* / *former student* from my university. He was part of the business club and graduated two years before me.

ō-jī

OG

オージー

Meaning in Japan:

This is an abbreviation of "Old Girl" and refers to a female alumna of your school/ college/university who was older and graduated before you

Example Japanglish Sentence:

彼女は私の大学のOGだ。
経営学クラブに入っていて、私より2年早く卒業した。

She's an *OG* from my university. She was part of our business management club and graduated two years before me.

Translated to English:

She's an *alumna* / *former student* from my university. She was part of our business management club and graduated two years before me.

Output

au-to-put-to

アウトプット

Meaning in Japan:

This is only used in regards to language learning. *Output* refers to speaking, writing, and expressing your thoughts and opinions through language.

Example Japanglish Sentence:

多くの学生はアウトプットが苦手だが、インプットは得意だ。

Many students are bad at doing *output* but are great at *input.*

Translated to English:

Many students are bad at *speaking and writing* but are great at reading and listening.

Zemi

ze-mi

Meaning in Japan:

An academic seminar, especially in college/university

Example Japanglish Sentence:

私は、坂本先生のゼミに所属している。

I belong to Dr. Sakamoto's *Zemi*.

Translated to English:

I'm part of Dr. Sakamoto's *seminar*.

Accessories

アクセサリー

2

Accessory

a-ku-se-sa-rī

アクセサリー

Meaning in Japan:

This only includes everyday jewelry like necklaces, rings and earrings. It does not include expensive jewelry with gems or diamonds. It does not refer to bags, belts, and other types of accessories. The word アクセサリ is used to talk about accessories for a phone, computer, car, etc.

Example Japanglish Sentence:

この<u>アクセサリー</u>は全部手づくりだ。

All of these <u>*accessories*</u> are handmade.

Translated to English:

All of this <u>*jewelry*</u> is handmade.

Bag

bag-gu

バッグ

Meaning in Japan:

A purse, crossbody, handbag, or personal bag. This is not used to talk about bags in general and does not include things like a paper bag or plastic bag.

Example Japanglish Sentence:

私は買った食料品を<u>バッグ</u>に入れるのが好きじゃない。

I don't like putting my groceries in a <u>*bag*</u>.

Translated to English:

I don't like putting my groceries in a <u>*purse*</u>.

chak-ku

Chack

チャック

Meaning in Japan:

Zipper, zip (UK)

Example Japanglish Sentence:

チャックが壊れた。

My *chack* is broken.

Translated to English:

My *zipper* is broken.

i-ya-rin-gu

Earrings

イヤリング

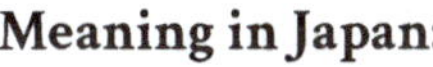

Meaning in Japan:

Clip-on earrings

Example Japanglish Sentence:

これは、ピアスだけど、
イヤリングがいるのよ。

These are *pierce*, but I need *earrings*.

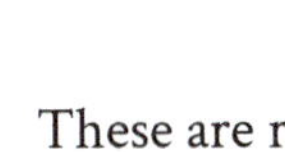

Translated to English:

These are regular earrings, but I need *clip-on earrings*.

Fastener

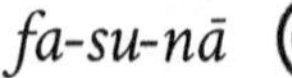

ファスナー

Meaning in Japan:

Zipper, zip (UK)

Example Japanglish Sentence:

ファスナーが壊れた。
My *fastener* is broken.

Translated to English:

My *zipper* is broken.

Gom

go-mu

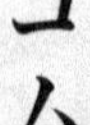

Meaning in Japan:

Rubber band; Rubber (the material)

Example Japanglish Sentence:

東南アジアにはゴムの木がたくさんある。
Southeast Asia has a lot of *gom* trees.

Translated to English:

Southeast Asia has a lot of *rubber* trees.

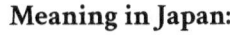

he-a ban-do

Hair Band

ヘアバンド

Meaning in Japan:

Headband

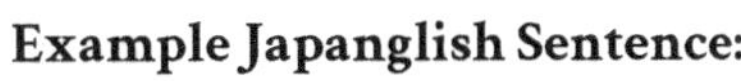

Example Japanglish Sentence:

あのヘアーバンドを買いたい。

I want to buy that *hair band* for my sister. She will love it!

Translated to English:

I want to buy that *headband* for my sister. She will love it!

he-a-go-mu

Hair Gom

ヘアゴム

Meaning in Japan:

Hair tie, hair band, ponytail holder

Example Japanglish Sentence:

私の猫は毎晩、ナイトスタンド（ベッドのサイドテーブル）からヘアゴムを盗んでいく！

My cat always steals my *hair gom* at night from my nightstand!

Translated to English:

My cat always steals my *hair band* at night from my nightstand!

Hair Pin

he-a-pin

ヘアピン

Meaning in Japan:

Hair clip, bobby pin, barrette

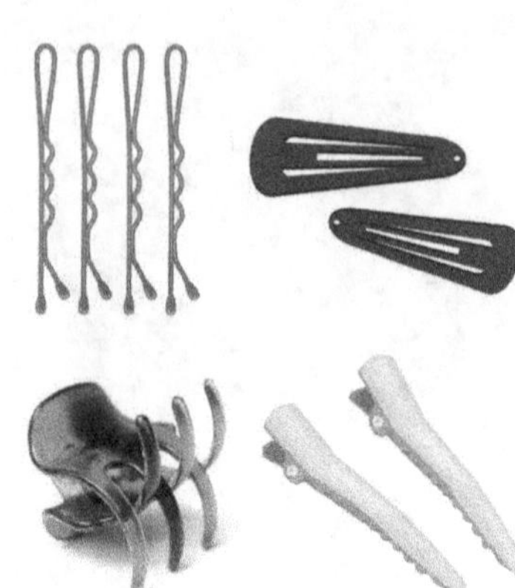

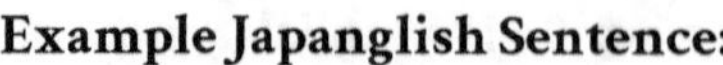

Example Japanglish Sentence:

あなたのヘアピン、すごく素敵だね。

Your *hair pin* is so cool!
I've never seen one in that shape!

Translated to English:

Your *hair clip* is so cool! I've never seen one in that shape!

Jewelry

ju-e-rī

ジュエリー

Meaning in Japan:

Only expensive jewelry with real diamonds and precious gems

Example Japanglish Sentence:

夫はジュエリーを買ってくれない。
アクセサリーしか買ってくれない。

My husband never buys me *jewelry*, only *accessories.*

Translated to English:

My husband never buys me *expensive diamond jewelry*, only fashion jewelry.

ma-jik-ku-tē-pu

Magic Tape

マジックテープ

Meaning in Japan:

Velcro, hook and loop

Example Japanglish Sentence:

私の息子は、マジックテープの靴が好きだ。

My son loves *magic tape* shoes since he doesn't know how to tie shoelaces.

Translated to English:

My son loves *Velcro* shoes since he doesn't know how to tie shoelaces.

ne-ku-tai-pin

Necktie Pin

ネクタイピン

Meaning in Japan:

Tie clip

Example Japanglish Sentence:

夫が誕生日に新しいネクタイピンが欲しいって言ってた。

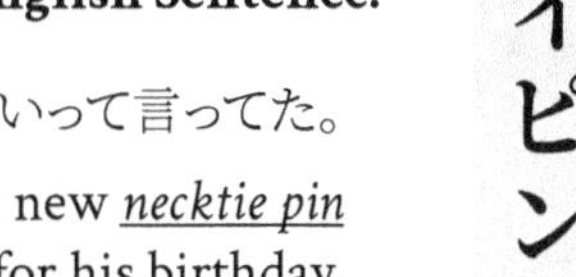

My husband said he wants a new *necktie pin* for his birthday.

Translated to English:

My husband said he wants a new *tie clip* for his birthday.

Pierce

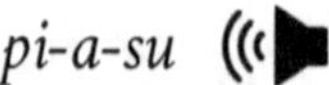

pi-a-su

ピアス

Meaning in Japan:

Earrings for pierced ears

Example Japanglish Sentence:

彼女の誕生日にピアスを買おうと思っている！

I think I'll buy her some *pierce* for her birthday!

Translated to English:

I think I'll buy her some *earrings* for her birthday!

Purse

pā-su

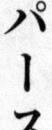

パース

Meaning in Japan:

Wallet (US), purse (UK)

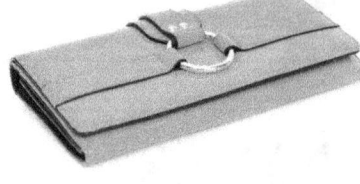

Example Japanglish Sentence:

バッグじゃなくて、パースだけ持っていくつもり。

I'm only going to bring my *purse*, not a *bag*.

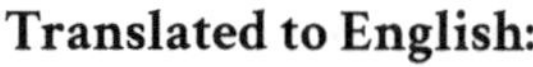

Translated to English:

I'm only going to bring my *wallet*, not a purse.

Business, Government, Economics

ビジネス 政府・経済

3

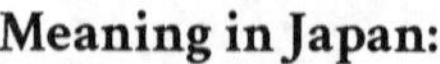

CAMPAIGN

キャンペーン

kyan-pēn

Meaning in Japan:

This only refers to a marketing or sales campaign in business and marketing; however, to consumers and those outside of business operations, it can also refer to a limited time sale or promotion. *Campaign* does not refer to political, military, or other types of campaigns as it does in English.

Example Japanglish Sentence:

日頃のご愛顧に感謝し、会員様限定の半額キャンペーンを実施いたします。人気メーカーの商品も対象です。ぜひこの機会にお買い求めください。

We appreciate our valued members and are offering an exclusive half-price *campaign* just for you. This *campaign* includes products from popular manufacturers, so please don't miss this chance to make a purchase!

彼らの新しいビジネス・マーケティング・キャンペーンでは、過去の政治活動や軍事作戦で成功を収めた際に撮影された写真や映像クリップを斬新な形でビジネスに応用している。

Their new *business marketing campaign* ビジネス・マーケティング・キャンペーン *(bijinesu māketingu kyanpēn)* innovatively uses old photos and video clips from successful *political campaigns* 政治活動 *(seiji katsudō)* and *military campaigns* 軍事作戦 *(gunji sakusen)*.

Translated to English:

We appreciate your continued patronage and are offering a half-price *special offer* exclusively for members. This *promotion* includes products from popular manufacturers, so please take advantage of this limited opportunity!

Their new business marketing *campaign* innovatively uses old photos and video clips from successful political *campaigns* and military *campaigns.*

kyat-chi-fu-rē-zu CATCHPHRASE

キャッチフレーズ

Meaning in Japan:

A company's tagline or slogan

Example Japanglish Sentence:

会社の<u>キャッチフレーズ</u>は、「Just go with it/流れに乗ろう」だ。

The company's *<u>catchphrase</u>* is "Just go with it."

Translated to English:

The company's *<u>tagline</u>* is "Just go with it."

ku-rē-mu CLAIM

クレーム

Meaning in Japan:

To complain; A complaint or demand

Example Japanglish Sentence:

新しいウェブサイトについて<u>クレーム</u>が来たよ。

We got a *<u>claim</u>* about our new website.

ええ、またカレンか。彼女は、いつもマネージャーに<u>クレーム</u>を言うんだよなあ。

Oh no, Karen is here again. She always *<u>claims</u>* to the manager!

Translated to English:

We got a *<u>complaint</u>* about our new website.

Oh no, Karen is here again. She always *<u>complains</u>* to the manager.

CLAIMER

ku-rē-mā

Meaning in Japan:

A demanding customer, usually one who complains often; a "Karen"

Example Japanglish Sentence:

うわあ。カレンがまた店に来てるよ。クレーマーだ！
今日マネージャーは居ないって言って。

Oh no, Karen is in the store again today. She's a *claimer*!
Tell her the manager isn't here today.

Translated to English:

Oh no, Karen is in the store again today. She's *a demanding customer who complains a lot*! Tell her the manager isn't here today.

CONTAINER

kon-te-na 

コンテナ・コンテナー

Meaning in Japan:

Only a shipping container

Example Japanglish Sentence:

日本からカナダへ荷物をコンテナーで運ぶ必要がある。

We need to use a *container* to bring our items from Japan to Canada.

Translated to English:

We need to use a *shipping container* to bring our items from Japan to Canada.

de-fu-re

Defle

デフレ

Meaning in Japan:

Deflation

Example Japanglish Sentence:

デフレは、ほとんどの現代経済においてインフレほど一般的ではない。

Defle is less common than *infla* in most modern economies.

Translated to English:

Deflation is less common than inflation in most modern economies.

de-mo

Demo

デモ

Meaning in Japan:

This means a public protest, the same as in British English. It does not refer to the demonstration of a product or way of doing something.

Example Japanglish Sentence:

政治家の行動に抗議して、
大規模なデモが行われた。

They had a big *demo* because of the politician's actions.

Translated to English:

They had a big *protest* because of the politician's actions.

Eco (Echo)

e-ko

エコ

Meaning in Japan:

Eco can be used as an adjective before many words to show that something is eco-friendly or environmentally conscious (e.g., eco car, eco life, eco goods, eco activity, eco tourism)

Example Japanglish Sentence:

カリフォルニアは、とてもエコな州だ。

California is so *eco*. California is an *eco* state.

Translated to English:

California is so *eco-friendly*.
California is such an *environmentally conscious* state.

Food Loss

fū-do-ro-su

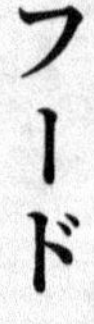

フードロス

Meaning in Japan:

Food waste

Example Japanglish Sentence:

地球を守るために、フードロスをなくすべきだ。先進国にはフードロスが多いようなので、私たちのNPOは人々や地域がフードロスを減らせるよう支援している。

Developed countries seem to have a lot of *food loss*, so our non-profit is devoted to helping people and communities reduce their *food loss*.

Translated to English:

Developed countries seem to *waste a lot of food*, so our non-profit is devoted to helping people and communities reduce their *food waste*.

IMAGE UP

イメージアップ

i-mē-ji-ap-pu

Meaning in Japan:

To improve one's image or reputation, especially a company's image

Example Japanglish Sentence:

その会社は、昨年の悪い評判を挽回しようとイメージアップを図っている。

The company is trying to *image up* after all the bad publicity it got last year.

Translated to English:

The company is trying to *improve its image* after all the bad publicity it got last year.

INFLA

インフレ

in-fu-re

Meaning in Japan:

Inflation

Example Japanglish Sentence:

インフレがひどいと、人々は必要なものを買う余裕がなくなる。

If *infla* is too high, people can't afford to buy what they need.

Translated to English:

If *inflation* is too high, people can't afford to buy what they need.

Infra

in-fu-ra

インフラ

Meaning in Japan:

Infrastructure

Example Japanglish Sentence:

その政治家は、国のインフラを改善したいと言った。

The politician promised he would improve our country's *infra*.

Translated to English:

The politician promised he would improve our country's *infrastructure*.

Long Seller

ron-gu-se-rā 

ロングセラー

Meaning in Japan:

A book or movie that sells well for a long time, an all-time best seller

Example Japanglish Sentence:

その著者は大きな成功を収め、
いくつものロングセラーを生み出した。

The author was so successful and had several *long sellers*.

Translated to English:

The author was so successful and had several *all-time best sellers*.

mai-na-su-i-mē-ji

Minus Image

マイナスイメージ

Meaning in Japan:

Bad reputation or negative public image

Example Japanglish Sentence:

その会社は、最新の3つの製品が発火によるリコールとなり、マイナスイメージを持たれるようになった。

The company got a *minus image* after all three of its latest products were recalled for catching on fire.

Translated to English:

The company got a *bad reputation* after all three of its latest products were recalled for catching on fire.

mo-de-ru-chen-ji

Model Change

モデルチェンジ

Meaning in Japan:

When a company updates an older model or releases a new model (e.g., a tech company releases its newest phone model, a car company releases this years' vehicle which has some obvious updates to the previous years' similar models)

Example Japanglish Sentence:

その会社は毎年モデルチェンジをしている。すべての製品についていくのは少し大変だ。

The company does *model change* every year. It's kind of hard to keep up with all of its products.

Translated to English:

The company releases *a new updated model* every year. It's kind of hard to keep up with all of its products.

Name Value

nē-mu-bar-yu

ネームバリュー

Meaning in Japan:

This refers to name recognition or brand recognition. Typically if name value is "high," that means the brand, product, school, company, etc., is well-known and generally highly trusted or respected.[1]

Example Japanglish Sentence:

多くの人が「ネームバリューのある(名前の通った)大学」に行くことが大切だと考えている。

Many people think it's important to go to a university with a good *name value*.

Translated to English:

Many people think it's important to go to a *well-known* university *with a good reputation*.

Nego

ne-go

Meaning in Japan:

Negotiation

Example Japanglish Sentence:

今、仕事がめちゃくちゃ忙しい。大きなネゴ（交渉）の真っ最中なんだ。

Work is so busy right now; we're in the middle of a huge *nego*.

Translated to English:

Work is so busy right now; we're in the middle of a huge *negotiation*.

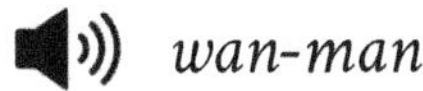

wan-man

One Man

ワンマン

Meaning in Japan:

One man refers to the owner of a company who runs it like a one-man show. This typically has negative connotations and the feeling that the man in charge runs the business like he's a dictator, ultimately making all final decisions himself without considering input from others.

Example Japanglish Sentence:

その会社で2年間働いていた。
オーナーがワンマンな人で、職場環境はすごく悪かった。

I worked at that company for two years.
The owner is *one man*, so the work environment was really unpleasant.

Translated to English:

I worked at that company for two years, but it's basically a one man show. The owner *makes all the decisions and won't take input from anyone else*, so the work environment was really unpleasant.

pē-pā-kan-pa-nī

Paper Company

ペーパーカンパニー

Meaning in Japan:

Shell company

Example Japanglish Sentence:

その会社は、ペーパーカンパニーみたいで、
実際のオーナーが誰なのか分からない。

It's difficult to tell who really owns the company because it seems to be a *paper company*.

Translated to English:

It's difficult to tell who really owns the company because it seems to be a *shell company*.

Recall

ri-kō-ru

リコール

Meaning in Japan:

Recall only means to remove someone from office before their term finishes, usually in local government, and does not have any of the additional meanings that recall can have in English.

Example Japanglish Sentence:

製品の発火が相次いだため、全製品をリコールせざるを得なかった企業について、市長は、公共の場で虚偽の発言をしたことで、解任された。

The mayor was *recalled* リコール *(rikōru)* after he lied about the company that was forced to *recall* 解任された *(kainin sa reta)* all of its products that kept catching on fire.

Translated to English:

The mayor was *recalled* after he lied about the company that was forced to *recall* all of its products that kept catching on fire.

Sales Point

sē-ru-su-poin-to 

セールスポイント

Meaning in Japan:

Selling point

Example Japanglish Sentence:

「御社の新製品のセールスポイントは何ですか？」とセールスマネージャーに聞いた。

I asked the sales manager, "What is the *sales point* of your company's new product?"

Translated to English:

I asked the sales manager, "What's the *selling point* of your company's new product?"

sō-rā-shi-su-te-mu

Solar System

ソーラーシステム

Meaning in Japan:

Solar panel energy system

Example Japanglish Sentence:

最近、社内でソーラーシステムを導入したところ、電気料金の大幅な削減につながっている。

Our office recently installed a *solar system*, and it's saving a ton of money on energy costs!

Translated to English:

Our office recently installed *solar panels*, and they're saving a ton of money on energy costs.

su-to

St / Suto

スト

Meaning in Japan:

Worker's strike

Example Japanglish Sentence:

日本では、あまりストを見かけない。

St is not very common in Japan.

Translated to English:

Workers' strikes are not very common in Japan.

Summit

sa-mit-to 

サミット

Meaning in Japan:

Summit only refers to a meeting of world leaders, not the top of a mountain.

Example Japanglish Sentence:

<u>サミット</u>は東京で開催されるので、その翌週に富士山の<u>頂上</u>まで登りたいと考えている人も何人かいる。

The <u>*summit* サミット *(samitto)*</u> is in Tokyo, so some of us hope to climb to the <u>*summit* 頂上 *(chōjō)*</u> of Mt. Fuji in the week afterwards.

Translated to English:

The <u>*summit*</u> is in Tokyo, so some of us hope to climb to the <u>*summit*</u> of Mt. Fuji in the week afterwards.

Tenant

te-nan-to 

テナント

Meaning in Japan:

Available for rent, vacant

Example Japanglish Sentence:

ショッピングモールで<u>テナント</u>を探す必要があるね。

We need to find a place that's <u>*tenant*</u> in the mall.

Translated to English:

We need to find a place that's <u>*available for rent*</u> in the mall.

Cars & Transportation

4

車・交通

Accel

a-ku-se-ru

アクセル

Meaning in Japan:

Accelerator, gas pedal

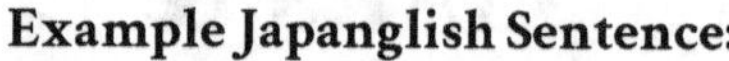

Example Japanglish Sentence:

車の調子がおかしいよ。
アクセルを踏んでも動かないんだ。

There is a problem with my car.
When I press the *accel*, my car doesn't move.

Translated to English:

There is a problem with my car.
When I press the *accelerator* / *give it gas*, my car doesn't move.

All Rai

ō-rai 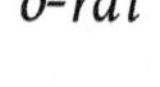

オーライ

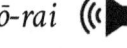

Meaning in Japan:

This phrase is an abbreviation of "all right" but is only used when backing up a car. Someone outside of the car will guide you saying, "All rai. All rai. Back, all rai..."

Example Japanglish Sentence:

車をバックさせるのを手伝ってもらえるかな。
もちろん。バック、バック、バックオーライ。

"Can you please help me back up my car?"
"Of course. Back. Back. Backu. *All rai*. *All rai*."

Translated to English:

"Can you please help me back up my car?"
"Of course. *Back. Back. More. Keep going*."

ō-to-bai

AUTOBI

オートバイ

Meaning in Japan:

Motorcycle, motorbike (UK)

Example Japanglish Sentence:

オートバイに乗るのは楽しい

It's fun to ride an *autobi*!

Translated to English:

It's fun to ride a *motorcycle*!

ō-to-ma

AUTOMA

オートマ

Meaning in Japan:

Automatic transmission

Example Japanglish Sentence:

今の日本では、ほとんどの車がオートマ車だ。

Most cars in Japan nowadays are *automa*.

Translated to English:

Most cars in Japan nowadays have *automatic transmissions*.

Back Mirror

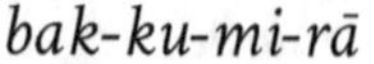

バックミラー

Meaning in Japan:

Rearview mirror

Example Japanglish Sentence:

私は、<u>バックミラー</u>越しに子どもたちを見た。
I looked at my kids in the <u>*back mirror*</u>.

Translated to English:

I looked at my kids in the <u>*rearview mirror*</u>.

Back Monitor

bak-ku-mo-ni-tā 

バックモニター

Meaning in Japan:

Backup camera in a car

Example Japanglish Sentence:

あなたの車には<u>バックモニター</u>が付いてる?
Does your car have a <u>*back monitor*</u>?

Translated to English:

Does your car have a <u>*backup camera*</u>?

bai-ku

Bike

バイク

Meaning in Japan:

Motorcycle, motorbike (UK)
Bike never means "bicycle" in Japan

Example Japanglish Sentence:

私は、田舎をバイクで走るのが大好きだ。

I love riding my *bike* in the countryside!

Translated to English:

I love riding my *bicycle* in the countryside!

kyan-pin-gu-kā

Camping Car

キャンピングカー

Meaning in Japan:

Camper, RV, Small "carstay" van, Caravan (UK), Campervan (UK), Motorhome (UK)

Example Japanglish Sentence:

新しいキャンピングカーでキャンプに行こう!

Let's go camping in our new *camping car*!

Translated to English:

Let's go camping in our new *RV*!

Claxon / Klaxon

ku-ra-ku-shon

クラクション

Meaning in Japan:

Car horn

Example Japanglish Sentence:

ここで運転するのは、嫌だなあ。いつでも皆がクラクションを鳴らすから。

I hate driving here because people always use the *Claxon*.

Translated to English:

I hate driving here because people always honk the *horn*.

Driveway

do-rai-bu-wei 

Meaning in Japan:

Highway or motorway or any road for driving, especially for scenic highways. *Driveway* is commonly used in names of roads (E.g., Mount Ibuki Driveway, Okuhiei Driveway)

Example Japanglish Sentence:

その町へ行くには新しくできた良いドライブウェイがある。昔の道を使うより速いよ。

There is a good new *driveway* to get to that city. It's faster than using the old roads.

Translated to English:

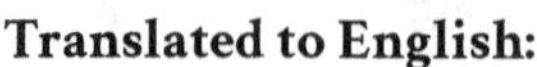

There is a good new *highway* to get to that city. It's faster than using the old roads.

Dump Car

dan-pu-kā

ダンプカー

Meaning in Japan:

Dump truck, tip lorry (UK)

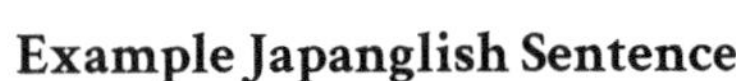

Example Japanglish Sentence:

私の息子は、おもちゃのダンプカー
で遊ぶのが好きだ。

My son really likes to play with toy *dump cars*.

Translated to English:

My son really likes to play with toy *dump trucks*.

Front Glass

fu-ron-to-ga-ra-su

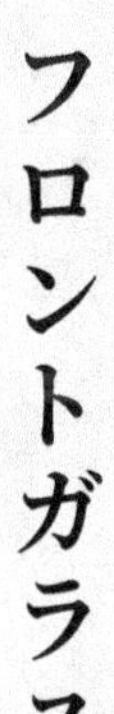

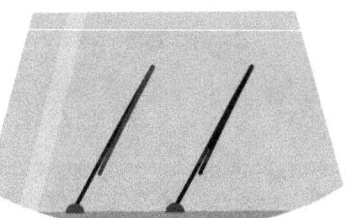

Meaning in Japan:

Windshield, windscreen (UK)

Example Japanglish Sentence:

石がフロントガラスに当たり、
現在は大きなひびが入っている。

A rock hit my *front glass* yesterday while I was driving, and now it has a huge crack.

Translated to English:

A rock hit my *windshield* yesterday while I was driving, and now it has a huge crack.

Gasoline Stand

ga-so-rin-su-tan-do 

ガソリンスタンド

Meaning in Japan:

Gas station, petrol station (UK)

Example Japanglish Sentence:

テキサスの田舎を3時間走ったのに、ガソリンスタンドが1軒もなかった!

In rural Texas, we drove for three hours and didn't even see one *gasoline stand*!

Translated to English:

In rural Texas, we drove for three hours and didn't even see one *gas station*!

Handle

han-do-ru

ハンドル

Meaning in Japan:

Steering wheel

Example Japanglish Sentence:

ハンドルに不具合がでたので、車を修理に出した。

I took my car to the auto shop because there was a problem with my *handle*.

Translated to English:

I took my car to the auto shop because there was a problem with my *steering wheel*.

HANDLE KEEPER

han-do-ru-kī-pā

ハンドルキーパー

Meaning in Japan:

Designated driver

Example Japanglish Sentence:

今夜は飲まないようにするね。ハンドルキーパーになるから。

I prefer not to drink alcohol tonight, so I can be our *handle keeper*!

Translated to English:

I prefer not to drink alcohol tonight, so I can be our *designated driver*!

HELI

he-ri

Meaning in Japan:

Helicopter

Example Japanglish Sentence:

私たちは、昨日大きなヘリを見た。

We saw the biggest *heli* yesterday!

Translated to English:

We saw the biggest *helicopter* yesterday!

Idling Stop *ai-do-rin-gu-su-top-pu*

アイドリングストップ

Meaning in Japan:

Continuing to run the engine of your car while it is stopped (For example, you are stopped at a light, but your car engine is still running; you are sitting in a parking lot waiting to pick up a friend, but the car engine running so you can continue to use the A/C.)

Example Japanglish Sentence:

日本では、一部の都市でアイドリングストップは違法だ。

In Japan, it's illegal in some cities to do an *idling stop*.

Translated to English:

In Japan, it's illegal in some cities to *leave your car running while you're stopped*.

Kickboard *kik-ku-bō-do* 

キックボード

Meaning in Japan:

A non-motorized scooter

Example Japanglish Sentence:

私の子供たちはキックボードに乗って友達の家へ行く。

My kids ride their *kickboards* to their friend's house.

Translated to English:

My kids ride their *scooters* to their friend's house.

My Car

mai-kā

マイカー

Meaning in Japan:

Privately owned car, a personal car that belongs to you (i.e. not a company car, not a rental car, not a borrowed car, not your sister's car that you often use)

Example Japanglish Sentence:

先月、マイカーを買ったんだ。

I just got *my car* last month.

Translated to English:

I just got *my own car* last month.
I just *bought a car* last month.

Number Plate

nan-bā-pu-rē-to

ナンバープレート

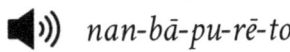

Meaning in Japan:

License plate (US);
Number plate (UK),
Registration plate (UK)

Example Japanglish Sentence:

「私たちの車のナンバーって何だったっけ?
ナンバープレートが見えない。」

What's our *back number*? I can't see our *number plate*.

Translated to English:

What's our license plate number? I can't see our *license plate*.

Open Car

ō-pun-kā

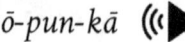

オープンカー

Meaning in Japan:

Convertible car

Example Japanglish Sentence:

私の父は、私が子どもの時、<u>オープンカー</u>を持っていた。

My dad had an <u>*open car*</u> when I was a kid.

Translated to English:

My dad had a <u>*convertible*</u> when I was a kid.

Paper Driver

pē-pā-do-rai-bā 

ペーパードライバー

Meaning in Japan:

A person who holds a valid driver's license but doesn't drive

Example Japanglish Sentence:

ニューヨークのような大都市には、便利な交通手段が豊富にあるため、<u>ペーパードライバー</u>が多い。

There are many <u>*paper drivers*</u> in big cities like NYC since there are so many good alternative transportation options.

Translated to English:

There are many <u>*people who have a driver's license but don't drive*</u> in big cities like NYC since there are so many good alternative transportation options.

pa-to-kā

Pat Car

パトカー

Meaning in Japan:

This is an abbreviation of "patrol car" and means police car.

Example Japanglish Sentence:

建物の外にパトカーがたくさん来ていたけれど、何があったのだろう。

There were a lot of *pat cars* outside the building; I wonder what happened.

Translated to English:

There were a lot of *police cars* outside the building; I wonder what happened.

pan-ku

Punc

パンク

Meaning in Japan:

This is an abbreviation of "puncture" and means a flat tire (US), flat tyre (UK), or puncture (UK).

Example Japanglish Sentence:

今朝、タイヤがパンクしたので、彼女は、授業に遅れる。

She had a *punc* this morning, so she'll be late to class.

Translated to English:

She had a *flat tire* the morning, so she'll be late to class.

Rush

ras-shu

ラッシュ

Meaning in Japan:

Rush hour

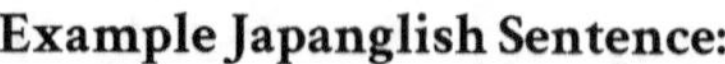

Example Japanglish Sentence:

通勤ラッシュの運転って本当に嫌いだ。
最悪だよね。

I hate driving in *rush*! It's the worst!

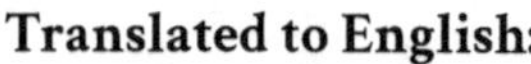

Translated to English:

I hate driving in *rush hour*! It's the worst!

RV

ā-ru-bui

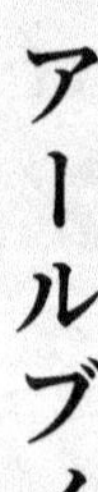

アールブイ

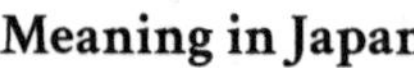

Meaning in Japan:

SUV

Example Japanglish Sentence:

どんな車に乗ってるんだい。
小型のRVだよ。

What kind of car do you have?
I have a small *RV*.

Translated to English:

What kind of car do you have?
I have a small *SUV*.

sai-do-bu-rē-ku

Side Brake

サイドブレーキ

Meaning in Japan:

Parking brake, emergency brake, handbrake (UK)

Example Japanglish Sentence:

車を停めるときは<u>サイドブレーキ</u>を使う。

When I park my car, I use my <u>*side brake*</u>.

Translated to English:

When I park my car, I use the <u>*parking brake*</u> / <u>*emergency brake*</u>.

e-su-e-ru

SL

エスエル

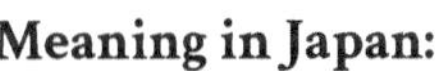

Meaning in Japan:

Steam train/locomotive

Example Japanglish Sentence:

祖父は昔の<u>*SL*（蒸気機関車）</u>が走っていた史跡を訪れるのが大好きだ。

My grandfather loves visiting historical locations with <u>*SL*</u>.

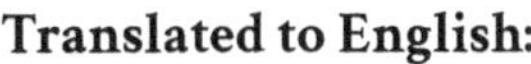

Translated to English:

My grandfather loves visiting historical locations with <u>*old steam trains/locomotives*</u>.

WINKER

ウインカー

u-in-kā

Meaning in Japan:

Blinker, turn signal,
indicator (UK)

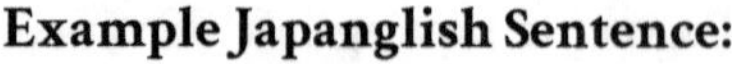

Example Japanglish Sentence:

曲がるときは、<u>ウインカー</u>をちゃんと使ったほうがいい。

You should always use your *winker* when you want to turn.

Translated to English:

You should always use your *blinker* when you want to turn.

CLOTHING & FASHION

衣服・ファッション

5

CONSERVA

コンサバ

kon-sa-ba 

Meaning in Japan:

This is an abbreviation of the word "conservative;" however, it does not describe one's politics or values. Instead, it describes a fashion style that is usually feminine, clean, and timeless[2]. It's similar to a fashionable, classy business casual style with muted colors, often paired with heels.

Example Japanglish Sentence:

彼女は、本当に<u>コンサバ</u>だ。彼女の服装は、いつもコンサバ系だ。

She's really <u>*conserva*</u> and wears a lot of <u>*conserva*</u> clothes.

Translated to English:

She has a <u>*classic, timeless style*</u> and wears a lot of <u>*elegant business casual*</u>.

DRESS

ドレス

do-re-su 

Meaning in Japan:

Only a formal dress like a wedding dress or evening gown, not an everyday dress

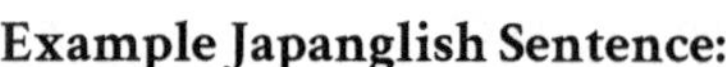

Example Japanglish Sentence:

カジュアルなレストランには<u>ドレス</u>を着て
行かないほうがいいよ

You shouldn't wear a <u>*dress*</u> to a casual restaurant.

Translated to English:

You shouldn't wear a <u>*formal dress*</u> to a casual restaurant.

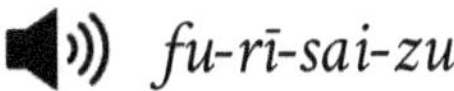

FREE SIZE

フリーサイズ

Meaning in Japan:

One size fits all

Example Japanglish Sentence:

このワンピースは、フリーサイズだ。

These one pieces are *free size*.

Translated to English:

These dresses are *one size fits all*.

Free Size Dresses

One time, I was shopping in Hawaii at a swap meet or market while on vacation. I came across a little shop with cute dresses. I loved the designs. I asked the owner, "What sizes do you have in these?"

"*Free size*," he answered. Confused, I looked at my husband expecting him to know. He's Japanese Hawaiian. I thought maybe it was a Hawaiian phrase, but he didn't know either.

"Only one size," the shop owner said," One size for everybody." I understood. He meant "one size fits all."

The next week, a student said the same phrase, "*free size*." This time, I knew what it meant.

G Jan

jī-jan

Meaning in Japan:

Jean jacket, denim jacket

Example Japanglish Sentence:

今夜はGジャンを着ようと思う。
暖かいし、おしゃれだからね。

I think I'll wear my *G jan* tonight.
It's pretty warm but also stylish.

Translated to English:

I think I'll wear my *denim jacket* tonight.
It's pretty warm but also stylish.

G Pan

jī-pan

Meaning in Japan:

Jeans

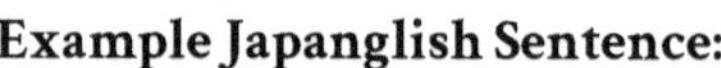

Example Japanglish Sentence:

アメリカでは毎日ジーパンを履いて出勤する人がいると知って驚いた。

I was surprised that in the U.S. some people wear *G pan* to their office every day.

Translated to English:

I was surprised that in the U.S. some people wear *jeans* to their office every day.

gya-ru

Gal / Girl

ギャル

Meaning in Japan:

Gal refers to a very specific fashion trend and Japanese subculture. It can have both negative and positive connotations. Within gal culture, there are several sub-categories and eras that have had different characteristics, so a gal from the '90s may look different from a gal in 2025.[3] Some of the consistent features of gal culture and fashion throughout the years are the following:[4]

Eye makeup: All eras have included heavy use of eye makeup. Trends have included very dark, thick eyeliner, multiple layers of false eyelashes, and making the entire area around the eyes either totally black or totally white (*reverse panda* makeup fad in the early 2000s).

Blond hair: While not all gals have blond hair, this is one of the most iconic features - long, beach blond hair.

Bright, flashy, trendy, revealing clothing: Fashion choices are often extremely trendy and don't necessarily match with the current weather (e.g., wearing miniskirts with bare legs in the middle of winter). Short skirts, miniskirts, high heels, thick platform shoes, flashy accessories are all features of gal style. Modern gals are bringing back a trend from '90s gals, loose socks, similar to leg warmers in the American '80s era.

Long nails: Most gals love their extremely long nails with unique, brightly colored, glittery, intricate designs!

Very white or very dark skin: In the past, gals who focused on getting their skin as light as possible were called *white gals,* while those who focused on getting as dark as possible with tanning bed were called *black gals.* Today, gals with "healthy" skin are called *latte gals.*[5]

Cheerful, positive, bubbly attitude: Gals should have a *gal mindset* and modern gals interpret this to mean don't worry about what others think, and be positive; trust that everything will work out somehow.[6]

Example Japanglish Sentence:

ギャルに会いたいなら、SHIBUYA109が一番のスポットだ!

SHIBUYA109 is the best place to go if you want to see gals!

Translated to English:

SHIBUYA109 is the best place to go if you want to see gyaru girls.

Gothic Lolita (Goth Loli)

ゴシックロリータ（ゴスロリ）

go-su-ro-ri
gos-hik-ku-ro-ri-ta 

Meaning in Japan:

Gothic lolita, also known as *goth loli,* is a specific type of Japanese fashion. It's a mixture of gothic fashion and lolita fashion. *Lolita fashion* includes cutesy, frilly, Victorian-style dresses with ribbons and bows evoking the image of the clothing on a porcelain Victorian doll. *Gothic fashion* brings heavier, darker, more mysterious elements. *Gothic lolita* blends these two styles together into its unique special style: dainty, intricate Victorian ruffles and lace, black, crimson and white colors, corsets, crosses, skulls, ribbons, pearls, large bows, frilly socks, long gloves, and dark eye liner.[7]

Example Japanglish Sentence:

ゴスロリは、コスプレじゃなくて、ファッションスタイルだ。

Goth loli isn't a Halloween a costume; it's a fashion style.

Translated to English:

Gothic lolita fashion isn't a Halloween costume; it's a fashion style.

Gown

ga-un

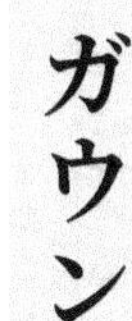

Meaning in Japan:

Bathrobe, dressing gown (UK)

Example Japanglish Sentence:

そのホテルでは、宿泊客向けに無料のガウンが用意されている。

The hotel has free *gowns* for guests.

Translated to English:

The hotel has free *bathrobes* for guests.

High Neck

ha-i-nek-ku

ハイネック

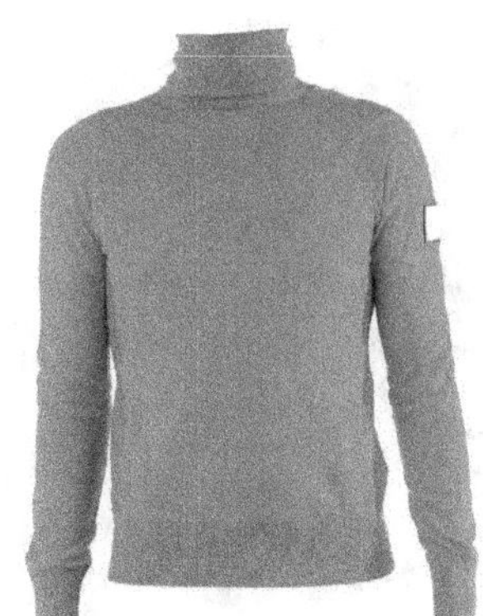

Meaning in Japan:

Turtleneck

Example Japanglish Sentence:

ハイネックはおしゃれだと思う人もいるが、そう思わない人もいる。

Some people think *high neck* is fashionable, but others disagree.

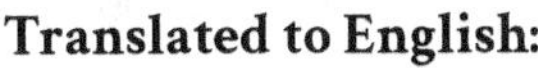

Translated to English:

Some people think *turtlenecks* are fashionable, but others disagree.

JACQUE (CHOKKI)

chok-ki

チョッキ

Meaning in Japan:

This word varies in meaning depending on generation. For older people, *chokki* means a fishing vest, a safety vest, or a bulletproof vest. Younger generations tend to think of it as an out-dated men's suit vest or waistcoat (UK).

Example Japanglish Sentence:

父は<u>チョッキ</u>を着るのが大好きだ。私は何度も「古くさいよ」と言っているのに。

My dad still wears <u>*chokki*</u> even though I told him they're old-fashioned.

Translated to English:

My dad still wears <u>*vests*</u> even though I told him they're old-fashioned.

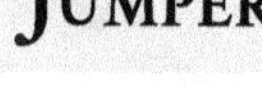

JUMPER

jan-pā

ジャンパー

Meaning in Japan:

Jacket, coat

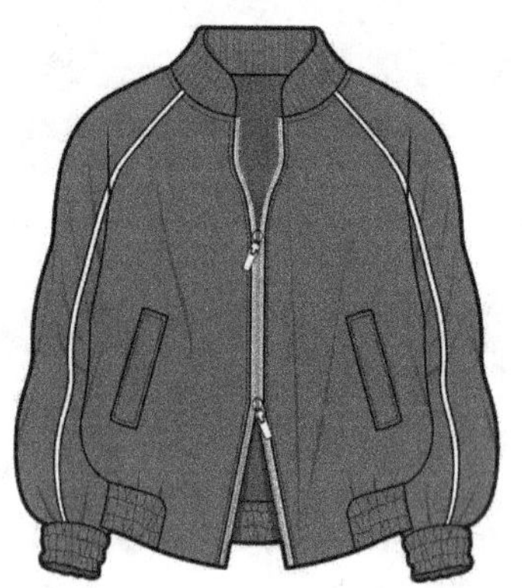

Example Japanglish Sentence:

その<u>ジャンパー</u>とても素敵ね。
どこで買ったの？

I really like your <u>*jumper*</u>.
Where did you get it?

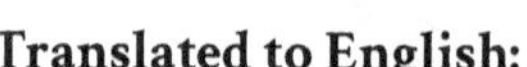

Translated to English:

I really like your <u>*jacket*</u>.
Where did you get it?

jan-pā-su-kā-to

Jumper Skirt

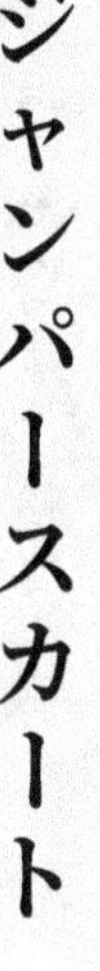
ジャンパースカート

Meaning in Japan:

Jumper (US), pinafore dress (UK)

Example Japanglish Sentence:

彼女は制服の<u>ジャンパースカート</u>
を着て学校へ行った。

She wore a *<u>jumper skirt</u>* to school
as part of her uniform.

Translated to English:

She wore a *<u>jumper</u>* to school as part of her uniform.

mi-shin

Machine / Mishin

ミシン

Meaning in Japan:

Sewing machine

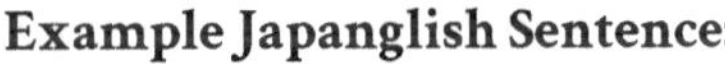
Example Japanglish Sentence:

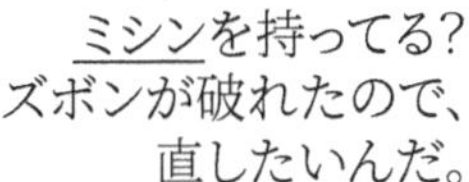
<u>ミシン</u>を持ってる?
ズボンが破れたので、
直したいんだ。

Do you have a *<u>mishin</u>*?
I have a rip in my pants that I need to fix.

Translated to English:

Do you have a *<u>sewing machine</u>*? I have a rip in my pants that I need to fix.

Muffler

ma-fu-rā

マフラー

Meaning in Japan:

1. Winter scarf
2. Car muffler, silencer (UK)

Example Japanglish Sentence:

私は、彼女の誕生日に
マフラーをあげるつもりだ。

I'm going to give her a
muffler for her birthday.

Translated to English:

I'm going to give her a *scarf* for her birthday.

Muffler in the Mail

In college, I had a great friend from Asia. One year, for my birthday, she told me that she had asked her mom to mail me a special gift, but it hadn't arrived on time. She said she couldn't find the style in the U.S. that she liked, so she had her mom pick a *muffler* out for me back home. I smiled and thanked her for her kind thought and reassured her that I didn't mind waiting for it to arrive.

When I thought about it later that evening, all I could think was, "What is a *muffler*?" The only kind of *muffler* I knew about was the kind that is in your car. I wasn't even totally sure what *that muffler* was. I just knew that you didn't want it to break. Obviously, she wasn't mailing me a car part for my birthday. Maybe it was a special kind of mittens for the winter?

Later when the gift arrived, I opened the box and found a beautiful winter scarf.

wan-pī-su

One Piece

ワンピース

Meaning in Japan:

A casual dress

Example Japanglish Sentence:

彼女はパーティーにワンピースを着て行った。

She's wearing a *one piece* to the party.

Translated to English:

She's wearing a *dress* to the party.

What Kind of Party?

Here is a conversation I once had with a student:

Me - What are you going to wear to the party tomorrow?

Student - I'm going to wear a *one piece.*

Me - Oh? It's a swimming party?

Student *(confused)* - No. It's not a swimming party.

Me *(confused)* - It's not? Then why are you wearing a swimsuit if it's not a swimming party?

Student *(more confused)* - I'm not wearing a swimsuit tomorrow!

Me *(even more confused)* - What? I'm confused. You said you were wearing a *one piece* tomorrow...

No Sleeve

nō-su-rī-bu

ノースリーブ

Meaning in Japan:

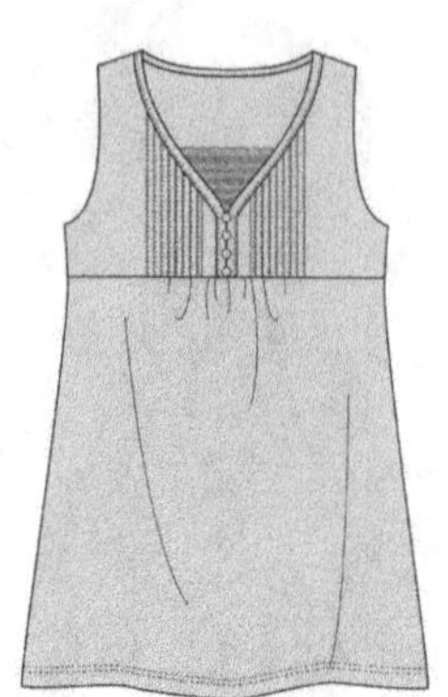

Sleeveless top/shirt

Example Japanglish Sentence:

彼女は、ノースリーブを着て登校して、
校則違反で家に帰された。

She wore *no sleeve* to school and got sent home for breaking the dress code.

Translated to English:

She wore a sleeveless top to school and got sent home for breaking the dress code.

Pair Look

pe-a-ruk-ku

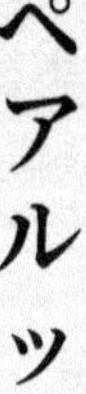

Meaning in Japan:

When a couple matches their clothes, outfits, and all-around look. This is quite common for young couples.

Example Japanglish Sentence:

わあ、かわいい！
ふたりのペアルック、いい感じ！

Oh cute! I like their *pair look*!

Translated to English:

Oh cute! They are *matching*! I like it!
Oh cute! I like their *matching outfits*!

pan-tsu

Pants

パンツ

Meaning in Japan:

Men's underwear, men's pants (UK), or a term kids use for undergarments

Example Japanglish Sentence:

私は、夫に自分でパンツを買うように言った。私が選びたくないから。

I told my husband to buy his own *pants*; I don't want to choose them.

Translated to English:

I told my husband to buy his own *underwear*; I don't want to choose them.

pan-tsu su-tai-ru

Pants Style

パンツスタイル

Meaning in Japan:

Any time a woman wears pants or trousers (UK), especially a pantsuit, to work or in a professional setting

Example Japanglish Sentence:

私は、たいていパンツスタイルだ。

I am usually *pants style*.

Translated to English:

I usually *wear pants/slacks* to the office.
I usually *wear a pantsuit* to the office.

Parker

パーカー

pā-kā

Meaning in Japan:

A hoodie, hooded jumper (UK)

Example Japanglish Sentence:

学校では<u>パーカー</u>は禁止されているが、家ではよく着る。

My school doesn't allow *<u>parkers</u>*, but I love wearing them at home.

Translated to English:

My school doesn't allow *<u>hoodies</u>*, but I love wearing them at home.

Recruit Suit

リクルートスーツ

ri-ku-rū-to-sū-tsu 

Meaning in Japan:

A plain and simple suit that young people wear when they first start job hunting. This *recruit suit* is typically worn during interviews, company information sessions, resumé/CV photos (common in Japan), internships, training, and more.[8]

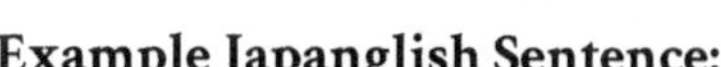

Example Japanglish Sentence:

教授は卒業生たちに、「<u>リクルートスーツ</u>を一着はクローゼットに入れておきなさい」と助言した。

The professor advised the graduates to make sure they have a good *<u>recruit suit</u>* in their closets.

Translated to English:

The professor advised the graduates to make sure they have *<u>a good, simple, professional, solid-color suit</u>* in their closets for their job hunt.

ran-nin-gu-sha-tsu

Running Shirt

ランニングシャツ

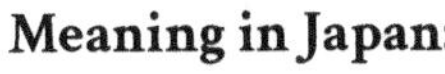
Meaning in Japan:

Sleeveless undershirt, tank top, muscle shirt

Example Japanglish Sentence:

ランニングシャツを着て庭仕事をしたから、日焼けした。

I got a sunburn because I wore a *running shirt* to do yard work.

Translated to English:

I got a sunburn because I wore a *tank top* to do yard work.

e-su-sai-zu

S Size

エスサイズ

Meaning in Japan:

Small

Example Japanglish Sentence:

彼女はSサイズを着ている。

She wears *S size*.

Translated to English:

She wears a *small*.

M Size

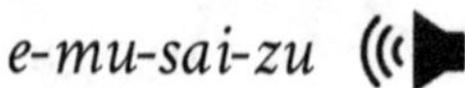

エムサイズ

Meaning in Japan:

Medium

Example Japanglish Sentence:

私は、シャツはMサイズが欲しい。
I need *M size* for shirts.

Translated to English:

I need a *medium* for shirts.

L Size

e-ru-sai-zu

エルサイズ

Meaning in Japan:

Large

Example Japanglish Sentence:

私の父にLサイズを買ってくれる?
Can you buy *L size* for my dad?

Translated to English:

Can you buy a *large* for my dad?

LL Size

エルエルサイズ

e-ru-e-ru-sai-zu

Meaning in Japan:

Extra large, XL

Example Japanglish Sentence:

このシャツのLLサイズはありますか?

Do you sell this shirt in *LL size*?

Translated to English:

Do you sell this shirt in *XL*?

3L Size

スリーエル

su-rī-e-ru

Meaning in Japan:

Extra extra large, XXL, 2XL

Example Japanglish Sentence:

彼のシャツのサイズは3Lだ。

His shirt size is *3L*.

Translated to English:

His shirt size is *XXL*.

Sense

センス

sen-su

Meaning in Japan:

Sense of fashion, design, or coordination of color, styles, design or clothing elements; Taste

Example Japanglish Sentence:

あなたのセンス、すごく素敵！

Your *sense* is so good!

彼のセンスは、最高！色の組み合わせが特に好き！

His *sense* is so good! I love the colors!

Translated to English:

Your *fashion sense* is so good!

He has great *taste*! I love the color scheme!

Short Pants

shō-to-pan-tsu 

ショートパンツ

Meaning in Japan:

Shorts (US), short trousers (UK)

Example Japanglish Sentence:

今日、新しいショートパンツで動物園に行くといいよ。

You should wear your new *short pants* to the zoo today.

Translated to English:

You should wear your new *shorts* to the zoo today.

shō-tsu

Shorts

ショーツ

Meaning in Japan:

Panties or underwear for women, knickers (UK)

Example Japanglish Sentence:

その女性は新しいピンクのショーツが気に入っている。

The woman loves her new pink *shorts*.

Translated to English:

The woman loves her new pink *underwear*.

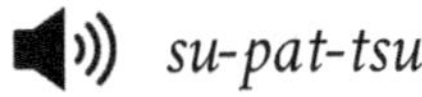

su-pat-tsu

Spats

スパッツ

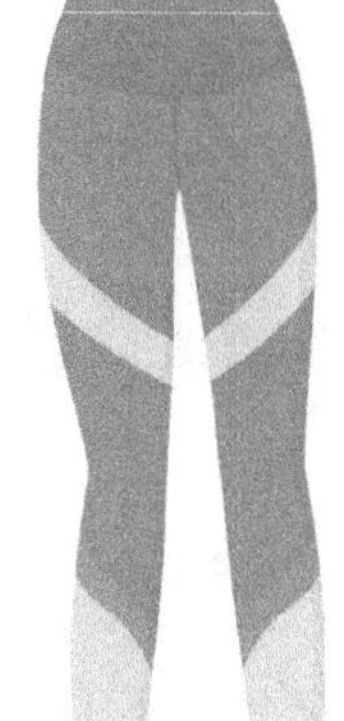

Meaning in Japan:

Workout pants, yoga pants, tights, leggings

Example Japanglish Sentence:

お店でスパッツを履いてる人を見て、すごく驚いた。

I was really surprised when I saw people wearing *spats* at the store.

Translated to English:

I was really surprised when I saw people wearing *yoga pants* at the store.

Sta Jan

su-ta-jan 

スタジャン

Meaning in Japan:

This is an abbreviation of "stadium jumper" and means a letter jacket (US) or varsity jacket (UK)

Example Japanglish Sentence:

チームのみんなは、パーティーにスタジャンを着てきた。

Everyone on our team wore their *sta jan* to the party.

Translated to English:

Everyone on our team wore their *letter jackets* to the party.

Stadium Jumper

su-ta-ji-a-mu-jan-pā 

スタジアムジャンパー

Meaning in Japan:

Letter jacket (US),
varsity jacket (UK)

Example Japanglish Sentence:

チームのみんなは、パーティーに
スタジアムジャンパーを着てきた。

Everyone on our team wore their *stadium jumpers* to the party.

Translated to English:

Everyone on our team wore their *letter jackets* to the party.

sū-wet-to

Sweat

スウェット

Meaning in Japan:

Sweat pants, sweat shirt, joggers (UK)

Example Japanglish Sentence:

彼は夏でもいつもスウェットを履いている。

He always wears *sweat*, even in the summer.

Translated to English:

He always wears *sweatpants*, even in the summer.

su-rī-sai-zu

Three Size

スリーサイズ

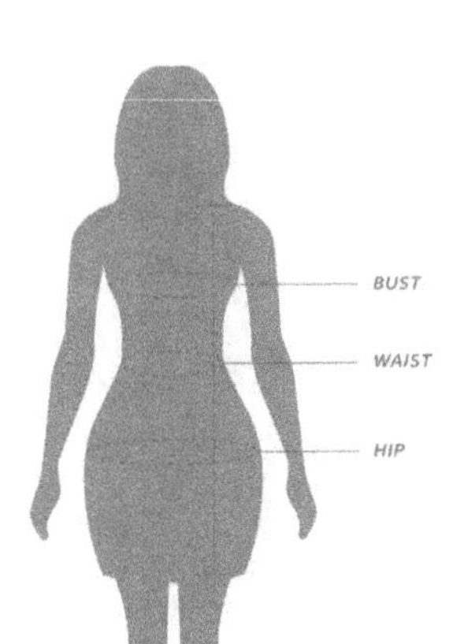

Meaning in Japan:

Body measurements of the bust, waist, hips

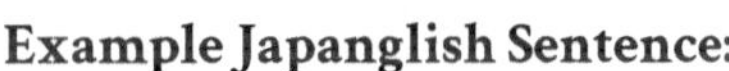

Example Japanglish Sentence:

自分のスリーサイズを知っておくと、
体に合った服を選びやすくなる。

You can choose clothes that suit you
by referring to your *three size*.

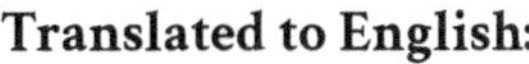

Translated to English:

Using your *body measurements* will make it
easier to choose clothes that fit well.

TRAINER

to-rē-nā

トレーナー

Meaning in Japan:

A sweatshirt that's usually better quality or from a more luxury brand than *sweat*

Example Japanglish Sentence:

彼は夏でもいつもトレーナーを着ている。

He always wears a *trainer*, even in the summer.

Translated to English:

He always wears a *sweatshirt*, even in the summer.

Y SHIRT

wai-sha-tsu 

ワイシャツ

Meaning in Japan:

White button-up dress shirts that men in Japan usually wear to work

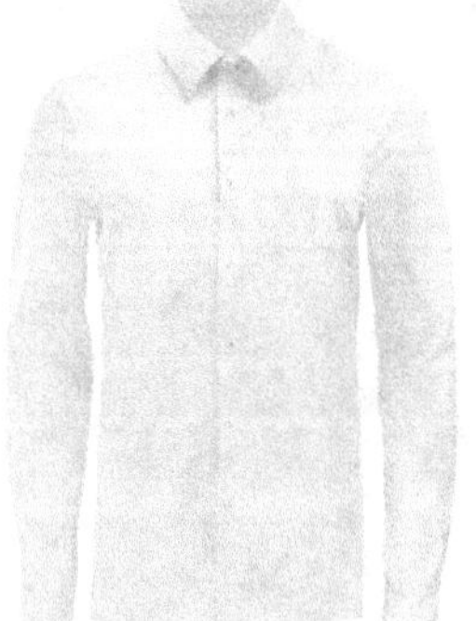

Example Japanglish Sentence:

ワイシャツが見つからない…
明日仕事なのに。

I can't find my *Y shirt*.
I need it for work tomorrow.

Translated to English:

I can't find my *white dress shirt*. I need it for work tomorrow.

Describing People

人物描写

6

All Back

ō-ru-bak-ku 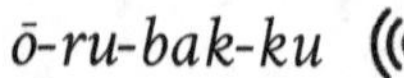

オールバック

Meaning in Japan:

Slicked-back hairstyle

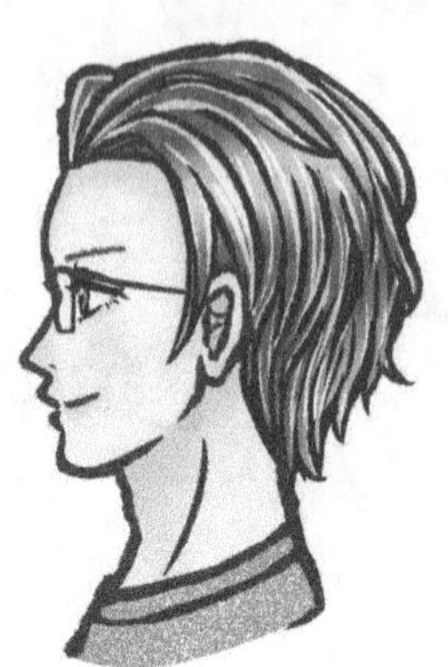

Example Japanglish Sentence:

彼は有名なセレブで、いつも<u>オールバック</u>の髪型をしている。

He's a famous celebrity who always has *<u>all back</u>*.

Translated to English:

He's a famous celebrity who always has his hair in a *<u>slicked-back style</u>*.

Aro Fo

a-ra-fō

アラフォー

Meaning in Japan:

Around 40 years old

Example Japanglish Sentence:

彼女は、<u>アラフォー</u>だ。

I think he's *<u>aro fo</u>*.

Translated to English:

I think he's *<u>around 40</u>*.

Aro Sa

a-ra-sā

アラサー

Meaning in Japan:

Around 30 years old

Example Japanglish Sentence:

彼女は、<u>アラサー</u>だ。

I think she's <u>*aro sa*</u>.

Translated to English:

I think she's <u>*around 30*</u>.

Barcode Hair

bā-kō-do-he-a

Meaning in Japan:

Comb-over hairstyle

Example Japanglish Sentence:

新しいプロジェクトの一環で、<u>バーコードヘア</u>のおじさんを撮影する写真家に会った。

I met a photographer who photographs older men with <u>*barcode hair*</u> as part of her new project.

Translated to English:

I met a photographer who photographs older men with <u>*comb-overs*</u> as part of her new project.

Charm Point

chā-mu-po-in-tu

チャームポイント

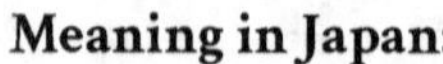

Meaning in Japan:

Attractive physical quality or attractive personality quality; best physical feature or attribute

Example Japanglish Sentence:

彼女のチャームポイントは、目だ。

Her *charm point* is her eyes.

Translated to English:

Her eyes are *her best physical feature.*
Her eyes are *really beautiful*/*attractive*.

Charming

chā-min-gu

チャーミング

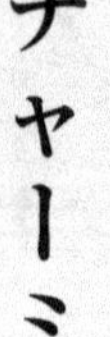

Meaning in Japan:

Physically attractive

Example Japanglish Sentence:

彼はとてもチャーミングだ。彼はとても魅力的だ。

He is so *charming*!

Translated to English:

He is so *attractive*/*good-looking*/*handsome*!

gu-ra-mā

Glamour

グラマー

Meaning in Japan:

A curvy, voluptuous woman

Example Japanglish Sentence:

最近、人々はグラマーな女性を好む。

People love *glamour* women nowadays.

Translated to English:

People love *curvy* women nowadays.

hā-fu

Half

ハーフ

Meaning in Japan:

Anyone of mixed race/ethnicity

Example Japanglish Sentence:

彼はハーフだ。
母親はアイルランド人で、父親は日本人とマレーシア人のハーフだ。

He's *half*.
His mom is Irish, and his dad is half Japanese and half Malaysian.

Translated to English:

He's *Irish, Japanese, and Malaysian*.
He's 1/2 Irish, 1/4 Japanese, and 1/4/ Malaysian.

Image Change

i-me-chen

イメチェン

Meaning in Japan:

A new look, a change to one's appearance, get a makeover

Example Japanglish Sentence:

今週末ゆかに会ったよ。イメチェンして、
ショートカットにして髪を染めたので、ずっと若く見えるよ!

I saw Yuka this weekend. She got *image change*.
She did *short cut* and *hair color* and looks so much younger now!

Translated to English:

I saw Yuka this weekend. She *totally changed her look*.
She cut her hair short and dyed it and looks so much younger now!

Intelli

in-te-ri

Meaning in Japan:

Very intelligent, usually someone with advanced academic degrees, such as a doctor

Example Japanglish Sentence:

新しい上司はとてもインテリで、私は彼女を尊敬している。

The new boss is extremely *intelli*; I really admire her.

Translated to English:

The new boss is extremely *intelligent*; I really admire her.

ma-ni-a

Mania

マニア

Meaning in Japan:

A big fan of something, connoisseur, enthusiast, a fanatic, a maniac, obsessed with something. *Mania* can have both positive or negative connotations depending on the person and situation.

Example Japanglish Sentence:

彼女はコーヒーマニアだ。暇なときにはスペシャルティコーヒーのテイスティングに出かけ、週末にはコーヒー豆のさまざまな焙煎方法を試している。

She is a coffee *mania*. She goes to specialty coffee tastings in her free time and experiments with different ways of roasting coffee beans on the weekends.

Translated to English:

She is a coffee *enthusiast*. She goes to specialty coffee tastings in her free time and experiments with different ways of roasting coffee beans on the weekends.

mi-su-kon

Miss Con

ミスコン

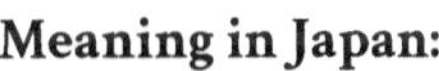
Meaning in Japan:

Beauty pageant

Example Japanglish Sentence:

彼女はきれいだ。
まるでミスコンで優勝したみたいに見える。

She's beautiful! She looks like she won the *miss con*!

Translated to English:

She's beautiful! She looks like she won a *beauty pageant*!

Miss Contest

mi-su-kon-te-su-to 

ミスコンテスト

Meaning in Japan:

Beauty pageant

Example Japanglish Sentence:

彼女はきれいだ。
まるでミスコンテストで優勝したみたいに見える。
She's beautiful!
She looks like she won the *miss contest*!

Translated to English:

She's beautiful! She looks like she won a *beauty pageant*!

Naive

na-ī-bu

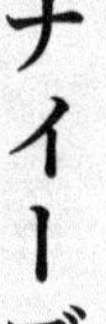

Meaning in Japan:

Overly sensitive; often used to describe someone who gets their feelings hurt easily or is easily bothered

Example Japanglish Sentence:

彼女はいつもすぐに気を悪くする。
何も言えない感じだ。本当にナイーブ(繊細)だ。

She always gets offended so easily.
I feel like I can't say anything around her. She's so *naive*.

Translated to English:

She always gets offended so easily.
I feel like I can't say anything around her. She's so *overly sensitive*.

Nice Guy

nai-su-gai

ナイスガイ

Meaning in Japan:

A good-looking, attractive guy

Example Japanglish Sentence:

新しい彼氏の写真見せてくれてありがとう！すごくナイスガイだね！

Thanks for showing me the picture of your new boyfriend! He's such a *nice guy*!

Translated to English:

Thanks for showing me the picture of your new boyfriend! He's so *good-looking*!

Outlook

au-to-ruk-ku

アウトルック

Meaning in Japan:

Physical appearance

Example Japanglish Sentence:

今日、彼のアウトルックは冴えないね。シャワーは、浴びたのかな。

His *outlook* is bad today. Did he even take a shower?

Translated to English:

He *looks* bad today. Did he even take a shower?

Rough

ra-fu

ラフ

Meaning in Japan:

1. When used to describe personality, *rough* means easy-going, laid back, or doesn't get caught up on minor details.

2. When used to describe appearance, *rough* means plain, casual, informal and does not have negative undertones as it does in English

Example Japanglish Sentence:

彼みたいにもっとラフに生きたいな。

I wish I was more like him; he's so *rough*.

彼女、在宅勤務だから服装もすごくラフでうらやましいよ。

She dresses really *rough* since she works from home. I'm so jealous.

Translated to English:

I wish I was more like him; he's so *laid back*.

She dresses really *casually* since she works from home. I'm so jealous.

ro-man-su-gu-rē **ROMANCE GRAY**

Meaning in Japan:

A man with salt and pepper hair; a "silver fox"

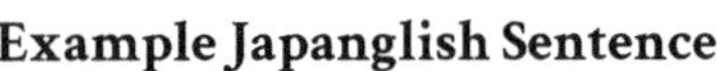

Example Japanglish Sentence:

夫に「髪は染めないで」って言ったの。
今のロマンスグレーがいい感じだから。

I told my husband not to dye his hair because right now he's a *romance gray*!

Translated to English:

I told my husband not to dye his hair because right now he's a *silver fox*!

shō-to-kat-to **SHORT CUT**

Meaning in Japan:

Short hair cut or hair style

Example Japanglish Sentence:

週末ユカに会ったんだけど、イメチェンして、髪をショートカットにしてカラーもしてて、すごく若返って見えた！

I saw Yuka this weekend. She got *image change*. She did *short cut* and *hair color* and looks so much younger now!

Translated to English:

I saw Yuka this weekend. She totally changed her look. She *cut her hair short* and dyed her hair and looks so much younger now!

Smart

su-mā-to

スマート

Meaning in Japan:

Thin, slim

Example Japanglish Sentence:

彼女は、とてもスマートになったね。ダイエットしたの?

She became *smart*! Did she diet?

Translated to English:

She became really *slim*! Did she go on a diet?

Unique

yu-nī-ku

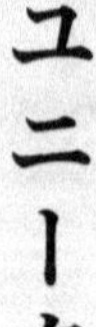

ユニーク

Meaning in Japan:

Peculiar, odd (with a generally negative connotation)

Example Japanglish Sentence:

私の生物の先生は、とてもユニークだ。

My biology teacher is really *unique*.

Translated to English:

My biology teacher is really *peculiar* / *odd* / *strange*.

be-rī-shō-to

Very Short

ベリーショート

Meaning in Japan:

Very short hair cut or style like a pixie cut

Example Japanglish Sentence:

彼女の髪はベリーショートだ。

She has *very short*.

Translated to English:

She has a *pixie cut* / *very short hair cut*.

yan-kī

Yankee

Meaning in Japan:

A young punk, delinquent, hooligan, thug

Example Japanglish Sentence:

彼は、高校生の時ヤンキーだった。

He was a *yankee* when he was a high school student.

Translated to English:

He was a *hooligan* / *punk* when he was in high school.

Feelings , Emotions, Encouragement

感情表現・励まし

7

Attack

a-tak-ku

アタック

Meaning in Japan:

This is used as a phrase of encouragement when someone is taking on a challenge or something difficult. It's similar to "Go for it!" or "Go get it!" A common use that can sound shocking to outsiders is in the world of romance: "If you like the girl, you should *attack* her!" To be clear, this simply means to "go for it" and pursue her or ask her out!

Example Japanglish Sentence:

そのインターンを取りたいなら、アタックすべきだよ！

If you want that internship, then you should *attack (it)*!

Translated to English:

If you want that internship, then you should *go for it*!

Capa

kya-pa 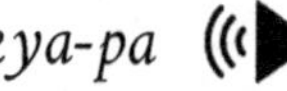

キャパ

Meaning in Japan:

1. Capacity
2. Personal mental or physical capacity or the limits of one's ability

Example Japanglish Sentence:

このスタジアムのキャパは1万人だ。

This stadium has a *capa* of 10,000.

今日は仕事が多すぎて、完全にキャパオーバーだ。

I have too much work today - I'm totally over my *capa*.

Translated to English:

This stadium has a *capacity* of 10,000.

I have too much work today - I'm totally *overwhelmed*.

don mai DON MI

ドンマイ

Meaning in Japan:

This is an abbreviation of "Don't mind" and is used as encouragement after a failure like, "It's okay! Shake it off! You'll do better next time!"

Example Japanglish Sentence:

(バレーボールの試合でチームメイトがボールをミスする)
チームメイト:「ドンマイ! ドンマイ!次頑張ろう!」

(Teammate in a volleyball game misses the ball)
Teammate: "*Don mi*! *Don mi*! Next time!"

Translated to English:

(Teammate in a volleyball game misses the ball)
Teammate: "*It's okay*! *Good try*! You'll get it next time!"

fai-to FIGHT

ファイト

Meaning in Japan:

You can do it! Good luck! Way to go! Let's go team! Give it your all! Often said while raising a closed fist in the air for inspiration and oomph, *Fight!* is a general shout or cheer of encouragement or rally to cheer on your friend or your favorite sports team.

Example Japanglish Sentence:

ファイト!君なら、できるよ!

Fight! You can do it!

Translated to English:

Go team! You can do it!
You got this! You can do it!

Goo

gū

Meaning in Japan:

An abbreviation of "good" and used to express approval

Example Japanglish Sentence:

5品のコース料理はとても<u>グー</u>だった！

That five course meal was so *<u>goo</u>*!

Translated to English:

That five course meal was so *<u>good</u>*!

Guts Pose

gat-tsu-pō-zu

Meaning in Japan:

Fist pump in the air typically used to say "YES!" to celebrate a win or accomplishment

Example Japanglish Sentence:

チームは<u>ガッツポーズ</u>をして、大勝利を祝う写真を撮った。

The team took a picture with *<u>guts pose</u>* celebrating after their big win.

Translated to English:

The team took a picture *<u>pumping their fists in the air</u>* celebrating after their big win.

hā-do HARD

ハード

Meaning in Japan:

1. Busy or hectic
2. Hardware

Example Japanglish Sentence:

私は、教授に「宿題ができなくてすみませんでした。今週末は、とても<u>ハード</u>だったんです」と詫びた。

I apologized to my professor, "I'm sorry, I didn't do my homework. This weekend was very *<u>hard</u>*."

Translated to English:

I apologized to my professor, "I'm sorry, I didn't do my homework. This weekend was very *<u>busy</u>*."

hī-rin-gu HEALING

ヒーリング

Meaning in Japan:

Relaxing, stress-relieving, calming. *Healing* is slightly deeper in meaning than just the English word relaxing. *Healing* seems to hold an idea of bringing balance to the mind and body and is often used to described the relaxing, or stress-relieving benefits often found in nature or the arts that enhance one's well-being.[9]

Example Japanglish Sentence:

この音楽には<u>ヒーリング</u>効果がある。

This music has *<u>healing</u>* effect!

Translated to English:

This music is so *<u>relaxing</u>*!

High Tension

hai-ten-shon 

ハイテンション

Meaning in Japan:

Excited, overexcited, high energy, enthusiastic

Example Japanglish Sentence:

学校の最終日はみんな<u>ハイテンション</u>だった。

Everyone was so *<u>high tension</u>* on the last day of school.

Translated to English:

Everyone was so *<u>excited</u>* on the last day of school.

High Touch

hai-tat-chi 

ハイタッチ

Meaning in Japan:

High five

Example Japanglish Sentence:

私たちは、好きなチームが決勝ゴールを決めた後、みんなで<u>ハイタッチ</u>した。

We all did *<u>high touch</u>* after our favorite team scored the winning goal.

Translated to English:

We all did *<u>high fives</u>* after our favorite team scored the winning goal.

hi-su-te-rī

Hysterie

ヒステリー

Meaning in Japan:

Hysterie comes from the German word hysterie and has two main meanings in Japanglish. The first is a diagnosable condition like a conversion disorder or dissociative personality disorder.[10]

The second meaning translates more similarly to hysterical but is slightly different than how the word is used in English. *Hysterie* has a similar literal translation to hysterical, meaning showing an uncontrollable outpouring of emotions, especially in women. However, in a Japanese context, this could mean simply having a bad temper, losing one's temper, losing control of one's emotions, expressing too much emotion, showing anger openly, losing one's cool over something trivial, or simply reacting in an unreasonable manner.[11, 12] In modern culture, this meaning of *hysterie* is considered a sexist and dismissive term.

Example Japanglish Sentence:

何人かの女子は、新しいチームメイトが<u>ヒステリー</u>を起こしていると文句を言っていた。

Some of the girls complained that their new teammate was <u>*hysterie*</u>.

Translated to English:

Some of the girls complained that their new teammate had a <u>*bad temper*</u>.

JINX *jin-ku-su*

ジンクス

Meaning in Japan:

Jinx can be used to mean something that causes either bad luck or good luck and includes curses as well as good luck charms.

Example Japanglish Sentence:

この試合に勝つために、私のジンクスを教えてあげるよ！

I'll give you my *jinx* to win the game!

Translated to English:

I'll give you my *good luck charm* to win the game!

NEUROSE *noi-rō-ze*

Meaning in Japan:

Postpartum depression, OCD, anxiety[13, 14, 15]

Example Japanglish Sentence:

彼女は出産後にノイローゼになって、今は専門家に相談している。

She got *neurose* after having the baby,
so she's started seeing a professional to get some help.

Translated to English:

She struggled with some *postpartum depression* after having the baby, so she's started seeing a professional to get some help.

nō-tat-chi — NO TOUCH

ノータッチ

Meaning in Japan:

To purposefully ignore or avoid discussing a problem or issue. Friends may *no touch* about a sensitive topic, or a boss may *no touch* about a past problem that he is already aware of.

Example Japanglish Sentence:

彼らが海外に引っ越すことはまだ他の人には言ってないから、今夜のパーティーではこの話題には、ノータッチで頼むよ。

They haven't told anyone else that they are moving abroad yet, so please *no touch* about this topic at the party tonight.

Translated to English:

They haven't told anyone else that they are moving abroad yet, so *please don't bring up this topic* at the party tonight.

ro-man — ROMAN

ロマン

Meaning in Japan:

A far-fetched dream, romanticized hypothetical adventure, pipe dream

Example Japanglish Sentence:

自分で会社を立ち上げてお金持ちになって早期リタイアするのが、男のロマンなのかもしれない。

It seems like every man's *roman* is to start his own company, become rich, and retire early.

Translated to English:

It seems like every man's *pipe dream* is to start his own company, become rich, and retire early.

Tension

ten-shon

Meaning in Japan:

Tension describes a heightened emotional state. It's often expressed as *high tension* or *low tension. High tension* is typically excitement in situations with friends while *low tension* is typically sadness, slowness, or lack of energy due to stress or fatigue.

Example Japanglish Sentence:

息子はいつもテンションが高めなんだけど、
娘は大学の願書のストレスでよくテンションが低くなってるんだ。

My son is usually *high tension*, but my daughter is often *low tension* due to her stress from the college application process.

Translated to English:

My son is usually really *energetic*, but my daughter is often *down and tired* due to her stress from the college application process.

Touch

tat-chi

Meaning in Japan:

To tap

Example Japanglish Sentence:

彼女が私にタッチしたから、
何かあるのかなと思って振り向いた。

She *touched* me, so I turned around to see what she wanted.

Translated to English:

She *tapped* me on the shoulder,
so I turned around to see what she wanted.

Food & Drinks

食べ物・飲み物

AMERICAN COFFEE

a-me-ri-kan-kō-hī

アメリカンコーヒー

Meaning in Japan:

American coffee refers to a very specific way of preparing coffee. It can often simply mean brewed coffee, but it has a few distinguishing features.

The first characteristic is that *American coffee* should be made with only lightly roasted beans.

Second, it should be made with a higher water to coffee ratio so the result will be a much weaker cup/pot of coffee. As an example, if you usually brew your scoop of ground coffee with eight ounces of water, to make *American coffee,* you would use the same amount of ground coffee beans but increase the water to 10 or 11 ounces. *American coffee* also typically uses hotter water than in a usual brewing process.

The alternative method to this is to simply brew your usual cup of coffee and then dilute it with hot water before drinking it.

Although it may sound similar to Americano, *American coffee* has its own unique taste since the brewing process, bean roast, and grind size differ.[16]

Example Japanglish Sentence:

アメリカ人は、エスプレッソではなく、アメリカンコーヒーを飲む。

Americans drink *American coffee*, not espresso.

Translated to English:

Americans drink *(weak) drip coffee*, not espresso.

American Dog

a-me-ri-kan-dog-gu

アメリカンドッグ

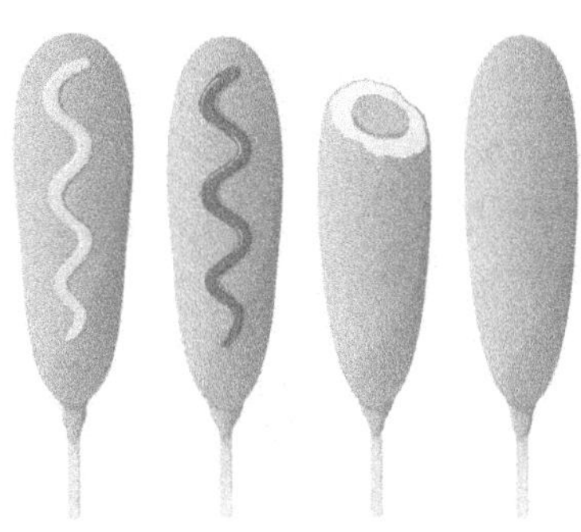

Meaning in Japan:

Corn dog

Example Japanglish Sentence:

アメリカンドッグは、とてもおいしい。

American dogs are so delicious!

Translated to English:

Corn dogs are so delicious!

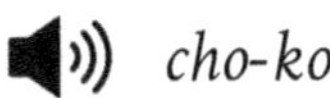

cho-ko

Choco

チョコ

Meaning in Japan:

Chocolate

Example Japanglish Sentence:

チョコ食べたい?

Do you want some *choco*?

Translated to English:

Do you want some *chocolate*?

CIDER

sai-dā

サイダー

Meaning in Japan:

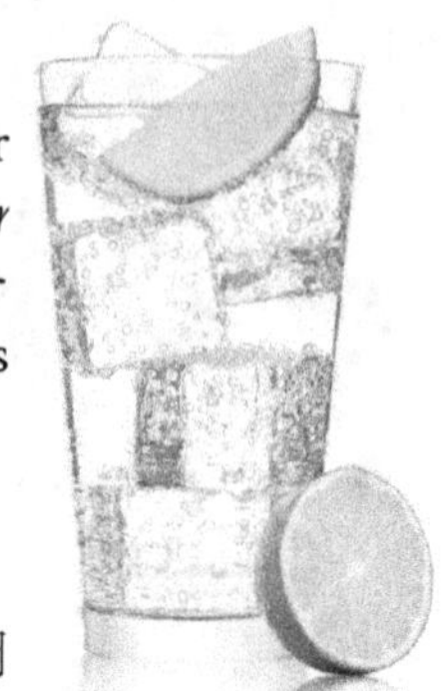

A non-alcoholic, fizzy, lemon-lime soda similar to Sprite and 7UP or lemonade in the UK. *Cider* usually means the brand Mistuya 三ツ矢サイダー but can also mean most similar carbonated drinks as well as sweetened club soda.

Example Japanglish Sentence:

サイダーはアルコールが入っていないので、胃の調子を整えるのにいいし、子供にもぴったりだ。アメリカでは、お腹の調子が悪いときにサイダーを飲むことがよくある。

Cider is great because it doesn't have alcohol and can help your stomach feel better. People often drink *cider* when they have an upset stomach.

Translated to English:

Sprite is great because it doesn't have alcohol and can help your stomach feel better. People often drink *Sprite* or *7UP* when they have an upset stomach.

The Advantage

I once had a student in the USA who was a businessman and often golfed with colleagues. They had an ongoing friendly competition. One particular day, he was determined to win, so he devised a simple plan. While all his colleagues ordered beer, he would order *cider*. "All my colleagues will be affected by the alcohol, but I will have an advantage since *cider* isn't alcoholic," he schemed proudly to himself. Believing he was ordering something akin to Sprite, he was surprised when he received a dark bottle with an apple on it and thought, "Wow, I guess *cider* in the U.S. is made with apples and served in a glass bottle! It must be much nicer here!" After several bottles, he noticed that his score wasn't much better than usual, and he was feeling a little tipsy. "It must be the heat outside today," he guessed. He had no idea that *cider* in the United States wasn't a Sprite-like drink and can sometimes have around 4-5% alcohol. Needless to say, he didn't have much of an advantage in golfing that day!

🔊 *kō-hī-fu-res-shu* — Coffee Fresh

コーヒーフレッシュ

Meaning in Japan:

Non-dairy coffee creamer cups

Example Japanglish Sentence:

コーヒーに<u>コーヒーフレシュ</u>いる?

Would you like some *<u>coffee fresh</u>* to put in your coffee?

Translated to English:

Would you like some *<u>creamer</u>* to put in your coffee?

🔊 *kō-hī-mi-ru-ku* — Coffee Milk

コーヒーミルク

Meaning in Japan:

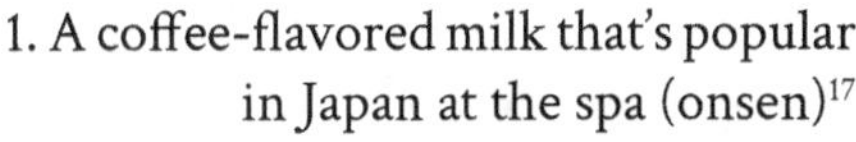

1. A coffee-flavored milk that's popular in Japan at the spa (onsen)[17]
2. Non-dairy coffee creamer cups

Example Japanglish Sentence:

スパや温泉で沢山の人が、<u>コーヒーミルク</u>を楽しんでいる。

Many people enjoy drinking *<u>coffee milk</u>* after a day at the onsen.

コーヒーに<u>コーヒーミルク</u>をいれる?

Would you like some *<u>coffee milk</u>* in your coffee?

Translated to English:

Many people enjoy *<u>Japanese coffee-flavored milk</u>* after a day at the spa.

Would you like some *<u>creamer</u>* in your coffee?

Cone

kōn

コーン

Meaning in Japan:

1. Corn
2. Ice cream cone

Example Japanglish Sentence:

日本では、ピザに<u>コーン</u>が乗っていることがある。

In Japan, sometimes it's common to find <u>*cone*</u> on pizza.

Translated to English:

In Japan, sometimes it's common to find <u>*corn*</u> on pizza.

Cream Pasta

ku-rī-mu-pa-su-ta

Meaning in Japan:

Alfredo pasta, Fettuccine Alfredo, or any pasta dish with a cream-based sauce

Example Japanglish Sentence:

あのレストランの<u>クリームパスタ</u>は、おいしい。

That restaurant has good <u>*cream pasta*</u>.

Translated to English:

That restaurant has good <u>*Alfredo pasta*</u>.

Cream Soda

ku-rī-mu-sō-da

クリームソーダ

Meaning in Japan:

An ice cream float that is made using green-colored, melon-flavored soda

Example Japanglish Sentence:

クリームソーダはおいしい。
緑の色とアイスクリームが大好き。

Cream soda is so good!
I love the green color and the ice cream!

Translated to English:

Melon soda ice cream float is so good!
I love the green color and the ice cream together!

Cup Ramen

kap-pu-rā-men

カップラーメン

Meaning in Japan:

Instant ramen, microwave ramen, cup noodles, instant noodles in a cup, pot noodles (UK). This typically refers to the simplest form of ramen where you simply add water to the container, not usually the kind cooked on the stove.

Example Japanglish Sentence:

旅行するときはいつもカップラーメンを持っていく。

We always bring some *cup ramen* when we travel.

Translated to English:

We always bring some *instant microwave ramen* when we travel.

Curry Rice

ka-rē-rai-su

カレーライス

Meaning in Japan:

Japanese-style curry eaten with rice. *Curry rice* differs from other curries in that it is typically sweeter, thicker, and less spicy than many other varieties of curry. The most typical ingredients are meat, onions, carrots, and potatoes.

Example Japanglish Sentence:

カレーライスに豆腐を入れるの?! それって伝統的じゃないよ!

You put tofu in your *curry rice*?! That is definitely not traditional!

Translated to English:

You put tofu in your *Japanese curry*?! That is definitely not traditional!

Curry Roux

ka-rē-rū

Meaning in Japan:

Japanese curry sauce mix used to make *curry rice* or Japanese curry, often sold in boxes or pouches

Example Japanglish Sentence:

カレーを作るのにカレーのルーを使う?それとも、一から作るの?

Do you use *curry roux* or make your *curry rice* from scratch?

Translated to English:

Do you use *(Japanese) curry mix* or make your Japanese curry from scratch?

do-rai-ka-rē

Dry Curry

ドライカレー

Meaning in Japan:

This type of Japanese curry, as you might guess from its name, has less liquid than curry rice. It is typically made with ground meat, and vegetables are often chopped into smaller pieces. *Dry curry* is served mixed with rice, with an end result somewhat similar to a pilaf.

Example Japanglish Sentence:

夫は、毎週火曜日ドライカレーを作ってくれる。

My husband cooks *dry curry* for us every Tuesday!

Translated to English:

My husband cooks *Japanese dry curry pilaf* for us every Tuesday!

e-ki-su

Ex

エキス

Meaning in Japan:

An herbal or exotic extract often used as a home remedy or for medical purposes

Example Japanglish Sentence:

このハーブエキスを身体に塗ると痒みが治まる。

Applying this herbal *ex* to the body will help stop the itching.

Translated to English:

Applying this *herbal extract* to the body will help stop the itching.

Fami Res

fa-mi-res

ファミレス

Meaning in Japan:

Fami res is an abbreviation of "family restaurant." This describes a type of casual, affordable family-friendly restaurant, similar to a fast casual restaurant. Many offer unlimited refills on their self-service drinks (which is not so common in Japan.) *Fami res* are popular for families, students, friend groups, or any other casual eating occasion but would be considered an unacceptable choice for a date or a business meeting.

Example Japanglish Sentence:

私の家族は、毎週土曜日に<u>ファミレス</u>に行く。

My family usually goes to <u>*fami res*</u> on Saturdays together.

Translated to English:

My family usually goes to <u>*casual dining restaurants*</u> on Saturdays.

Frankfurt

fu-ran-ku-fu-ru-to 

フランクフルト

Meaning in Japan:

Sausage on a stick

Example Japanglish Sentence:

晩ごはんに<u>フランクフルト</u>を食べよう。

Let's eat <u>*Frankfurt*</u> for dinner!

Translated to English:

Let's eat <u>*sausage*</u> (on a stick) for dinner!

Free Drink

fu-rī-do-rin-ku

フリードリンク

Meaning in Japan:

Drinks are free and included in the price of entrance to a restaurant or venue, or as part of a promotion

Example Japanglish Sentence:

あのカラオケは、フリードリンク制だ。

That karaoke has a *free drink* system.

Translated to English:

That karaoke place *includes free drinks in the price*.

Fried Potato

fu-rai-do-po-te-to

フライドポテト

Meaning in Japan:

French fries, Chips (UK)

Example Japanglish Sentence:

アメリカ人は、いつもハンバーガーと
フライドポテトを食べてるの？

Do Americans always eat *fried potatoes* with their burgers?

Translated to English:

Do Americans always eat *fries* with their burgers?

Fruit Punch

fu-rū-tsu-pon-chi

フルーツポンチ

Meaning in Japan:

1. Fruit punch フルーツポンチ *(furūtsuponchi)* is most similar to a fruit salad
2. Fruit punch フルーツパンチ *(furūtsupanchi)* is similar to the drink fruit punch

Example Japanglish Sentence:

デザートにフルーツポンチを食べるのが好きだ。

I love eating *fruit punch* for dessert!

Translated to English:

I love eating *fruit salad* for dessert!

Green Tea

gu-rīn-tī

グリーンティー

Meaning in Japan:

Only matcha green tea, often served iced and sweetened

Example Japanglish Sentence:

グリーンティーではなく、
煎茶を飲む方が好きだ。

I prefer to drink sencha, not *green tea*.

Translated to English:

I prefer to drink sencha, not *matcha tea*.

ha-mu-eg-gu — HAM EGG

ハムエッグ

Meaning in Japan:

Fried ham and eggs: fried ham wrapped around a fried egg, or fried ham with a fried egg on top

Example Japanglish Sentence:

アメリカ人は朝食にハムエッグを食べると思っていたので、友達に「食べたことがない」と言われて驚いた。

I thought Americans ate *ham egg* for breakfast, so I was really surprised when my friends told me they had never had it.

Translated to English:

I thought Americans ate *fried ham with fried eggs* for breakfast, so I was really surprised when my friends told me they had never had it.

han-bā-gu — HAMBURG

ハンバーグ

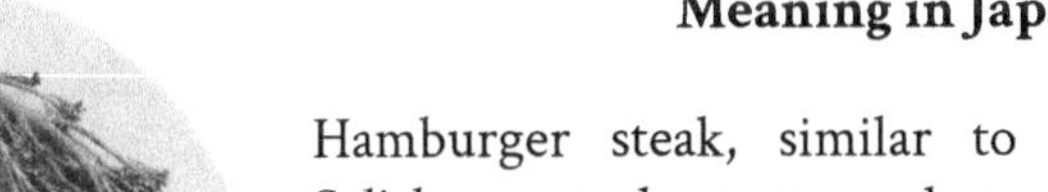

Meaning in Japan:

Hamburger steak, similar to a Salisbury steak: a ground meat hamburger patty made with onion, egg, breadcrumbs, often topped with cheese, egg, or sauce or gravy

Example Japanglish Sentence:

私のいとこはハワイに住んでいが、
そこでもハンバーグは人気があると言っていた！

My cousin lives in Hawaii and told me *hamburg* is popular there too!

Translated to English:

My cousin lives in Hawaii and told me *hamburger steak* is popular there!

Hash(ed) Potatoes

has-shu-do-po-te-to 

ハッシュドポテト

Meaning in Japan:

Hash browns

Example Japanglish Sentence:

ファストフード店で朝食にハッシュドポテトを食べるのが好きだ。

I love eating *hash potatoes* for breakfast at fast food restaurants!

Translated to English:

I love eating *hash browns* for breakfast at fast food restaurants!

Hot Tea

hot-to-tī 

ホットティー

Meaning in Japan:

Usually English black tea, not other various types of teas

Example Japanglish Sentence:

私は緑茶ではなく、ホットティーを飲むのが好きだ。

I prefer to drink *hot tea*, not *green tea.*

Translated to English:

I prefer to drink *hot black tea*, not matcha green tea.

HOTCAKE

ホットケーキ

hot-to-kē-ki

Meaning in Japan:

Pancake, American pancake (UK)

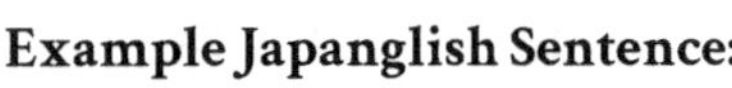

Example Japanglish Sentence:

日本のホットケーキは、アメリカのホットケーキよりもふわふわしていることが多い。

Hotcakes in Japan are usually fluffier and more airy than *hotcakes* in the USA.

Translated to English:

Pancakes in Japan are usually fluffier and more airy than *pancakes* in the USA.

ICE

アイス

a-i-su

Meaning in Japan:

Ice cream bar

Example Japanglish Sentence:

アイスとアイスキャンディー、どちらが好き?

Do you prefer *ice* or *ice candy?*

Translated to English:

Do you prefer *ice cream bars* or popsicles?

Ice Candy

アイスキャンディー

a-i-su-kyan-dī

Meaning in Japan:

Popsicle

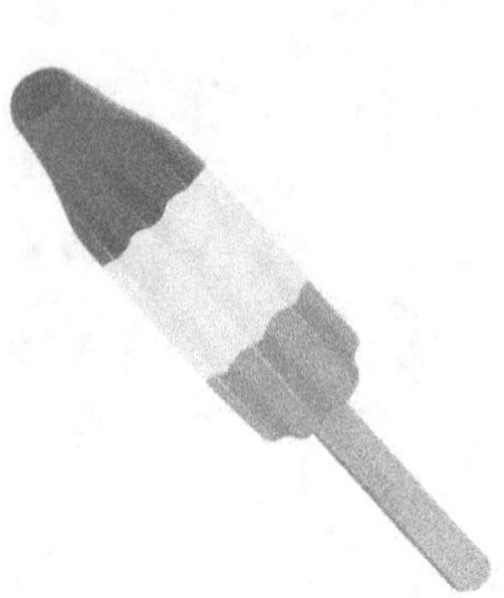

Example Japanglish Sentence:

アイスとアイスキャンディー、どちらが好き？

Do you prefer *ice* or *ice candy*?

Translated to English:

Do you prefer ice cream bars or *popsicles*?

Jelly / Jello

ゼリー・ジェロ

ze-rī / je-ro

Meaning in Japan:

Jello, gummies, jelly (UK), jelly sweets (UK)

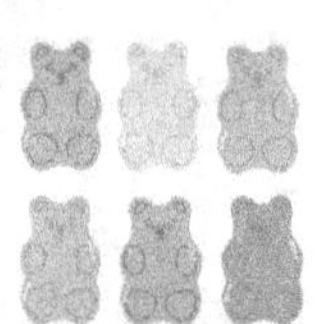

Example Japanglish Sentence:

子供たちはゼリーが大好きだ。

Kids love *jelly*.

私はゼリータイプのサプリを飲むのが好きだ。

I love taking *jelly* vitamins.

Translated to English:

Kids love *gummies/jello*.

I love taking *gummy* vitamins.

JOCKEY

jok-ki

ジョッキ

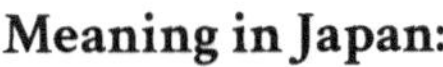

Meaning in Japan:

Beer mug

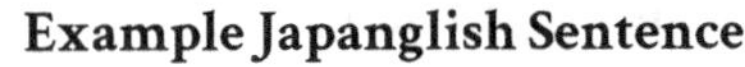

Example Japanglish Sentence:

私は<u>ジョッキ</u>でビールを飲むのが大好きだ。

Beer tastes the best in a *<u>jockey</u>*.

Translated to English:

Beer tastes the best in a *<u>beer mug</u>*.

KENTA

ken-ta

ケンタ

Meaning in Japan:

An abbreviation for KFC, Kentucky Fried Chicken, mainly used in the Tokyo area

Bon_man - stock.adobe.com

Example Japanglish Sentence:

日本人はクリスマスの時期、<u>ケンタ</u>が大好きだ！

Japanese people love *<u>Kenta</u>* at Christmas time.

Translated to English:

Japanese people love *<u>KFC</u>* at Christmas time.

KENTUCKY

ken-tak-kī

ケンタッキー

Meaning in Japan:

KFC, Kentucky Fried Chicken

LT - stock.adobe.com

Example Japanglish Sentence:

日本人はクリスマスの時期、
ケンタッキーが大好きだ！

Japanese people love *Kentucky* at Christmas time.

Translated to English:

Japanese people love *KFC* at Christmas time.

Christmas Chicken

Did you know that in Japan, people celebrate Christmas by eating KFC?! Every Christmas, millions of Japanese people pre-order the KFC Christmas dinner weeks in advance (or wait in line for hours hoping they haven't run out yet). The tradition started back in the 1970s when the manager of the first KFC in Japan overheard some American expats discussing how they missed eating turkey for Christmas. The savvy KFC manager, Takeshi Okawara, thought maybe chicken could be the next best thing, and captivated the nation with his Christmas fried chicken bucket and his creative slogan *Kentucky for Christmas* forever linking Christmas and KFC in the minds of the Japanese people! Although only about 1.1% of Japan identifies as Christian,[18] this tradition has taken root. Some locations even have Colonel Sanders dressed up as Santa Claus in December! Almost every Japanese student I've ever taught has mentioned ordering KFC for Christmas.[19, 20, 21]

🔊 *rō-ri-e*

Laurier

ローリエ

Meaning in Japan:

Bay leaf

Example Japanglish Sentence:

スープに風味をつけるために、
ローリエを2〜3枚入れてください。

Put two or three *laurier* to help season the soup.

Translated to English:

Put two or three *bay leaves* to help season the soup.

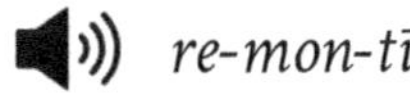

🔊 *re-mon-tī*

Lemon Tea

レモンティー

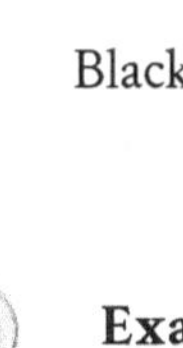

Meaning in Japan:

Black tea with lemon, not herbal lemon tea

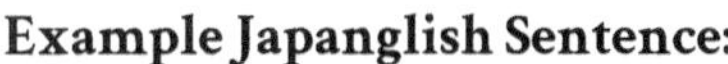

Example Japanglish Sentence:

レモンティーはおいしいし、
カフェイン効果も期待できる。

Lemon tea is great for your health and can also give you a good caffeine boost.

Translated to English:

Black tea with lemon is great for your health and can also give you a good caffeine boost.

Liver / Lever

re-bā

レバー

Meaning in Japan:

Liver only when eaten as food (e.g., chicken liver, beef liver)

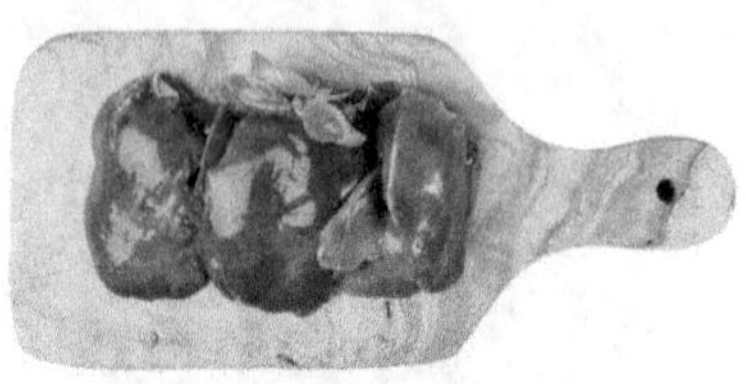

Example Japanglish Sentence:

「私の叔父は脂肪肝の病気を持っているので、
医者に鶏レバーや牛レバーを食べてはいけないと言われた。

My uncle has fatty *liver 肝 (kan)* disease, so his doctor told him he can't eat chicken *liver レバー (rebā)* and beef *liver レバー (rebā)* anymore.

Translated to English:

My uncle has fatty *liver* disease, so his doctor told him he can't eat chicken *liver* and beef *liver* anymore.

Mac / MacDo

mak-ku / ma-ku-do

Meaning in Japan:

Both are abbreviations of McDonald's. *Mac* is commonly used in the Tokyo area and Eastern part of Japan while *MacDo* is more common in the Western part of Japan.

Bon_man - stock.adobe.com

Example Japanglish Sentence:

日本のマック/マクドには、
てりやきバーガーがある。

Mac in Japan has a teriyaki burger.
MacDo in Japan has a teriyaki burger.

Translated to English:

McDonald's in Japan has a teriyaki burger.

ma-ka-ro-ni

Macaroni

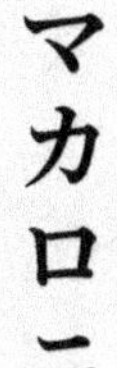

Meaning in Japan:

In some regions, *macaroni* can refer generally to any type of pasta

Example Japanglish Sentence:

晩御飯は、マカロニとミートボールだ。

We're having *macaroni* and meatballs for dinner.

Translated to English:

We're having *spaghetti* and meatballs for dinner.

mi-ru-ku-tī

Milk Tea

ミルクティー

Meaning in Japan:

Only black tea with milk, not other types of milk tea

Example Japanglish Sentence:

彼女はミルクティーではなく、ミルク入りのグリーンティーを欲しがっている。

She wants green tea with milk, not *milk tea*.

Translated to English:

She wants green milk tea, not *black milk tea*.

Minchi

min-chi

ミンチ

Meaning in Japan:

Ground meat, minced meat (UK)

Example Japanglish Sentence:

そのレシピでは、ミンチを2ポンド使う。

The recipe calls for two pounds of *minchi*.

Translated to English:

The recipe calls for two pounds of *ground beef*.

Morning

mō-nin-gu

モーニング

Meaning in Japan:

Breakfast served in a cafe and sometimes called *morning set*

Example Japanglish Sentence:

そのカフェには、モーニングセットがある。

The cafe near my house has a really good *morning* set.

Translated to English:

The cafe near my house serves a really good *breakfast*.

ma-gu-kap-pu

Mug Cup

マグカップ

Meaning in Japan:

Coffee mug

Example Japanglish Sentence:

あのカフェには、
本当に素敵なマグカップがある。

My wife and I enjoy collecting cool *mug cups* from the different places we travel.

Translated to English:

My wife and I enjoy collecting cool *coffee mugs* from the different places we travel.

mas-shu-rū-mu

Mushroom

マッシュルーム

Meaning in Japan:

Mushroom only refers to white button or cremini mushrooms. It is not used generally to refer to all types of mushrooms and fungi.

Example Japanglish Sentence:

「好きなキノコの種類は何？」「私はホワイトマッシュルーム、シイタケ、エリンギ、それとエノキが特に好き」。

What is your favorite type of *mushroom キノコ(kinoko)*? I especially like *mushrooms マッシュルーム (masshurūmu)*, *shiitake mushrooms シイタケ(shītake)*, *king oyster mushrooms エリンギ (eringire)*, and *enoki mushrooms エノキ(enoki)*.

Translated to English:

What is your favorite type of *mushroom*? I especially like *white mushrooms*, *shiitake mushrooms*, *king oyster mushrooms*, and *enoki mushrooms*.

Open Sand

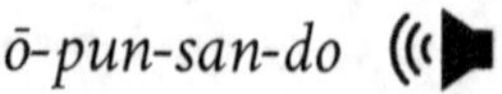

ō-pun-san-do

オープンサンド

Meaning in Japan:

Open-face sandwich served only with a bottom slice of bread

Example Japanglish Sentence:

新しいカフェのオープンサンドはとてもおいしい。

The new cafe has really good *open sands*.

Translated to English:

The new cafe has really good *open face sandwiches*.

Pan

pan

パン

Meaning in Japan:

Bread

Example Japanglish Sentence:

日本のカフェは、美味しいパンが多い。
私はメロンパンが一番好き!

Cafes in Japan have really good *pans*. Melon *pan* is my favorite!

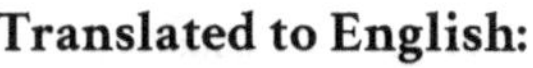

Translated to English:

Cafes in Japan have really good *bread and pastries*.
Melon *bread* is my favorite!

PINE JUICE

パインジュース

pa-in-jū-su

Meaning in Japan:

Pineapple juice, Pineapple soda

Example Japanglish Sentence:

夏は、パインジュースが大好きだ。

I love *pine juice* in the summer!

Translated to English:

I love *pineapple juice* in the summer!

POOCHI TOMATO

プチトマト

pu-chi-to-ma-to

Meaning in Japan:

Cherry tomato

Example Japanglish Sentence:

サラダにプチトマトをいれるつもり。

I'm going to add some *poochi tomatoes* to the salad.

Translated to English:

I'm going to add some *cherry tomatoes* to the salad.

Potato Fries

po-te-to-fu-rai

ポテトフライ

Meaning in Japan:

French fries, Chips (UK)
Depending on the generation,
fried potato may be more common

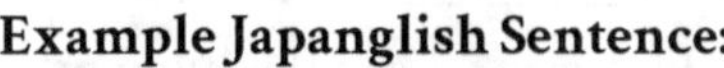

Example Japanglish Sentence:

アメリカ人は、いつもハンバーガーと
<u>ポテトフライ</u>を食べてるの？

Do Americans always eat <u>*potato fries*</u> with their burgers?

Translated to English:

Do Americans always eat <u>*French fries*</u> with their burgers?

Range Food

ren-ji-fū-do

レンジフード

Meaning in Japan:

Microwave meals

Example Japanglish Sentence:

息子たちには料理の仕方を教えた。ファストフードや<u>レンジフード（電子レンジ用食品）</u>ばかりに頼ったり、将来奥さんに全部まかせたりしてほしくないからだ。

I taught my sons how to cook because I don't want them relying on fast food or <u>*range food*</u> or expecting their wives to do all the cooking.

Translated to English:

I taught my sons how to cook because I don't want them relying on fast food or <u>*microwave meals*</u> or expecting their wives to do all the cooking.

🔊 *re-to-ru-to* — RETORTE

Meaning in Japan:

Pre-made food, sealed in a sterile package, pouch, or container, that needs to be heated to eat.

Example Japanglish Sentence:

おいしいレトルトカレーが見つかるよ。

You can find some delicious *retorte* curry roux.

Translated to English:

You can find some delicious *pouches* of curry mix.

🔊 *roi-ya-ru-mi-ru-ku-tī* — ROYAL MILK TEA

ロイヤルミルクティー

Meaning in Japan:

This is a Japanese variety of black milk tea typically made with at least 50% milk. Rather than simply adding a splash of milk into a brewed tea, royal milk tea requires simmering the hot water, milk, and tea together to create this special drink. It's somewhat comparable to an Indian masala chai with more milk and none of the additional spices.[22]

Example Japanglish Sentence:

アメリカではなかなか見つからないから、ロイヤルミルクティーの作り方を学びたい。

I want to learn how to make *royal milk tea* since it's really difficult to find in the USA.

Translated to English:

I want to learn how to make *Japanese royal milk tea* since it's really difficult to find in the USA.

Sand(o)

san-do

Meaning in Japan:

This is an abbreviation of "sandwich" and is typically used as part of the name of any specialty sandwich (e.g., egg sand, tofu sand, fruit sand, cream sand)

Example Japanglish Sentence:

ビーチでは美味しい卵サンドが売られている。

At the beach, they sell good egg sand.

Translated to English:

At the beach, they sell good egg *sandwiches*.

Shoe Cream

shū-ku-rī-mu

シュークリーム

Meaning in Japan:

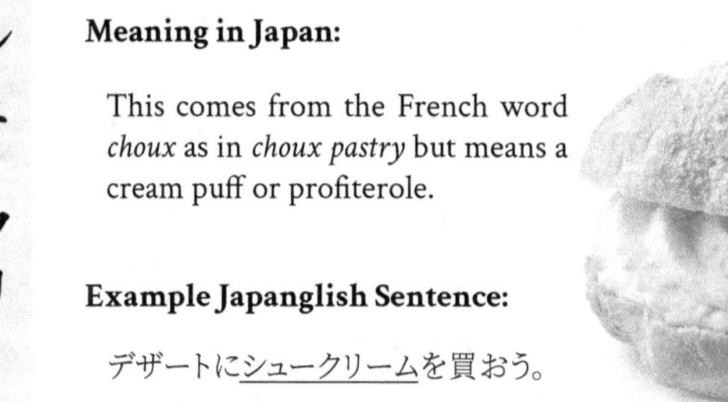

This comes from the French word *choux* as in *choux pastry* but means a cream puff or profiterole.

Example Japanglish Sentence:

デザートにシュークリームを買おう。

Let's get some *shoe cream* for dessert.

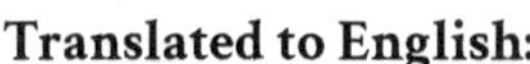

Translated to English:

Let's get some *cream puffs* for dessert.

su-nak-ku

Snack

スナック

Meaning in Japan:

This describes a small, cozy bar that serves drinks, opens only in the evening, and likely offers only a few salty appetizers or bar snacks. A *snack* typically offers karaoke and a fun local, conversational atmosphere.[23]

Example Japanglish Sentence:

このあたりに食べるところはないけれど、角にスナックがひとつだけあるよ。

There are no food places around here, only a *snack* on the corner.

Translated to English:

There are no food places around here, only *a local bar* on the corner *with some salty appetizers*.

so-fu-to-ku-rī-mu

Soft Cream

ソフトクリーム

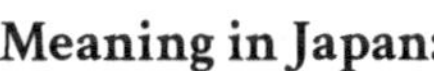

Meaning in Japan:

Soft serve ice cream

Example Japanglish Sentence:

ソフトクリームとアイス、どっちが好き？

Do you prefer *soft cream* or *ice*?

Translated to English:

Do you prefer *soft serve ice cream* or ice cream bars?

Soup Pasta

sū-pu-pa-su-ta

スープパスタ

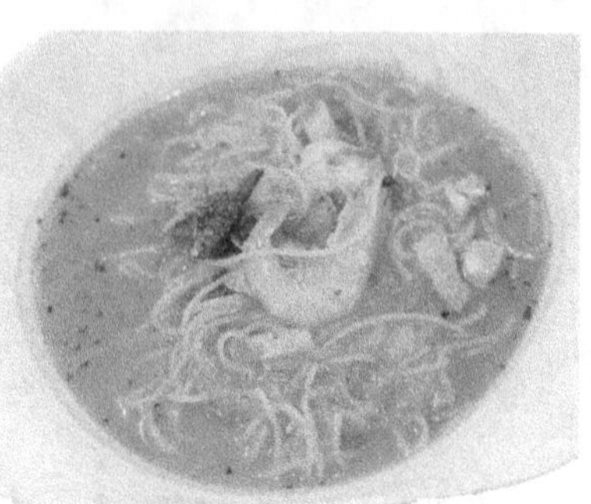

Meaning in Japan:

Pasta served with a soupy base

Example Japanglish Sentence:

私はスープパスタが大好きだけど、子どもたちはマカロニのほうが好きみたい。

I love *soup pasta*, but my kids prefer *macaroni.*

Translated to English:

I love *pasta with a soupy base*, but my kids prefer spaghetti.

Starbu

su-ta-ba

Meaning in Japan:

An abbreviation of "Starbucks"

Example Japanglish Sentence:

日本のスタバには、すごく美味しい抹茶ラテがある。

Starbu in Japan has a really delicious matcha latte.

Bon_man - stock.adobe.com

Translated to English:

Starbucks in Japan has a really good matcha latte.

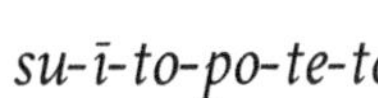

su-ī-to-po-te-to

Sweet Potato

スイートポテト

Meaning in Japan:

Sweet potato only refers to a specific dessert made mainly from sweet potatoes and is not used for the vegetable sweet potato *(satsuma imo)*.

Example Japanglish Sentence:

私の好きなデザートはスイートポテト。さつまいもから作られている。

My favorite dessert is sweet potato; it's made from *(satsumi imo)*.

Translated to English:

My favorite dessert is *Japanese sweet potato pastry*; it's made from sweet potatoes.

tī

Tea

ティー

Meaning in Japan:

Only hot English black tea

Example Japanglish Sentence:

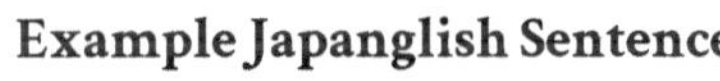

グリーンティーではなく、

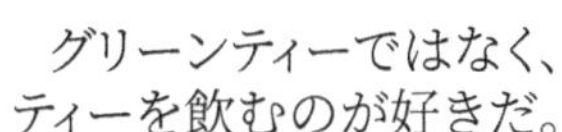

ティーを飲むのが好きだ。

I prefer to drink tea, not *green tea*.

Translated to English:

I prefer to drink *black tea*, not matcha.

Viking

bai-kin-gu

バイキング

Meaning in Japan:

Buffet

Example Japanglish Sentence:

結婚式の食事はバイキング
形式だった。

We had a *viking* at our wedding.

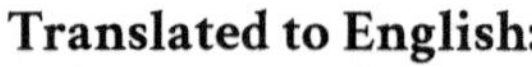

Translated to English:

We had a *buffet* at our wedding.

Whiskey Bonbon

wi-su-kī-bon-bon 

ウイスキーボンボン

Meaning in Japan:

Liquor-filled chocolates

Example Japanglish Sentence:

ウイスキーボンボンって、
子どもが食べても大丈夫かな？

Are these *whiskey bonbons* okay for children to eat?

Translated to English:

Are these *whiskey-filled chocolates* okay for children to eat?

Games, Toys, Hobbies

9

ゲーム おもちゃ・趣味

Ama

a-ma 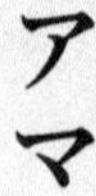

アマ

Meaning in Japan:

Amateur, non-professional

Example Japanglish Sentence:

私の息子は、バンドをしてるけど、アマなんだ。

My son is in a band, but it's just *ama*.

Translated to English:

My son is in a band, but it's *just a hobby*. They're *not professionals*.

Cosplay

ko-su-pu-re

コスプレ

Meaning in Japan:

Dressing up in costumes of any kind, including kids dressing up on Halloween. *Cosplay* is used very generally in Japan and is not directly associated with any role-playing subculture or comic conventions that a Westerner might assume.

Example Japanglish Sentence:

ハロウィンに、職場でコスプレをする。

We're going to do *cosplay* for Halloween at our office.

Translated to English:

We're going to *dress up* / *wear costumes* for Halloween at our office.

fa-mi-kon　**Fami Com**

ファミコン

Meaning in Japan:

This is an abbreviation of the term "family computer" but means a video game console, particularly a retro model

Example Japanglish Sentence:

ファミコンは持っていないけど、
いとこの家でN64の古いゲームで遊ぶのが大好きなんだ。

We don't have *fami com*, but we love playing old games at my cousins' house on their N64.

Translated to English:

We don't have a *video game console*, but we love playing old games at my cousins' house on their N64.

gē-sen　**Ga Cen**

ゲーセン

Meaning in Japan:

This is an abbreviation of "game center" and means a gaming arcade or video arcade

Example Japanglish Sentence:

10代の頃、私は放課後ほぼ毎日、
友達とゲーセンに行っていた。

When I was a teenager,
I went to the *ga cen* almost every day after school with my friends.

Translated to English:

When I was a teenager,
I went to the *arcade* almost every day after school with my friends.

GAME CENTER

gē-mu-sen-tā

ゲームセンター

Meaning in Japan:

A gaming arcade or video arcade

Example Japanglish Sentence:

10代の頃、私は放課後ほぼ毎日、
友達とゲームセンターに行っていた。

When I was a teenager,
I went to the *game center* almost every day after school with my friends.

Translated to English:

When I was a teenager,
I went to the *arcade* almost every day after school with my friends.

GAME SOFT

gē-mu-so-fu-to

ゲームソフト

Meaning in Japan:

The physical video game that needs to be placed into the *fami com* or video game console in order to play

Example Japanglish Sentence:

好きなゲームソフトは何？
私は、『Lauren's Kingdom of Ruins』.

What's your favorite *game soft*? Mine is *Lauren's Kingdom of Ruins.*

Translated to English:

What's your favorite *video game*? Mine is *Lauren's Kingdom of Ruins.*

mo-de-ru-gan — Model Gun

モデルガン

Meaning in Japan:

A cap gun or toy gun that is modeled after a real gun but is incapable of firing real bullets

Example Japanglish Sentence:

モデルガンで遊ぶことを許さない親もいるが、気にしない親もいる。

Some parents don't allow their children to play with *model guns*, but others have no issues with them.

Translated to English:

Some parents don't allow their children to play with *cap guns*, but others have no issues with them.

nan-pu-re — Num Play

ナンプレ

2			3		6			
6		5	9			4		8
						5		2
4		9		6	3			
			8			7		1
		1		4			9	
1		6	2	7				
	2					8		4
		4		1	8			7

Meaning in Japan:

Sudoku

Example Japanglish Sentence:

新聞のアプリで、
毎朝ナンプレやってるんだ。

I do the *num play* every morning in the newspaper *appli.*

Translated to English:

I do the *Sudoku* every morning in the newspaper app.

Pla Mo

pu-ra-mo

プラモ

Meaning in Japan:

This is an abbreviation of "plastic model" and refers to model kits of figures like airplanes, vehicles, and action figures, often put together and collected by hobbyists.

Example Japanglish Sentence:

彼は飛行機のプラモやアクションフィギュアを集めていて、
それらが50個以上並ぶ専用の部屋もあるんだ！

He collects *pla mo* of airplanes and actions figures
and has a room with over 50 of them!

Translated to English:

He collects *plastic airplane models and action figures*
and has a room with over 50 of them!

Pla Rail

pu-ra-rē-ru

プラレール

Meaning in Japan:

This is an abbreviation of "plastic rail" and means toy trains and railway tracks, usually made of plastic.

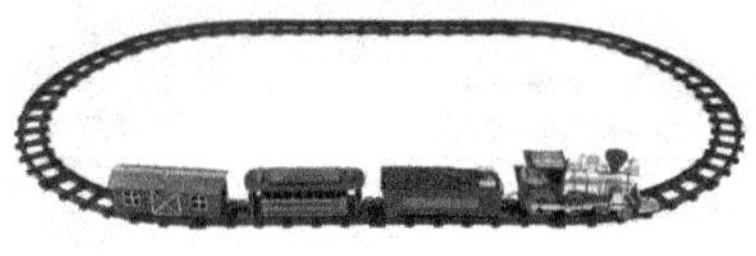

Example Japanglish Sentence:

私の叔父はプラレールを集めていて、
子どもの頃いとこと一緒によく遊んだ。

My uncle collects *pla rail*,
and we loved playing with them as kids with my cousins.

Translated to English:

My uncle collects *toy train sets*,
and we loved playing with them as kids with my cousins.

pu-ri-ku-ra

Prin Clu

プリクラ

Meaning in Japan:

This is an abbreviation of "print club" and means an automated, digital photo booth with a touch screen that allows quick editing before printing the photos out as stickers.

Example Japanglish Sentence:

東京のいくつかの駅には、
プリクラがあって、すごく楽しい!

In Tokyo, some of the train stations have *prin clu*. So fun!

Translated to English:

In Tokyo, some of the train stations have *photo booths that print out stickers*! So fun!

pu-rai-bē-to-tai-mu

Private Time

プライベートタイム

Meaning in Japan:

Free time, leisure time

Example Japanglish Sentence:

プライベートタイムに、バスケットボールをするのが大好きだ。

In my *private time*, I love to play basketball.

Translated to English:

In my *free time*, I love to play basketball.

Puzzle

pa-zu-ru

パズル

Meaning in Japan:

Only a jigsaw puzzle, not other types of puzzles

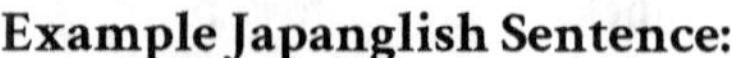

Example Japanglish Sentence:

ジグソーパズルは好きなんだけど、
それ以外のパズルは苦手なんだよね。

I like *jig-saw puzzles ジグソーパズル (jigusōpasuru)* but not other types of *puzzles パズル (pazuru)*.

Translated to English:

I like jig-saw *puzzles* but not other types of *puzzles*.

Seal

shī-ru

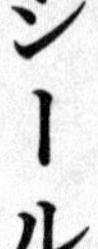

Meaning in Japan:

Sticker or decal

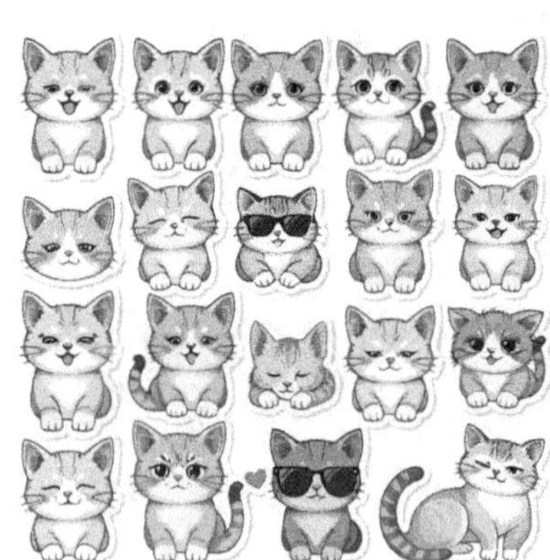

Example Japanglish Sentence:

私の甥と姪は、
シールで遊ぶのが好きだ。

My niece and nephew love to play with *seals*.

Translated to English:

My niece and nephew love to play with *stickers*.

TELEBI GAME

te-re-bi-gē-mu

テレビゲーム

Meaning in Japan:

Video game

Example Japanglish Sentence:

妹は彼氏と別れたんだ。彼がテレビゲームばっかりやってたから。

My sister broke up with her boyfriend because all he wanted to do was play *telebi games* all day.

Translated to English:

My sister broke up with her boyfriend because all he wanted to do was play *video games* all day.

WAPPEN

wap-pen

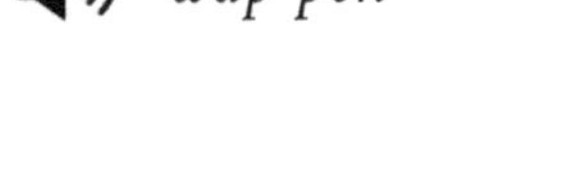

ワッペン

Meaning in Japan:

Iron-on patch

Example Japanglish Sentence:

旅行に行った所のワッペンを集めるのが好きだ。

I love collecting *wappens* from the places where I travel.

Translated to English:

I love collecting *iron-on patches* from the places where I travel.

Health & Body

健康·身体

10

Bodyline

bo-dī-ra-in 

ボディーライン

Meaning in Japan:

The shape of your body,
your figure

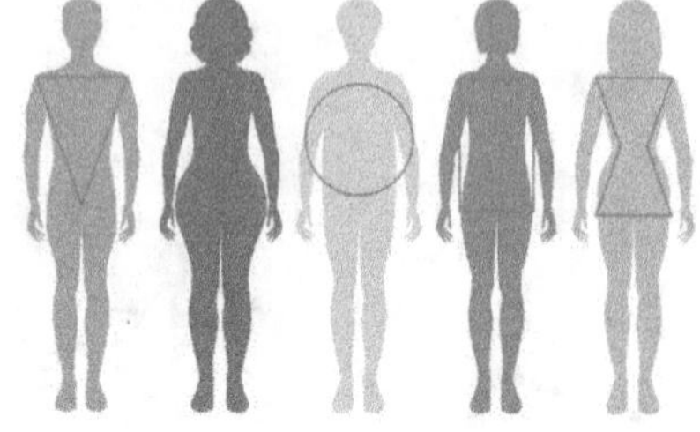

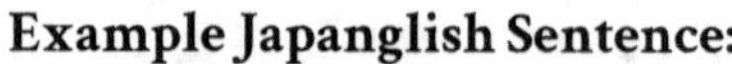

Example Japanglish Sentence:

「彼女はきれいなボディーラインをしている。」「ボディーラインを引き締めるために運動が必要だ。」

She has a good <u>*bodyline*</u>. I need to exercise to improve my <u>*bodyline*</u>.

Translated to English:

She has a good <u>*figure*</u>. I need to exercise to improve my <u>*figure*</u>.

Diet

dai-et-to

ダイエット

Meaning in Japan:

This refers to the whole process of losing weight, including diet and exercise. *Diet* it not used to mean the kind of food one usually eats.

Example Japanglish Sentence:

ダイエット中なので、ジムに行くよ。

I'm going to the gym because I'm on a <u>*diet*</u>.

Translated to English:

I'm going to the gym because I'm <u>*trying to lose weight*</u>.
I'm trying to get in shape.

do-ku-tā-su-top-pu Doctor Stop

ドクターストップ

Meaning in Japan:

An order or instructions from a doctor to stop doing something or to avoid a specific food or activity

Example Japanglish Sentence:

私は糖分についてドクターストップがかかっている。

I have a *doctor stop* about sugar.

今、ちょうどスポーツ/運動は、ドクターストップがかかっている。

Sports is a *doctor stop* for me right now.

Translated to English:

My doctor told me to cut sugar out of my diet.

My doctor told me I shouldn't do any strenuous activity right now.

hip-pu Hip

ヒップ

Meaning in Japan:

Hips and buttocks

Example Japanglish Sentence:

彼女のヒップは大きい。

She has a big *hip*.

Translated to English:

She has a big *butt/behind/bottom*.

Home Doctor

hō-mu-do-ku-tā 

ホームドクター

Meaning in Japan:

General practitioner, family medicine doctor, primary care physician

Example Japanglish Sentence:

子どもが体調を壊していると思うなら、
ホームドクター（かかりつけの医者）に診てもらったほうがいい。

You should take your kids to the *home doctor* if you think they are getting sick.

Translated to English:

You should take your kids to the *family medicine doctor* if you think they're getting sick.

Human Dock

nin-gen-dok-ku 

人間ドック

Meaning in Japan:

A very thorough annual medical checkup

Example Japanglish Sentence:

私は毎年夏に日本へ帰ったときに人間ドックを受ける。
アメリカよりもずっと安いので。

I always get my *human dock* when I go to Japan in the summer because it's so much cheaper than in the U.S.

Translated to English:

I always get my *annual checkup* when I go back to Japan in the summer because it's so much cheaper than in the U.S.

KARTE

ka-ru-te

カルテ

Meaning in Japan:

Medical records

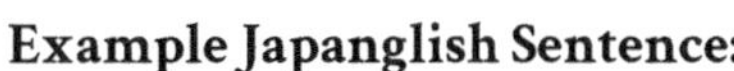

Example Japanglish Sentence:

新しい先生のところに持っていくために、カルテのコピーをもらえますか?

Can I get a copy of my *karte* to bring to my new doctor?

Translated to English:

Can I get a copy of my *medical records* to bring to my new doctor?

PILL

pi-ru

ピル

Meaning in Japan:

Pill only refers to birth control pills, not pills generally

Example Japanglish Sentence:

うちのおばあちゃん、1日に10錠も薬を飲まなきゃいけないの!更年期を過ぎてるから、唯一飲んでいない薬はピルくらいかな。

My grandma has to take 10 *pills 錠剤 (jōzai)* a day! Basically the only *pill 薬 (kusuri)* she doesn't take is *birth control ピル (piru)* since she's post-menopausal.

Translated to English:

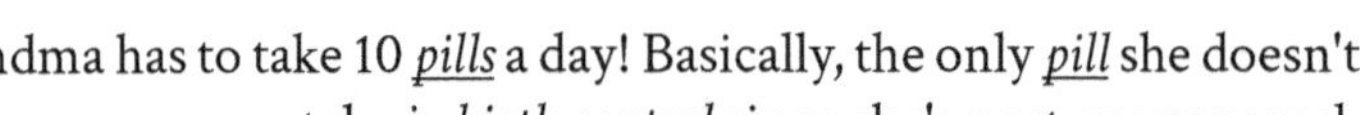

My grandma has to take 10 *pills* a day! Basically, the only *pill* she doesn't take is *birth control* since she's post-menopausal.

Proportion

pu-ro-pō-shon

プロポーション

Meaning in Japan:

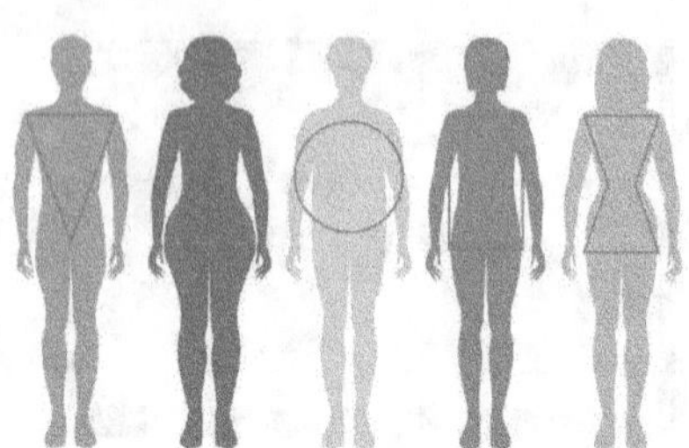

Proportion is a complex word attempting to describe the balance of one's physical features, especially of the bust, waist, and hips in relation to each other. One website classifies body type *proportions* into four main types or categories: V, X, I, and A.[24, 25] Here is a brief explanation of each along with its Western equivalent:

V - Bust dominant (inverted triangle)

I - Straighter body (rectangle)

X - Larger bust and hips with smaller middle (hourglass)

A - Hip dominant (pear/triangle)

Similarly, there are many websites and services offering to help people find their ideal *proportion* to look their best.

Example Japanglish Sentence:

日本では、自分にとって理想のプロポーション探しをサポートしてくれるサービスが数多く存在する。

In Japan, you can find many services that offer to help you find your ideal *proportion*.

Translated to English:

In Japan, you can find many services that offer to help you find your *ideal body shape*.

re-ha-bi-ri

Rehabili

リハビリ

Meaning in Japan:

Rehab, PT, Physical therapy, Occupational therapy

Example Japanglish Sentence:

彼はケガのあと、長期間にわたってリハビリに取り組まなければならなかった。

He had to do a lot of *rehabili* after the injury.

Translated to English:

He had to do a lot of *rehab/physical therapy* after the injury.

ri-bā-su

Reverse

Meaning in Japan:

To vomit or throw up

Example Japanglish Sentence:

「昨日は、飲み過ぎてリバースしたわ。」

I drank way too much last night and did *reverse* a lot.

Translated to English:

I drank way too much last night and *threw up* a lot.

Style

su-tai-ru

スタイル

Meaning in Japan:

Style is similar to *bodyline* and *proportion* but takes more of the body into account, not just the middle-most portion. Many services advertise that they can help you discover your "skeletal diagnosis" or "body style" in order to figure out what clothing style looks best on you or in order to improve your overall figure. It refers to your body structure, your bone structure, your figure, and overall body look based on both static biological and bone structural factors such as height as well as dynamic factors such as percentage of muscle versus fat. Most websites list three main body *styles*: straight, wave, and natural.[26, 27, 28, 29] Here are a few characteristics of each:

Straight - Often toned and muscular, sharper body lines, ability to build muscle quickly, shorter neck, higher chest and waist, slender knees, thin legs below the knees, firm skin

Wave - Thin bones, delicate and curvy body line, longer neck with a bony clavicle, lower bust and waist, a tendency to gain fat rather than muscle, thicker legs below the knees, soft fluffy skin

Natural - Long limbs, a strong bone structure with straighter lines, well balanced center of gravity, higher waist, larger limbs and knees, dry skin

If someone is said to have "good style," it usually means they have a good well-balanced figure. They are likely thin with good posture and a slightly toned, but not muscular, build.[30]

Example Japanglish Sentence:

自分のスタイルを理解すると、自分に合うファッションがわかってくるよ。

If you understand your *style*, then you can learn what kind of fashion looks best on your body.

Translated to English:

If you understand your *body shape*/*figure*/*type*, then you can learn what kind of fashion looks best on your body.

HOUSES, HOMES, & LIVING

家・住まい・生活

11

Air Con

e-a-kon

エアコン

Meaning in Japan:

Air conditioner and heater

Example Japanglish Sentence:

とても寒いから、エアコンつけてもいいかな。

It's so cold in here; can we turn on the *air con*?

Translated to English:

It's so cold in here; can we turn on the *heater*?

Apart

a-pā-to

Meaning in Japan:

Apart is an abbreviation of "apartment;" however, *apart* describes an affordable type of older, wooden, two-story apartment building with stairs outside. *Aparts* are considered affordable options for students, young people, and those who live alone.[31]

Example Japanglish Sentence:

私のアパートは、とても古い。

My *apart* is really old.

Translated to English:

My *apartment* is really old but affordable. It's not very big or fancy.

Apartment with Service

サービスアパートメント

sā-bi-su-a-pā-to-men-to

Meaning in Japan:

Apartment hotel, extended-stay hotel, or serviced apartment. In Japan this type of apartment usually targets affluent people looking for a long-term stay in a desirable area without the commitment of a traditional lease. These serviced apartments are typically furnished and provide hotel-like services like housekeeping that would not be included in the cost of a typical apartment.

Example Japanglish Sentence:

私たちはサービスアパートメントを探したい。

We want to find an *apartment with service*.

Translated to English:

We want to find a *luxury furnished apartment that provides special amenities like housekeeping*.

Bed Cover

ベッドカバー

bed-do-ka-bā

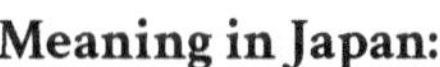

Meaning in Japan:

Bedspread, Comforter

Example Japanglish Sentence:

あの店は、本当に素敵なベッドカバーを売っている。

That store sells really nice *bed covers*.

Translated to English:

That store sells really nice *comforters*.

Bed Town

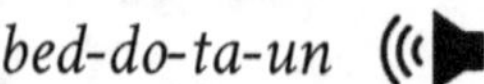

bed-do-ta-un

ベッドタウン

Meaning in Japan:

Commuter town, Bedroom community, Dormitory town (UK)

Example Japanglish Sentence:

東京の近くにたくさん<u>ベッドタウン</u>があるの?

Are there many <u>*bed towns*</u> near Tokyo?

Translated to English:

Are there many <u>*commuter towns*</u> near Tokyo?

Consent

kon-sen-to 

コンセント

Meaning in Japan:

Electrical outlet, Socket

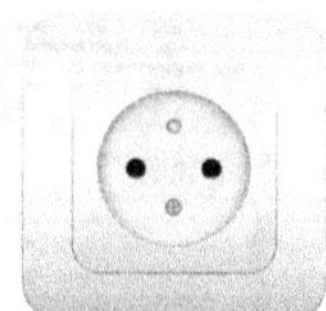

Example Japanglish Sentence:

この部屋の<u>コンセント</u>はどこ?
携帯の充電がしたいんだ。

Where is the <u>*consent*</u> in this room?
I need to charge my phone.

Translated to English:

Where is the <u>*outlet*</u> in this room?
I need to charge my phone.

kū-rā

Cooler

クーラー

Meaning in Japan:

Air conditioner

Example Japanglish Sentence:

今日は、とっても暑いね。アパートには、クーラーがついてるの?

It's so hot today! Do you have a *cooler* in your apart?

Translated to English:

It's so hot today! Do you have an *air conditioner* in your apartment?

fu-rō-rin-gu

Flooring

フローリング

Meaning in Japan:

Only hardwood flooring

Example Japanglish Sentence:

私の家には、フローリングがない。

I don't have any *flooring* in my house.

Translated to English:

I don't have any *wood flooring* / *hardwood floors* in my house.

IH

ai-ei-chi

アイエイチ

Meaning in Japan:

Induction cooktop

Example Japanglish Sentence:

家を出る前にIHコンロの
電源を消してください。

Please switch off the *IH*
before you go out.

Translated to English:

Please turn off the *stove* / *induction cooktop* before leaving the house.

INTERPHONE

in-tā-hon 

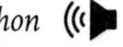

インターホン

Meaning in Japan:

The intercom box usually at the entrance of an apartment or building that guests use to call up so the resident can buzz them in when they arrive

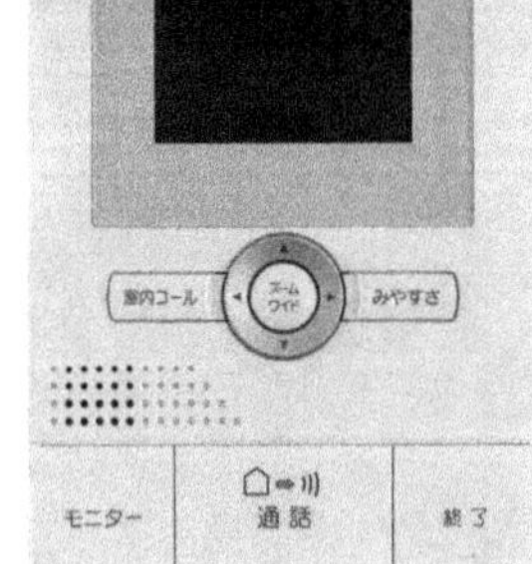

Example Japanglish Sentence:

到着したらインターホンで呼んでね。

Call me on the *interphone* when
you arrive.

Translated to English:

Call me on the *intercom* when you arrive.
Call me when you arrive, and I'll buzz you up.

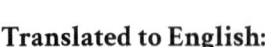

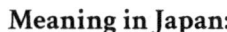

man-shon

MANSION

マンション

Meaning in Japan:

A *mansion* is an apartment in any building taller than three stories high. Many are in high-rise buildings and tend to be newer, nicer, and more expensive than other apartment types like *apart.*[32]

Example Japanglish Sentence:

5年間小さなDKに住んだ後、ついにマンションに引っ越しした。

After living in a *DK apart* for five years, we finally moved to a *mansion*.

Translated to English:

After living in a small studio apartment for five years, we finally moved to a *nice apartment*.

man-su-rī-man-shon

MONTHLY MANSION

マンスリーマンション

Meaning in Japan:

A furnished apartment rented by the month

Example Japanglish Sentence:

私の家族は、新しい街で自分たちの家を購入できるまで、マンスリーマンションに滞在する予定だ。

My family plans to stay in a *monthly mansion* in the new city until we can find our own place to buy.

Translated to English:

My family plans to rent *a furnished apartment on a monthly basis* in the new city until we can find our own place to buy.

My Home

マイホーム

mai-hō-mu

Meaning in Japan:

An owned or mortgaged house that belongs to you and is in your name; this does not refer to a home rented from another owner

Example Japanglish Sentence:

お家、綺麗ですね！ありがとう。マイホームなんだ。

- Wow, your house is beautiful!
- Thanks! It's *my home*!

Translated to English:

- Wow, your house is so beautiful!
- Thanks! *We bought it* last year!

One Room Mansion

ワンルームマンション

wan-rū-mu-man-shon 

Meaning in Japan:

A studio apartment in a *mansion* or building at least three stories high

Example Japanglish Sentence:

先週、ワンルームマンションに引っ越したんだ。
まだ狭いけど、前のアパートよりずっといいよ。

Last week we moved into a *one room mansion*.
It's still small, but it's much better than our old *apart*.

Translated to English:

Last week we moved into a *studio apartment in a nice building*.
It's still small, but it's much better than our old apartment.

ō-bun-ren-ji — **Oven Range**

オーブンレンジ

Meaning in Japan:

Microwave oven combo, like a convection microwave or a microwave that also has some features of a traditional convection oven like grilling and baking

Example Japanglish Sentence:

大抵のキッチンにはオーブンレンジしかなくて、ちゃんとしたオーブンはないんだよね。

Most kitchens in Japan only have an oven range, not an oven.

Translated to English:

Most kitchens in Japan only have a *convection microwave,* not an oven.

(den-shi) ren-ji — **(Denshi) Range**

（電子）レンジ

Meaning in Japan:

Microwave

Example Japanglish Sentence:

コンロとオーブンの両方が壊れてしまったので、最近は電子レンジを使っている。

My stove and oven are both broken,
so we have been using the *range* for everything.

Translated to English:

My stove and oven are both broken,
so we have been using the *microwave* for everything.

Reform

リフォーム

ri-fō-mu

Meaning in Japan:

To renovate, redecorate, remodel, or rearrange a room or building. This is typically not as extensive as a whole-home renovation, but would include changing and updating small details such as replacing old wallpaper, redoing the kitchen, replacing some outdated appliances or furniture with new, etc.

Example Japanglish Sentence:

彼らは、キッチンをリフォームしたばかりで、すごく素敵になってるね。

They just did *reform* in their kitchen, and it looks amazing!

Translated to English:

They just *remodeled* their kitchen, and it looks amazing!

Semi Double

セミダブル

se-mi-da-bu-ru 

Meaning in Japan:

A bed size in Japan that is bigger than a twin but smaller than a double bed. A *semi double* is often recommended for single sleepers who would like more space than a twin bed.[33]

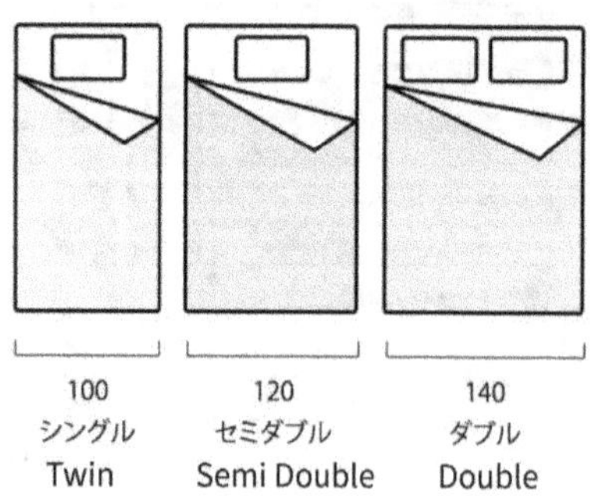

Example Japanglish Sentence:

ツインよりもセミダブルの方が少し広くて好きだ。

I prefer a *semi double* to a twin since it's a little more spacious.

Translated to English:

I prefer a *Japanese semi double, a bed that's bigger than a twin but smaller than a double*, since it's a little more spacious than a twin.

Stove

su-tō-bu

ストーブ

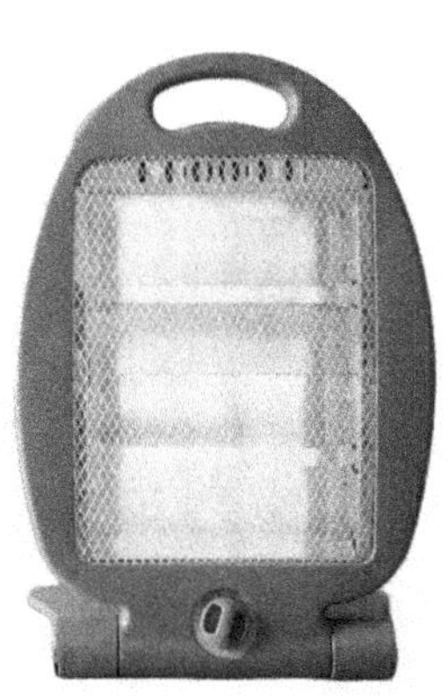

Meaning in Japan:

Space heater, portable heater, electric heater

Example Japanglish Sentence:

オフィスの建物がクーラーで寒すぎるときがあるから、暖かくするためにストーブを買ったんだ。

Sometimes my office building is so cold because of the *cooler*, so I bought a *stove* to warm me up.

Translated to English:

Sometimes my office building is so cold because of the air conditioner, so I bought a *space heater* to warm me up.

Towelket

ta-o-ru-ket-to

タオルケット

Meaning in Japan:

A large, thin blanket made from the material of a towel. These are common in hot, humid Japanese summers since they absorb moisture well and hold up against frequent washing.[34]

Example Japanglish Sentence:

旅行のときはいつもタオルケットを持って行くよ。いろんな用途に使えて便利なんだ。

I always bring my *towelket* when I travel because it's so versatile.

Translated to English:

I always use my *Japanese towel blanket* when I travel because it's so versatile.

Unit Bath

yu-nit-to ba-su

ユニットバス

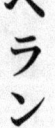

Meaning in Japan:

A *unit bath* is a bathroom where the toilet and bathtub are together in the same room. Traditional Japanese bathrooms almost always have the toilet and bathtub in separate rooms, so when a home has a *unit bath*, this is usually considered a cheap and undesirable living situation.

Example Japanglish Sentence:

ホテルの部屋には、ユニットバスがついている。

The hotel room has a *unit bath*.

Translated to English:

The hotel room has a *toilet and bathtub in the same room*.

Veranda

be-ran-da

ベランダ

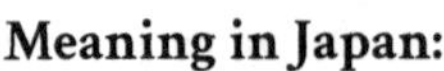

Meaning in Japan:

Balcony in an apartment

Example Japanglish Sentence:

ベランダで、
たくさんの植物を育てている。

I have a lot of plants on my *veranda*.

Translated to English:

I have a lot of plants on my *balcony*.

WASHLET

wo-shu-ret-to

ウォシュレット

Meaning in Japan:

A bidet toilet

Example Japanglish Sentence:

アジアの良いホテルには、
部屋ごとにウォシュレットが付いてる。

Many nice hotels in Asia have *washlets* in each room.

Translated to English:

Many hotels in Asia have *bidet toilets* in each room.

WEEKLY MANSION

wī-ku-rī-man-shon

ウィークリーマンション

Meaning in Japan:

Similar to a monthly mansion but rented by the week

Example Japanglish Sentence:

気に入ったLDKが見つかるまで、ウィークリーマンション
とマンスリーマンション、どっちに泊まるのがいいかな?

Is it better to stay at a *weekly mansion* or a *monthly mansion* while we try to find an *LDK* we like?

Translated to English:

Is it better to *rent an apartment by the week* or by the month while we try to find an apartment we like?

1R / 1K / 2K

Meaning in Japan:

1R and **1K** are two common types of studio apartment layouts in Japan. The number, 1 in this case, tells how many bedrooms are in the layout.

R stands for "room" and usually indicates the most basic style of apartment. It has a bathroom that may be a traditional style with separation of toilet and bathtub or perhaps just a simple *unit bath.* In this layout, there will be a small kitchen area (usually in the hallway), but there is no real wall or separation between the kitchen and the one remaining room (or bedroom) of the apartment.

K stands for "kitchen" and indicates that the apartment will have a kitchen that is at least somewhat separated from the rest of the living areas. Ideally, the bedroom and kitchen will be separated by a door and wall, but situations may vary. Because of the nature of a studio apartment, 2R doesn't really exist. However, **2K** apartments can be found. This would similar to the 1K layout below but would include a second bedroom.[35, 36, 37, 38]

1R Floor plan **1K Floor plan**

1DK / 2DK

Meaning in Japan:

A **1DK** is similar to but larger than a 1K.

D stands for "dining," so together DK means "dining kitchen." In a 1DK, or any apartment with a **DK** distinction rather than a K, the kitchen will be slightly larger than in a K and is typically big enough to be able to fit at least a small dining table. Like a 1K, a **1DK** may either have a *unit bath* or separate rooms for the bathtub and toilet. Additionally, 1DKs tend to have more closets and storage options than 1Ks typically have.

Similarly, a **2DK** is a two-bedroom apartment with a separate dining and kitchen area.[39, 40, 41, 42]

1DK Floor plan

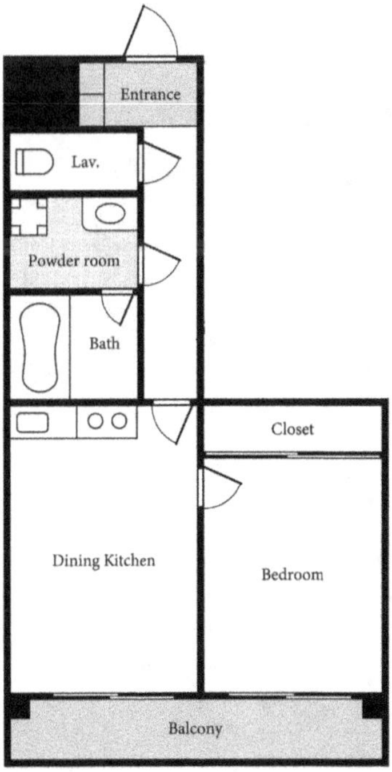

Entrance
Lav.
Powder room
Bath
Closet
Dining Kitchen
Bedroom
Balcony

2DK Floor plan

Entrance
Lav.
Master
Bedroom
Powder room
Bath
Strage
Closet
Closet
Dining Kitchen
Bedroom
Balcony

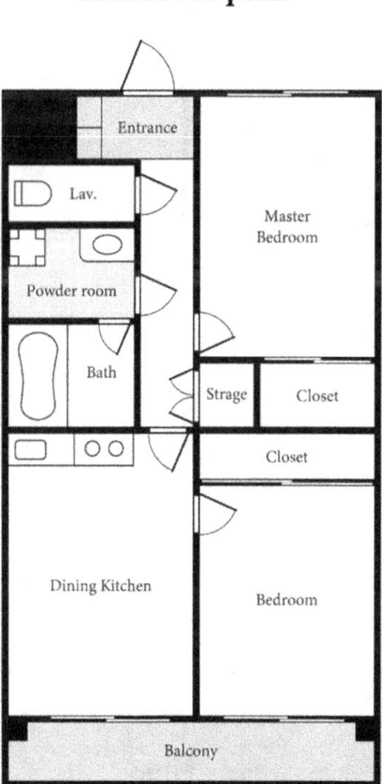

1LDK / 2LDK

Meaning in Japan:

A 1LDK is considered the most spacious (and most expensive) typical apartment layout.

L stands for "living" and refers to a space like to a living room or lounge (UK). **1LDK**s will have three mostly separate areas for the kitchen, dining area, and living room as well as an additional bedroom. This is the most similar layout to a Western one-bedroom apartment. LDKs typically have some closets and will usually have a separate toilet and bathtub area.

A **2LDK** is similar to a two-bedroom apartment with a kitchen, dining area, and living room, and a **3LDK** would be like a three-bedroom apartment.

Sometimes you will see the letter S, like **1SLDK**. **S** stands for "service room" and means any extra room that doesn't qualify as a bedroom for various reasons. Depending the size of this extra room, it could potentially be used as an extra closet or even an office or game room.[43, 44, 45, 46]

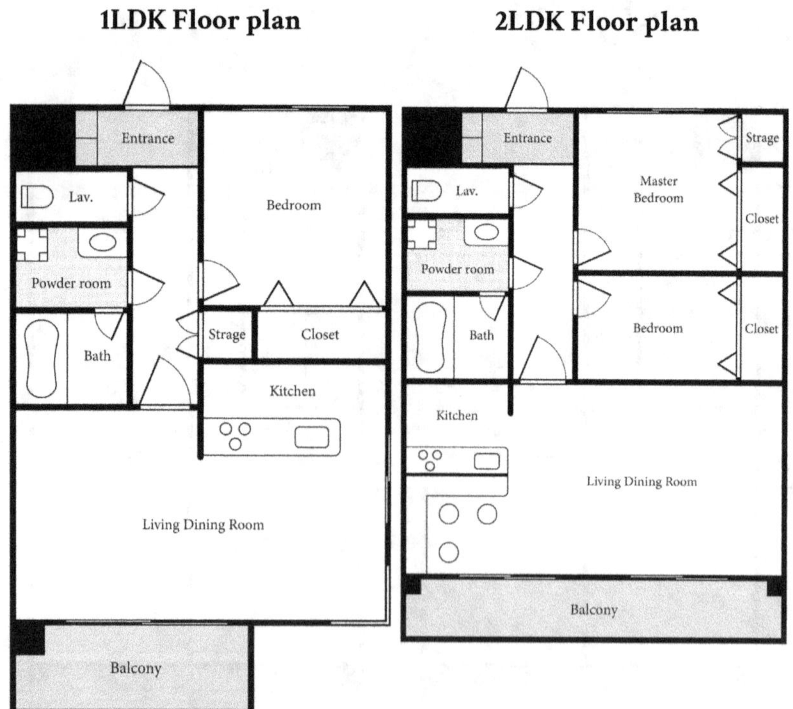

Hygiene, Makeup, Skincare, Haircare

12

衛生・メイクアップ
スキンケア・ヘアケア

Barikan (Barriquand)

ba-ri-kan

バリカン

Meaning in Japan:

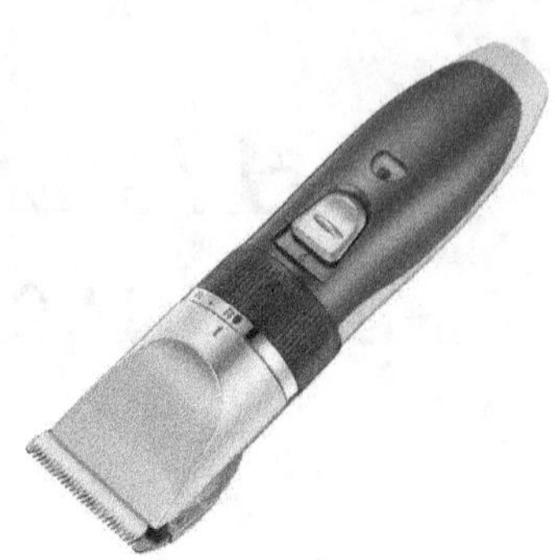

Electric hair trimmer/clippers

Example Japanglish Sentence:

彼は、クリスマスにひげ用のバリカンを頼んできたのに、全然使っていない。

He asked for a *barikan* for his beard for Christmas, but he never uses it.

Translated to English:

He asked for an *electric hair trimmer* for his beard for Christmas, but he never uses it.

Blow

bu-rō

ブロー

Meaning in Japan:

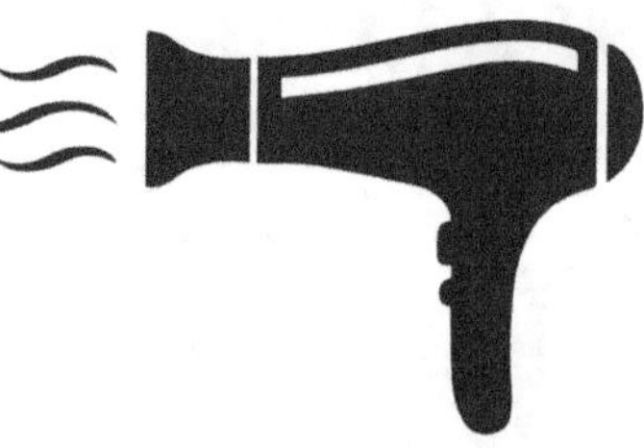

Blow dry

Example Japanglish Sentence:

美容院で、美容師は、私に「髪の毛をブローしていきますね」と言った。

In the beauty salon, the hairstylist said, “Now, I’m going to *blow* your hair.”

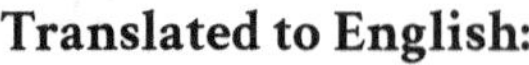

Translated to English:

In the beauty salon, the hairstylist said, “Now, I’m going to *blow dry* your hair.”

bo-dī-shan-pū

Body Shampoo

Meaning in Japan:

Body wash, Shower gel

Example Japanglish Sentence:

ホテルの<u>ボディーシャンプー</u>はとても香りが良かった。どこかで買えるかな？

The *<u>body shampoo</u>* at the hotel smelled so good! Do you think we can buy it somewhere?

Translated to English:

The *<u>body wash</u>* at the hotel smelled so good! Do you think we can buy it somewhere?

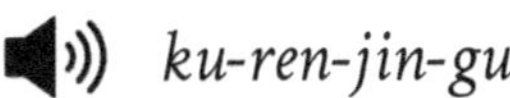

ku-ren-jin-gu

Cleansing

クレンジング

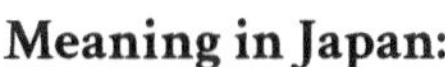

Meaning in Japan:

Makeup remover

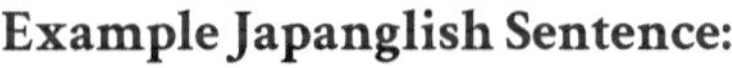

Example Japanglish Sentence:

<u>クレンジング</u>なしでメイクを落とすのは本当に嫌だ！

I hate trying to take off my makeup without *<u>cleansing</u>*.

Translated to English:

I hate trying to take off my makeup without *<u>makeup remover</u>*.

Dryer

do-rai-yā

ドライヤー

Meaning in Japan:

Hair dryer, blow dryer

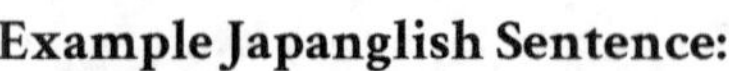

Example Japanglish Sentence:

髪をきれいに整えるために
<u>ドライヤー</u>を使わないといけない。

I need to use the *<u>dryer</u>* to make my hair look good.

Translated to English:

I need to use the *<u>hair dryer</u>* to make my hair look good.

Este

e-su-te 

エステ

Meaning in Japan:

A spa, med spa, or similar type of place one can go to get a facial, beauty treatments, hair removal, or sometimes various non-surgical weight loss procedures

Example Japanglish Sentence:

今週末<u>エステ</u>にいく。

I'm going to go to *<u>este</u>* this weekend.

Translated to English:

I'm going to get a facial at a *<u>med spa</u>* this weekend.

fan-dē-shon

Foundation

ファンデーション

Meaning in Japan:

Foundation only refers to foundation makeup; none of the other meanings, such as the base for a building, are called *foundation*

Example Japanglish Sentence:

私は新居の基礎工事を眺めながら、ファンデーションとマスカラをつけた。

I put on my *foundation ファンデーション (fandēshon)* and mascara while watching the workers pour the *foundation 基礎 (kiso)* of my new home.

Translated to English:

I put on my makeup *foundation* and mascara while watching the workers pour the *foundation* of my new home.

he-a-ka-rā

Hair Color

ヘアカラー

Meaning in Japan:

Only hair dye or hair coloring; *hair color* in Japan does not refer to the color of your hair.

Example Japanglish Sentence:

彼女は赤のヘアカラーにした。

She has red *hair color*.

Translated to English:

She dyed her *hair red*.

Hair Iron

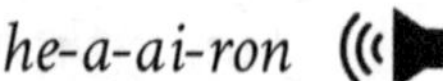
he-a-ai-ron

ヘアアイロン

Meaning in Japan:

Hair straightener, Flat iron

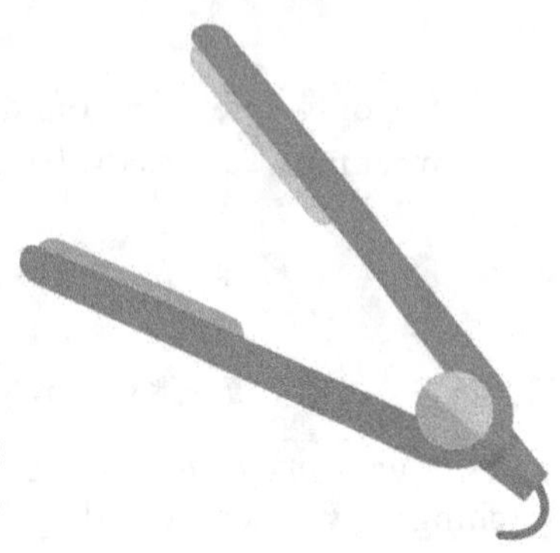

Example Japanglish Sentence:

ストレートヘアの女の子はコテを欲しがり、巻き髪の女の子はヘアアイロンを欲しがるようだ。

It seems like people with straight hair want a curling iron, and people with curly hair want a *hair iron*.

Translated to English:

It seems like people with straight hair want a curling iron, and people with curly hair want a *hair straightener* / *flat iron*.

Lip (Cream)

rip-pu-ku-rī-mu

リップクリーム

Meaning in Japan:

Chapstick, Lip balm

Example Japanglish Sentence:

あなたのリップ、すごくいい香りがするね。どんなのをつけてるの？

Your *lip* smells so good.
What kind is it?

Translated to English:

Your *chapstick* smells so good. What kind is it?

Make

メイク

mei-ku

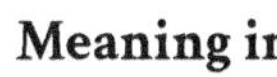

Meaning in Japan:

Makeup

Example Japanglish Sentence:

日本に行くのが大好き。人気のあるコスメブランドがたくさんあるし、メイクの仕上がりも素晴らしいから。

We love visiting Japan because they have a lot of popular *cosme brands* with great *make*!

Translated to English:

We love visiting Japan because they have a lot of popular makeup brands with great *makeup*!

Makeup

メイクアップ

mei-ku-ap-pu

Meaning in Japan:

To put on makeup

Example Japanglish Sentence:

「まあ！今日は、メイク(メイクアップ)してるんだ！」

Wow! You *made up* today!

Translated to English:

Wow! You *put on makeup* today!

Manicure

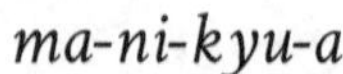

マニキュア

Meaning in Japan:

Nail polish

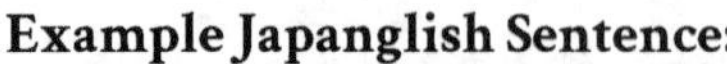

Example Japanglish Sentence:

あなたの<u>マニキュア</u>の色、
とても素敵！

I love your *<u>manicure</u>* color!

Translated to English:

I love your *<u>nail polish</u>* color!

No Make

nō-mei-ku 

ノーメイク

Meaning in Japan:

Not wearing makeup

Example Japanglish Sentence:

今週ずっと私は、<u>ノーメイク</u>だったんだ。すごく解放感があったわ。

I did *<u>no make</u>* all week, and it was so freeing!

Translated to English:

I *<u>didn't wear makeup</u>* all week, and it was so freeing!

pak-ku

Pack

パック

Meaning in Japan:

1. (Noun) Facial mask
2. (Verb) To use a facial mask
3. (Noun) A pre-made and packaged food like a salad

Example Japanglish Sentence:

あのブランドのパック製品はとても質がいい。

That brand sells really good *packs*.

昨日の夜、友達と一緒に顔にパックした。

My friend and I *packed* our faces last night.

このあたりのスーパーでは、パック入りのサラダとか、美味しい惣菜がたくさん売っている。

Most grocery stores around here sell some really good *packed* foods like *packed* salads.

Translated to English:

That brand sells really good *facial masks*.

My friend and I *did facial masks* last night.

Most grocery stores around here sell some really good *pre-packaged foods* like salads.

PINCETTO

ピンセット

pin-set-to 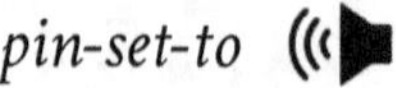

Meaning in Japan:

Tweezers

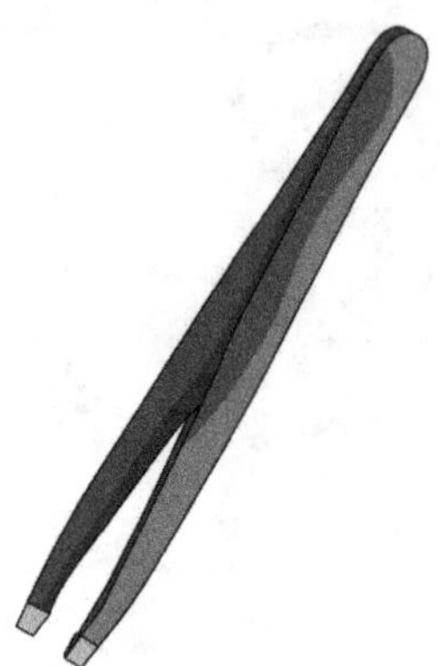

Example Japanglish Sentence:

ピンセットある？
足にトゲが刺さったみたいなんだ。

Did you bring the *pincetto*?
I think I have a splinter in my foot.

Translated to English:

Did you bring the *tweezers*? I think I have a splinter in my foot.

RINSE

リンス

rin-su

Meaning in Japan:

Hair conditioner

Example Japanglish Sentence:

リンスを使わない男性もいる。

Some people don't use *rinse* for their hair.

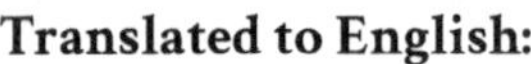

Translated to English:

Some people don't use *conditioner* for their hair.

Kids, Family, Relationships

子ども・家族・人間関係

13

Baby Bed

ベビーベッド

be-bī-bed-do

Meaning in Japan:

Crib, cot (UK)

Example Japanglish Sentence:

シ〜！赤ちゃんが<u>ベビーベッド</u>で寝ているわ。

Shh. The baby is sleeping on the *<u>baby bed</u>* in the room next to us.

Translated to English:

Shh. The baby is sleeping in the *<u>crib</u>* in the room next to us.

Baby Car

ベビーカー

be-bī-kā

Meaning in Japan:

Stroller, pushchair (UK), pram (UK)

Example Japanglish Sentence:

もしよかったら、明日うちの<u>ベビーカー</u>を動物園で使ってもいいよ。

You can use our extra *<u>baby car</u>* at the zoo tomorrow if you'd like!

Translated to English:

You can use our extra *<u>stroller</u>* at the zoo tomorrow if you'd like!

be-bī-sā-ku-ru — Baby Circle

ベビーサークル

Meaning in Japan:

Pack and play, playpen for babies

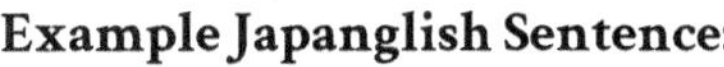

Example Japanglish Sentence:

晩ごはんを作るとき<u>ベビーサークル</u>はとても便利。

Our <u>*baby circle*</u> is so helpful when I need to cook dinner.

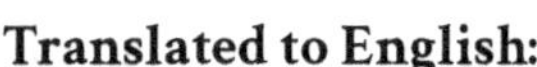

Translated to English:

Our <u>*playpen*</u> is so helpful when I need to cook dinner.

be-bī-shi-tā — Babysitter

ベビーシッター

Meaning in Japan:

A nanny who provides ongoing and often full-time childcare. A babysitter, as used in many Western cultures for occasional sporadic childcare such as on a date night, is very uncommon in Japan.

Example Japanglish Sentence:

<u>ベビーシッター</u>は、私が仕事をしている間、平日は毎日うちの子の世話をしてくれている。

The <u>*babysitter*</u> takes care of our toddler every day during the week when I am working.

Translated to English:

The <u>*nanny*</u> takes care of our toddler every day during the week when I am working.

DV

dī-bu-i

ディーブイ

Meaning in Japan:

Domestic violence

Example Japanglish Sentence:

私たちの非営利団体は、DVに対する認識を高め、立ち向かうために、地域社会に情報を提供している。

Our non-profit helps provide information to the community to help bring awareness and fight against *DV*.

Translated to English:

Our non-profit helps provide information to the community to help bring awareness and fight against *domestic violence*.

Family Service

ka-zo-ku sā-bi-su 

家族サービス

Meaning in Japan:

Family service is a term for when a dad spends time with his kids or participates in family activities outside of work, usually on the weekends. Traditional Japanese culture expected men to focus solely on their work while most childcare and household responsibilities fell to the women. However, modern generations tend to think differently, and many expect fathers to be able to participate in *family service* outside of work.

Example Japanglish Sentence:

今週末は夫が家族サービスしてくれるので、
私はコーヒーでも飲みに行けそうよ。

My husband is doing *family service* this weekend,
so I should be free to meet you for coffee.

Translated to English:

My husband is *spending time with the kids* this weekend,
so I should be free to meet you for coffee.

gō-ru-in — GOAL IN

ゴールイン

Meaning in Japan:

This is used to express that people *finally* achieved something and is commonly used when people finally get married, somewhat similar to "tie the knot"

Example Japanglish Sentence:

メアリーとマイクは今週末ついにゴールインした!
5年間付き合って、ついに結婚したんだ。

Mary and Mike did *goal in* this weekend!
They dated for five years and finally got married.

Translated to English:

Mary and Mike finally *tied the knot* this weekend!
They dated for five years and finally got married.

ra-bu-ra-bu — LOVE LOVE

ラブラブ

Meaning in Japan:

Head over heels, passionately in love, all over each other

Example Japanglish Sentence:

彼らはラブラブだね。私は、二人が巡り会えたことを心から嬉しく思う。

They are *love love*. I'm so happy they found each other.

彼らはすごくラブラブだね。微笑ましいけど、ちょっと鬱陶しいかもね。

They are so *love love*; it's really sweet but also kind of annoying!

Translated to English:

They are *head over heels*. I'm so happy they found each other.

They are *all over each other all the time*.
It's really sweet, but also kind of annoying!

Manneri

man-ne-ri

Meaning in Japan:

Manneri describes the feeling of boredom or mundanity that many experience after a few years into a stable relationship. This word is a bit negative and expresses the lack of excitement that can be experienced by dull routine in a relationship.

Example Japanglish Sentence:

私たちの生活はマンネリ化しているので、
何か変化がいる。イメージチェンジでもしようかな！

Our life has become *manneri*, so we need some kind of change.
Maybe I'll do *image change* to spice things up!

Translated to English:

Our life and relationship has become boring and monotonous, so we need some kind of change. Maybe I'll change my look and get a new hairstyle!

Skinship

su-kin-ship-pu 

スキンシップ

Meaning in Japan:

Physical touch. This word can describe romantic physical touch but can also describe a person who casually touches someones arm while talking or forms friendly bonds with touch. This can also be used to describe how much physical affection one gives a pet.

Example Japanglish Sentence:

彼女はとてもフレンドリーで、よくスキンシップをする。

She's very friendly and does a lot of *skinship*.

寂しそうだから、もっと犬にスキンシップしてあげた方がいいかも。

You should do more *skinship* for the dog because he seems really lonely.

Translated to English:

She's very friendly and very *physically affectionate*.

You should *pet*/*hold* the dog more because he seems really lonely.

vu-ā-jin-rō-do

Virgin Road

Meaning in Japan:

The aisle that a bride walks down during her wedding as well as the act of walking down the aisle to get married

Example Japanglish Sentence:

友達はお父さんと一緒にヴァージンロードを歩いた。

My friend walked with her father on the *virgin road*.

私もヴァージンロードを歩いてみたい。

I want to walk the *virgin road*.

友だちは、ヴァージンロードで転んだ。

My best friend fell down on her *virgin road*.

Translated to English:

My friend *walked down the aisle* with her father on her wedding day.

I want to *get married and walk down the aisle*.

My best friend fell down when she was *walking down the aisle at her wedding*.

MISCELLANEOUS

14 その他

Case by Case

kē-su-bai-kē-su

ケースバイケース

Meaning in Japan:

Case by case is used in Japanglish similarly to how "it depends" is used in English

Example Japanglish Sentence:

「普段は車で通勤するの？」
「ケースバイケースだ。妻が車を使う必要があるときは、バスで行くよ」。

- Do you usually drive to work?
- *Case by case*. If my wife needs the car, I take the bus.

Translated to English:

- Do you usually drive to work?
- *It depends*. If my wife need the car, I take the bus.

Happening

ha-pu-nin-gu

ハプニング

Meaning in Japan:

Unexpected event, accident

Example Japanglish Sentence:

昨日、私のオフィスでハプニングがあった。

There was a *happening* at my office yesterday!

Translated to English:

Something crazy happened at my office yesterday!
There was an accident at my office yesterday!

i-mē-ji

Image

イメージ

Meaning in Japan:

Impression

Example Japanglish Sentence:

滞在中ずっと天気が悪かったので、あの町にはあまりいいイメージがない。

I don't have a good *image* of that city because the weather was terrible the whole time I was there.

Translated to English:

I don't have a good *impression* of that city because the weather was terrible the whole time I was there.

mo-ru-mot-to

Marmot

モルモット

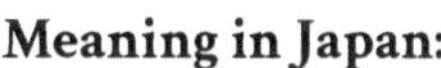

Meaning in Japan:

A guinea pig, especially when referring to an animal used in experiments. Some older generations may interpret *marmot* to mean a mouse or rat instead.

Example Japanglish Sentence:

子供の頃、親友がモルモットをペットとして飼っていた。

When I was a kid, my best friend had a *marmot* as a pet.

Translated to English:

When I was a kid, my best friend had a *guinea pig* as a pet.

Miss / Misutta

mi-su / mi-sut-ta

ミス・ミスった

Meaning in Japan:

Miss ミス means a mistake or error.

Careless miss ケアレスミス is a careless mistake.

Misutta ミスった means to make a mistake, mess up, or screw up in the context of a friendship or relationship.

Near miss ニアミス means to run into someone unexpectedly.

Example Japanglish Sentence:

「試験でミスをした」

I made a *miss* on the exam!

宿題でいつもケアレスミスをしてしまう。
もっと気をつけないと！

I always make *careless miss* on my homework.
I need to be more careful.

ヤバイ、ミスった。完全にミスった。

Oh no, I *misutta*! I totally *misutta*!

昨日スーパーでユキコを見かけたけど、ニアミスだった！
昨日スーパーでユキコとニアミスしたんだ。

I had a *near miss* with Yukiko at the grocery store yesterday!

Translated to English:

I made a *mistake* on the exam!

I always make *careless mistakes* on my homework.
I need to be more careful.

Oh no, I *messed up*! I totally *screwed up*!

I *ran into* Yukiko at the grocery store yesterday!

e-nu-jī

NG

エヌジー

Meaning in Japan:

An abbreviation for "no good," meaning not good, not allowed, inappropriate, unacceptable, taboo

Example Japanglish Sentence:

飛行機では離陸時の席の移動は<u>NG</u>行動とされている。

Getting out of your seat during takeoff is <u>*NG*</u> on an airplane.

ゴールデンタイムのテレビ番組では、<u>NG</u>とされる言葉もある。

Some words are <u>*NG*</u> on golden time TV.

Translated to English:

Getting out of your seat during takeoff is <u>*not allowed*</u> on an airplane.

Some words are <u>*not allowed*</u> on prime time TV.

on-pa-rē-do

On Parade

オンパレード

Meaning in Japan:

1. A continuous display of something
2. A similar line of things or actions happening one after another

Example Japanglish Sentence:

その新作映画は、スターの<u>オンパレード</u>だ。

The new movie is an <u>*on parade*</u> of stars.

A社が値上げし、今月は他社も次々値上げの<u>オンパレード</u>だ。

Company A raised its prices, and now there's been an <u>*on parade*</u> of mark ups this month.

Translated to English:

The new movie has an <u>*all-star cast*</u>.

Company A raised its prices, and many other businesses <u>*have followed suit*</u>.

ONE PATTERN

wan-pa-tān

ワンパターン

Meaning in Japan:

Repetitive

Example Japanglish Sentence:

会議は<u>ワンパターン</u>だった。
もっといろんな話題が出るかと思ってたんだけどね。

The conference was really *<u>one pattern</u>*.
I was hoping there would be more of a variety of topics.

Translated to English:

The conference was really *<u>repetitive</u>*.
I was hoping there would be more of a variety of topics.

PLUS ALPHA

pu-ra-su-a-ru-fa

プラスアルファ

Meaning in Japan:

Extra or additional

Example Japanglish Sentence:

あのインターナショナルスクール、とても高い!
年間2万ドルで、しかもそれに<u>プラスアルファ</u>があるんだ!

The international school is so expensive!
It's like $20,000 per year *<u>plus alpha</u>*!

Translated to English:

The international school is so expensive!
It's like $20,000 per year *<u>plus additional fees</u>*!

pu-chi

Poochi

プチ

Meaning in Japan:

Poochi means small, petite, tiny and is often used as part of a short phrase, such as a ***poochi trip*** プチ旅行 (a short trip or a quick getaway) or a ***poochi luxury*** プチ贅沢 (a small indulgence or guilty pleasure)

Example Japanglish Sentence:

友達は、「週末は、プチ旅行で温泉に行く予定よ」と言った。

My friend said, "I'm planning a *poochi* trip to a hot spring this weekend!"

Translated to English:

My friend said, "I'm planning a *short* trip to a hot spring this weekend!"

po-su-to

Post

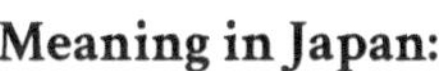

Meaning in Japan:

ポスト

Mailbox, postbox (UK)

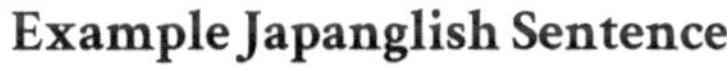

Example Japanglish Sentence:

ポストを確認しなくては。
友達が大事なものを送ったと言ったので。

I need to check my *post*. My friend said he sent me something important.

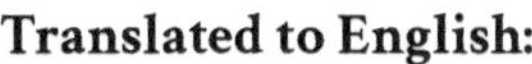

Translated to English:

I need to check my *mailbox*.
My friend said he sent me something important.

SF

e-su-e-fu

エスエフ

Meaning in Japan:

Science fiction, sci-fi

Example Japanglish Sentence:

SF小説が大好きだ。

I love *SF* novels.

Translated to English:

I love *science fiction (sci-fi)* novels.

Spam

su-pa-mu

スパム

Meaning in Japan:

Junk mail that constitutes a crime, like phishing or a scam

Example Japanglish Sentence:

彼は迷惑メール(スパム)を送信したことで刑務所に入った。

He went to jail for *spam*.

Translated to English:

He went to jail for a *phishing scam*.

Office Items

15

オフィス用品

Ball Pen

bō-ru-pen

ボールペン

Meaning in Japan:

A ballpoint pen

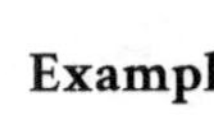

Example Japanglish Sentence:

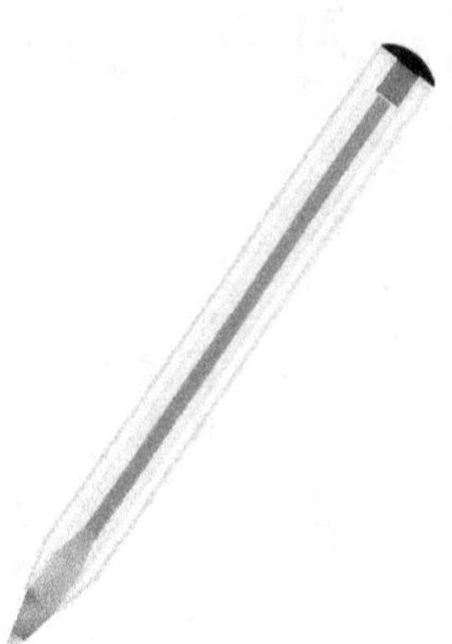

ボールペンを貸してもらえますか?

Do you have a *ball pen* I can borrow?

Translated to English:

Do you have a *pen* I can borrow?
Do you have a *ballpoint pen* I can borrow?

Bond

bon-do 

ボンド

Meaning in Japan:

Strong glue, superglue

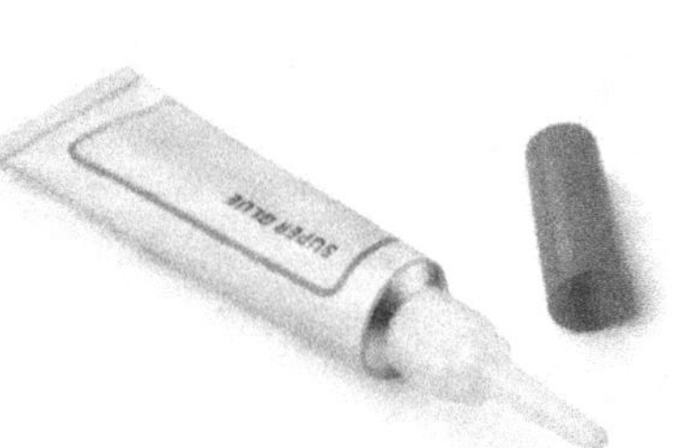

Example Japanglish Sentence:

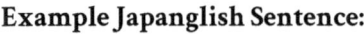

そのボンド、どこで買った?

Where did you get that *bond*?

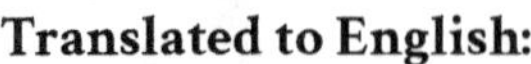

Translated to English:

Where did you get that *superglue*?

dī-e-mu

DM

ディーエム

Meaning in Japan:

Junk mail, spam

Example Japanglish Sentence:

今週、私のメールにたくさんディーエムが届いてる。

I've been getting so many *DMs* this week in my email!

Translated to English:

I've been getting so much *spam*/*junk mail* this week in my email!

hat-chin-gu

Hatching

ハッチング

HIGHLIGHTER

Meaning in Japan:

Highlighting or highlighted area

Example Japanglish Sentence:

ページのハッチング部分をご覧ください。

Please look at the *hatching* area on the page.

Translated to English:

Please look at the *highlighted* area on the page.

Hotchkiss

ホッチキス

hot-chi-ki-su

Meaning in Japan:

Stapler

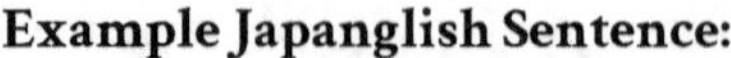

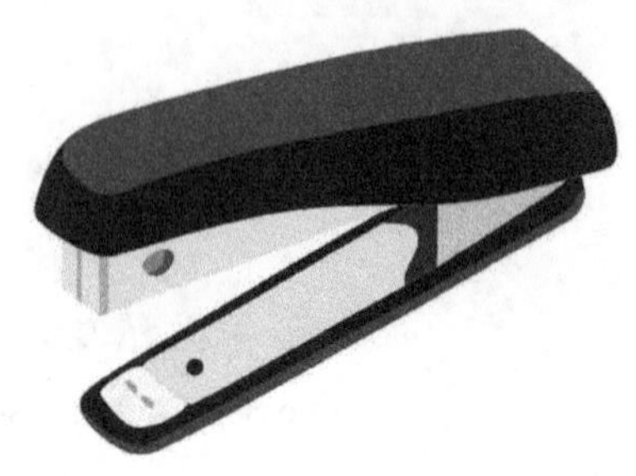

Example Japanglish Sentence:

うわー！君のホチキスは金でできてるなんて信じられない。

Wow, I can't believe your *Hotchkiss* is made of gold.

Translated to English:

Wow, I can't believe your *stapler* is made of gold.

Magic

マジック

ma-jik-ku

Meaning in Japan:

Magic marker, permanent marker, Sharpie

Example Japanglish Sentence:

マジックでこれを書きたい。

I'd like to write this with a *magic*.

Translated to English:

I'd like to write this with a *permanent marker*.

me-mo

Memo

メモ

Meaning in Japan:

A short note, especially like one written on a post-it note

Example Japanglish Sentence:

授業でノートにいくつかのメモを書き留めた。

I wrote some *memos* from the class in my *note.*

Translated to English:

I wrote some *notes* from the class in my notebook.

nō-to

Note

ノート

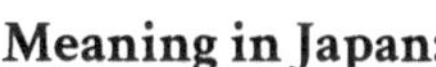

Meaning in Japan:

Notebook

Example Japanglish Sentence:

これを私のノートに書かせてください。

Let me write this in my *note*.

Translated to English:

Let me write this in my *notebook*.

Print

pu-rin-to 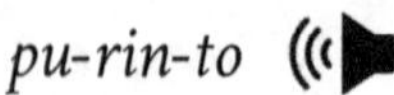

プリント

Meaning in Japan:

Handout, printout

Example Japanglish Sentence:

彼はミーティングでみんなにプリントを配った。

He brought *prints* for everyone at the meeting.

Translated to English:

He brought *handouts* / *printouts* for everyone at the meeting.

Punch

pan-chi

パンチ

Meaning in Japan:

1. Hole punch
2. Spicy or strong when describing food
3. Bold or bright when describing clothes

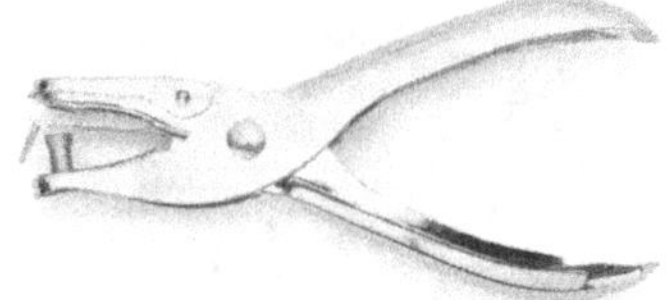

Example Japanglish Sentence:

ここにパンチがあるかな。Do we have a *punch* here?

この料理、パンチが効いてるね。This food has *punch*!

そのドレス、パンチが効いててかっこいい！Your dress really has *punch*!

Translated to English:

Do we have a *hole punch*?

This food is *spicy*!

Your dress has really *bold colors*!

Sharp Pen

shā-pen

シャーペン

Meaning in Japan:

An abbreviation of "sharp pencil," meaning a mechanical pencil

Example Japanglish Sentence:

私は、生徒たちに数学の課題には、シャーペンを使うように伝えた。

I asked my students to use *sharp pens* for their math assignments.

Translated to English:

I asked my students to use *mechanical pencils* for their math assignments!

Sign Pen

sa-in-pen

サインペン

Meaning in Japan:

A thin felt-tipped permanent marker often used for signing things

Example Japanglish Sentence:

市役所の人は私に「サインペンでこちらに署名をお願いします」と言った。

The city clerk said, "Please put your *sign* here with your *sign pen*."

Translated to English:

The city clerk said, "Please put your signature here with a *felt-tipped pen*."

Stamp

su-tan-pu

スタンプ

Meaning in Japan:

Postmark stamp showing the date

Example Japanglish Sentence:

この郵便物がいつ送られたかを確認するには消印を見る必要がある。
切手は貼られているが、日付印が見つからない。

We need to see the *stamp 消印 (keshiin)* to verify when this mail was sent. It has a (postage) *stamp 切手 (kitte)*, but I can't find the stamp of the *date日付印 (hizukein)*.

Translated to English:

We need to see the *stamp* to verify when this mail was sent. It has a *(postage) stamp*, but I can't find the *postmark stamp*.

White

ho-wai-to 

ホワイト

Meaning in Japan:

Whiteout, White out, Wite-out
Correction tape, Correction fluid

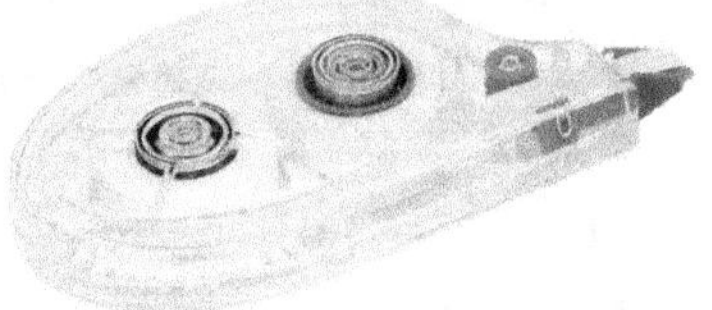

Example Japanglish Sentence:

間違った!ホワイトが要るわ。

I made a mistake. I need some *white*.

Translated to English:

I made a mistake. I need some *correction tape* / *whiteout*.

Schedules, Calendars, Timing

16

スケジュール カレンダー・時間調整

Appo

a-po 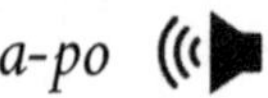

アポ

Meaning in Japan:

An informal abbreviation of "appointment"

Example Japanglish Sentence:

明日、午後2時にアポが入っているんだけど、その後は空いていると思う。
4時に会うのはどう?

I have an *appo* tomorrow at 2 p.m., but I should be available afterwards. How about meeting at 4 p.m.?

Translated to English:

I have an *appointment* tomorrow at 2 p.m., but I should be available afterwards. How about meeting at 4 p.m.?

Appoint

a-po-in-to 

アポイント

Meaning in Japan:

A more formal abbreviation of "appointment"

Example Japanglish Sentence:

明日、午後2時にアポイントが入っているんだけど、
その後は空いていると思う。
4時に会うのはどう?

I have an *appoint* tomorrow at 2 p.m., but I should be available afterwards. How about meeting at 4 p.m.?

Translated to English:

I have an *appointment* tomorrow at 2 p.m., but I should be available afterwards. How about meeting at 4 p.m.?

kō-nā — CORNER

コーナー

Meaning in Japan:

A time, space, place, or area devoted to a specific purpose or activity

Example Japanglish Sentence:

講義の後、質問<u>コーナー</u>がある。

After the lecture, we'll have a <u>*corner*</u> for questions.

そのフェスティバルでは、ふれあい動物園とピッグレースの<u>コーナー</u>がある。

At the festival, they have a <u>*corner*</u> for petting zoo and also pig races!

Translated to English:

After the lecture, we'll have some <u>*time*</u> for questions.

At the festival, they have an <u>*area*</u> with a petting zoo and an <u>*area*</u> for pig races!

dai-ya — DIA

ダイヤ

Meaning in Japan:

1. Diamond
2. An abbreviation of "diagram" meaning a train or bus timetable

Example Japanglish Sentence:

彼は彼女に大きな<u>ダイヤ</u>を買った。

He bought her a huge <u>*dia*</u>!

<u>ダイヤ</u>改正により、バスの運行本数が減ったので、不便だ。

Due to the <u>*dia*</u> revision, the number of bus services has decreased, making the bus inconvenient.

Translated to English:

He bought her a huge <u>*diamond*</u>!

Due to the change in <u>*bus schedule*</u>, the number of buses throughout the day has decreased, making the bus an inconvenient choice.

Go Sign

gō-sa-in

ゴーサイン

Meaning in Japan:

The metaphorical green light or go ahead to move forward with something

Example Japanglish Sentence:

そのプロジェクトにゴーサインをもらった。

We got the *go sign* for the new project.

Translated to English:

We got the *green light* / *go ahead* for the new project.

Golden Week

gō-ru-den wī-ku 

ゴールデンウィーク

Meaning in Japan:

This is the most important holiday week in Japan and takes place the first week of May from April 29 to May 5. During this time, there are four major public holidays:

Showa Day

昭和の日 *(Shōwa no Hi)* - April 29 Emperor Hirohito's birthday

Constitution Memorial Day

憲法記念日 *(Kenpō Kinenbi)* - May 3

Greenery Day

みどりの日 *(Midori no Hi)* - May 4

Children's Day

子供の日 *(Kodomo no Hi)* - May 5

ja-su-to

Just

ジャスト

Meaning in Japan:

Exactly at a specific time, On the nose, On the dot

Example Japanglish Sentence:

今、3時ジャストだ！

It's *just* 3 p.m.!

Translated to English:

It's *exactly* 3 p.m.!

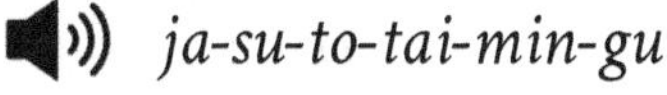

ja-su-to-tai-min-gu

Just Timing

ジャストタイミング

Meaning in Japan:

Perfect timing

Example Japanglish Sentence:

ジャストタイミングだよ！ちょうど午後3時だ！

Just timing! It's just 3 p.m.!

Translated to English:

Perfect timing! It's exactly 3 p.m.!

My Pace

mai-pē-su

マイペース

Meaning in Japan:

This comes from the expression "at one's own pace," however, if someone is described as *my pace*, it's usually negative and means they are usually slow, behind, and not punctual (all of which are considered generally negative traits in Japan).

Example Japanglish Sentence:

アメリカで働き始めたとき、多くの人がマイペースで仕事をしていることにとても驚いた。

When I started working in the U.S., I was really surprised that a lot of people are *my pace* at work.

Translated to English:

When I started working in the U.S., I was really surprised that a lot of people are *slow* / *behind on deadlines* / *not very punctual* at work.

Resc

ri-su-ke

Meaning in Japan:

Reschedule

Example Japanglish Sentence:

欧米の同僚は、日本の同僚に比べて会議をリスケすることがずっと多いと気づいた。

We noticed that our Western coworkers *resc* meeting much more often than our Japanese coworkers do.

Translated to English:

We noticed that our Western coworkers *reschedule* meetings much more often than our Japanese coworkers do.

su-ke-jū-ru

SCHEDULE

スケジュール

Meaning in Japan:

Plans or schedule

Example Japanglish Sentence:

月曜は予定があるので会えないんだ。
他の日で都合がつくかスケジュール帳で確認してみるよ。
I can't meet you on Monday. I have a *schedule*.
Let me look in my *scheduler* to see some other options.

Translated to English:

I can't meet you on Monday. I have *plans*.
Let me look at my calendar to see some other options.

su-ke-jū-ra

SCHEDULER

スケジューラ

Meaning in Japan:

Planner, calendar, schedule book, diary (UK)

Example Japanglish Sentence:

月曜は予定があるので会えないんだ。
他の日で都合がつくかスケジュール帳で確認してみるよ。
I can't meet you on Monday. I have a *schedule*. Let me look in my *scheduler* to see some other options.

Translated to English:

I can't meet you on Monday. I have plans. Let me look in my *calendar* to see some other options.

Silver Week

shi-ru-bā-wī-ku 

シルバーウィーク

Meaning in Japan:

Similar to Golden Week, *Silver Week* is the second busiest holiday week in Japan in September with a three-consecutive-day holiday break. It includes three main holidays:

Respect for the Aged Day

敬老の日 *(Keirō no Hi)* - third Monday of September

Autumnal Equinox Day

秋分の日 *(Shūbun no Hi)* - usually September 23

Citizen's Holiday

国民の祝日 *(kokumin no skukujitsu)* - May 4

Summer Time

sa-mā-tai-mu 

サマータイム

Meaning in Japan:

Daylight savings time

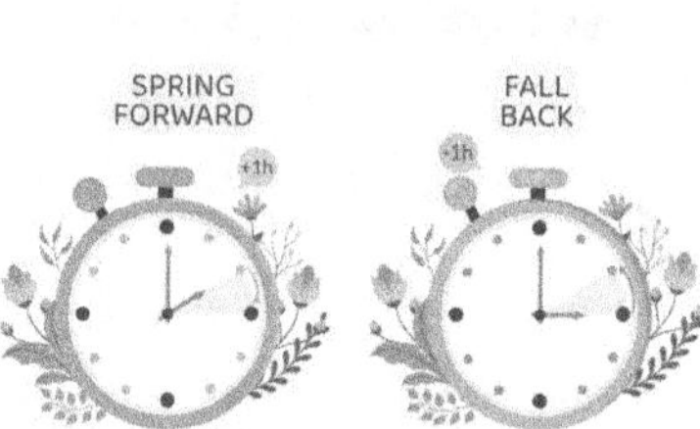

Example Japanglish Sentence:

ここの州には<u>サマータイム</u>ってある
の？ない州もあるって聞いたんだけど。

Does your state have <u>*summer time*</u>?
I heard some states don't have it.

Translated to English:

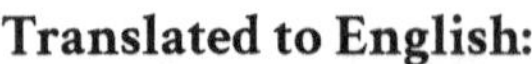

Does your state have <u>*daylight savings time*</u>?
I heard some states don't have it.

SHOPPING

17

After Service

a-fu-tā-sā-bi-su 

アフターサービス

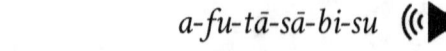

Meaning in Japan:

A warranty on a product or free help or service after purchasing a product; after-sales service; customer service, customer support

Example Japanglish Sentence:

「1週間前にスマホを買ったばかりなんだけど、
なんだか調子が悪くて。<u>アフターサービス</u>ってあるのかな」

I just bought this phone one week ago, but it is acting up a bit.
Do they have any <u>*after service*</u>?

「テレビを買おうと思っているんだけど。もし壊れたら困るし、<u>アフターサービス</u>がしっかりしてるおすすめの電気屋さんって、どこか知ってる?」

I'm planning to buy a TV, but if it breaks I'll be in trouble. Do you know any electronics store with good <u>*after service*</u> you could recommend?

Translated to English:

I just bought this phone one week ago, but it acting up a bit.
Does it have a <u>*warranty*</u>? Do they have any <u>*after-sales support*</u>?

I'm planning to buy a TV, but if it breaks, I'll be in trouble. Do you know any electronics stores with good <u>*customer support*</u> you could recommend?

After Service in the U.S.

I once had a student who moved to the United States and bought a couch. A week later, she found a small rip in one of the cushions. She went to the store and asked if they had *after service* on her sofa purchase. The store employees looked at her kind of strangely and eventually went to get a manager to help. "*After service*," she asked again, "Do you have after service for my couch?" Still, no one at the store understood. She left feeling sad and defeated and thought maybe her accent was too thick for people to understand. She was sure she was speaking correct English.

🔊 *an-ten-a-shop-pu* ANTENNA SHOP

アンテナショップ

Meaning in Japan:

A store that sells specialties from another region, area, or city (e.g., a store in Tokyo selling specialties from Hokkaido)

Example Japanglish Sentence:

北海道に行く時間がないなら、
東京のアンテナショップに連れていってあげるよ。

Since you don't have time to visit Hokkaido, let me take you to an *antenna shop* in Tokyo!

Translated to English:

Since you don't have time to visit Hokkaido, let me take you to *a shop in Tokyo that sells authentic specialties from Hokkaido*!

🔊 *ā-kei-do* ARCADE

アーケイド

Meaning in Japan:

A shopping arcade; a covered passageway or street with shops on both sides (e.g., Cleveland Arcade in Ohio, Piccadilly Arcade in London)

Example Japanglish Sentence:

私たちは、金曜日の午後アーケード商店街に行った。

We went to an *arcade* Friday afternoon.

Translated to English:

We went to a *covered outdoor shopping street* Friday afternoon.

BARGAIN

bā-gen

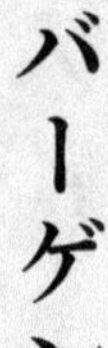

Meaning in Japan:

A sale

Example Japanglish Sentence:

その店は、今週末バーゲンだ。

My favorite store is having a *bargain* this weekend!

Translated to English:

My favorite store is having a *sale* this weekend!

CASHING

kyas-shin-gu

Meaning in Japan:

Cashing is similar to a cash advance on a credit card. The cash you withdraw is subject to your credit card's cash advance limit as well as the predetermined interest rate.

Cashing card loans function more like loans connected to your credit card. They require a quick application and are advertised by banks as a way to get money fast (some within 15 minutes), especially if you need more cash than your cash advance limit would otherwise allow.[47,48,49,50]

Example Japanglish Sentence:

キャッシング/カードローンは好きじゃない。利息が高すぎる。

I don't like *cashing*. The interest rates are too high.

Translated to English:

I don't like *cash advances*. The interest rates are too high.

kon-bi-ni

Conveni

コンビニ

Meaning in Japan:

Convenience store

Example Japanglish Sentence:

日本では、コンビニで何でもできる。公共料金の支払い、宅配便の発送・受け取り、ATMの利用、コピーやプリントサービスなど。

In Japan, *conveni* has everything! You can pay utility bills, send and receive packages, use ATM machines, make copies, print documents, and much more!

Translated to English:

In Japan, *convenience stores* have everything! You can pay utility bills, send and receive packages, use ATM machines, make copies, print documents, and much more!

de-pā-to

Depart

デパート

Meaning in Japan:

Department store

Example Japanglish Sentence:

日本のデパートの中には、10階建てのものもある。

Some *departs* in Japan are 10 floors high!

Translated to English:

Some *department stores* in Japan are 10 floors high!

Doz

dā-su

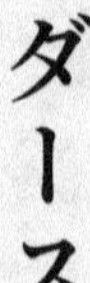

Meaning in Japan:

A dozen

Example Japanglish Sentence:

何個ドーナツが欲しい?
1<u>ダース。</u>

- How many donuts do you want?
- A *<u>doz</u>*.

Translated to English:

- How many donuts do you want?
- A *<u>dozen</u>*.

Eco (Echo) Bag

e-ko bag-gu

エコバッグ

Meaning in Japan:

Reusable, eco-friendly shopping bag

Example Japanglish Sentence:

日本で、<u>エコバッグ</u>は人気がある。
<u>Eco bags</u> are really popular in Japan.

Translated to English:

<u>Eco-friendly/reusable shopping bags</u> are really popular in Japan.

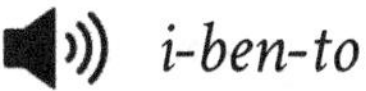 *i-ben-to*

Event

イベント

Meaning in Japan:

Sale

Example Japanglish Sentence:

今週末、私の好きな店でイベントがある!

My favorite store is having an *event* this weekend!

Translated to English:

My favorite store is having a *sale* this weekend!

han-do-mei-do

Handmade

ハンドメイド

Meaning in Japan:

Handmade, homemade, made from scratch

Example Japanglish Sentence:

私たちのスープは、すべてハンドメイドだ。

Our soup is *handmade*.

Translated to English:

Our soup is *made from scratch*.

High Grade

ハイグレード

hai-gu-rē-do

Meaning in Japan:

Good quality

Example Japanglish Sentence:

新しい食料品店はとても高級(ハイグレード)だ。

The new grocery store is really *high grade*.

Translated to English:

The new grocery store is really *good quality.*

Kiosk

キオスク

ki-o-su-ku

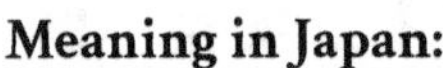

Meaning in Japan:

A small convenience store inside train stations

Example Japanglish Sentence:

日本のほとんどの駅にはキオスクがある。

Every every train station in Japan has *kiosk*.

Translated to English:

Nearly every train station in Japan has *a convenience store called Kiosk*.

mai-bag-gu

MY BAG

マイバッグ

Meaning in Japan:

Reusable shopping bag

Example Japanglish Sentence:

私は、<u>マイバッグ</u>を店に持って行くほうが好きなんだ。環境に良いからね。

I prefer to bring <u>*my bag*</u> to the store; it's better for the environment!

Translated to English:

I prefer to bring a <u>*reusable shopping bag*</u> to the store; it's better for the environment!

ō-dā-mei-do

ORDER MADE

オーダーメイド

Meaning in Japan:

Custom-made

Example Japanglish Sentence:

いつか<u>オーダーメイド</u>のスーツを作るのが夢だ。

My dream is to have an <u>*order made*</u> suit someday.

Translated to English:

My dream is to have a <u>*custom-made*</u> suit someday.

Recycle Shop

ri-sai-ka-ru shop-pu

リサイクルショップ

Meaning in Japan:

Second hand store, thrift store, resale shop, consignment shop

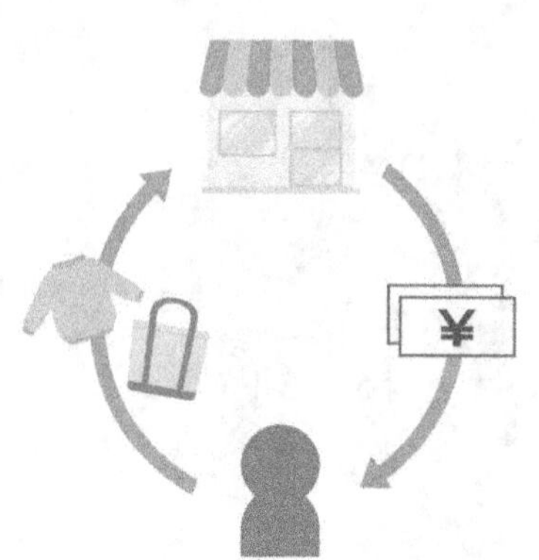

Example Japanglish Sentence:

リサイクルショップで
こんなものを見つけたよ!

Look what I found at the *recycle shop*!

Translated to English:

Look what I found at the *thrift store*!

Regi

re-ji

レジ

Meaning in Japan:

Cash register

Example Japanglish Sentence:

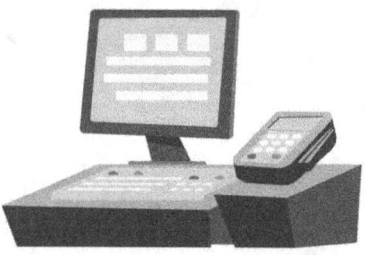

レジでチケットのことを聞いてみて。

You can ask for the tickets at the *regi*.

Translated to English:

You can ask for the tickets at the *(cash) register*.

Self

se-ru-fu

セルフ

Meaning in Japan:

Self-serve, self-service

Example Japanglish Sentence:

(日本では、カフェやレストランなどの接客でよく使われる)：
「水は、<u>セルフ</u>となっております。」

The water is *<u>self</u>*.

(Commonly used in customer service settings, such as restaurants or cafes in Japan. It means the customer should serve themselves water.)

Translated to English:

The water is *<u>self-serve.</u>*

Self-Regi

se-ru-fu-re-ji

セルフレジ

Meaning in Japan:

Self-checkout

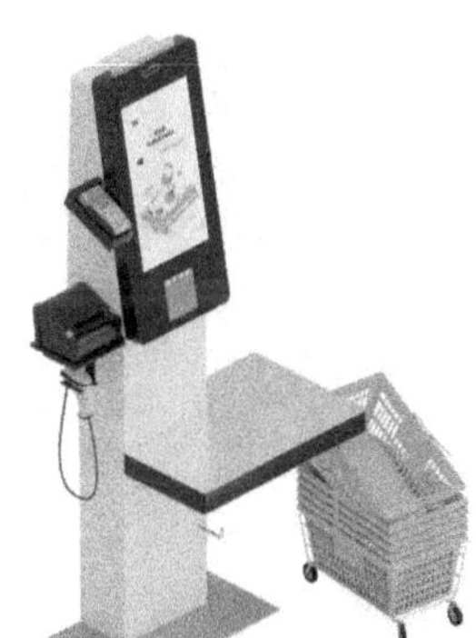

Example Japanglish Sentence:

一部のコンビニには<u>セルフレジ</u>がある。

Some *convenis* have *<u>self-reji</u>* now.

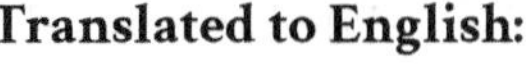

Translated to English:

Some convenience stores have *<u>self-checkout</u>* now.

サービス

Service

sā-bi-su

Meaning in Japan:

Free or complimentary items a manager might give customers at a restaurant or store

Example Japanglish Sentence:

こちらは、サービスでお出ししています。
（日本のレストランや居酒屋などで）

These appetizers are from our *service*.
(Common at Japanese restaurants and izakayas)

Translated to English:

These appetizers are *on the house*.

スーパー

Super

sū-pā

Meaning in Japan:

Supermarket, grocery store

Example Japanglish Sentence:

今週末、スーパーに行った。

I went to the *super* this weekend.

Translated to English:

I went to the *supermarket* this weekend.

tai-mu-sē-ru

Time Sale

タイムセール

Meaning in Japan:

Limited time offer

Example Japanglish Sentence:

今週、カフェが<u>タイムセール</u>をやっていて、コーヒーのおかわりが無料なんだ。

The cafe is having a *<u>time sale</u>* this week and offering free coffee refills all week.

Translated to English:

The cafe is having a *<u>limited time offer</u>* this week and offering free coffee refills all week.

SOCIAL LIFE & LOCAL COMMUNITY

社会生活・地域生活

18

At Home

at-to-hō-mu 

アットホーム

Meaning in Japan:

Cozy, relaxed, comfortable

Example Japanglish Sentence:

私は、あのカフェが大好き。アットホームな雰囲気だから。

I love that coffee shop; it's *at home*.

Translated to English:

I love that coffee shop; it has such a *cozy, relaxed, comfortable atmosphere*.

Barten

bā-ten 

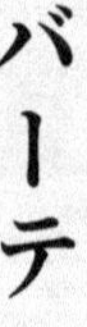

Meaning in Japan:

Bartender

Example Japanglish Sentence:

バーテンに頼めば、
ライムをもらえるよ。

We can ask *barten* for some limes.

Translated to English:

We can ask the *bartender* for some limes.

bū-mu

Boom

ブーム

Meaning in Japan:

Trend, Fad

Example Japanglish Sentence:

今、J-popは大<u>ブーム</u>だ。

J-pop is a big <u>*boom*</u> right now!

Translated to English:

J-pop is a huge <u>*trend*</u> right now!

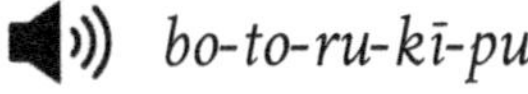

bo-to-ru-kī-pu

Bottle Keep

ボトルキープ

Meaning in Japan:

Bottle keep is a special option offered by some bars in Japan to their frequent patrons. If a customer orders and pays for an entire bottle of alcohol (such as a premium sake) but doesn't wish to finish the whole bottle in one sitting, the customer can ask the bar to keep the bottle. The bottle will be labeled and put away for safe keeping until the customer comes back to finish it later in the week (or whenever).[51]

Example Japanglish Sentence:

今夜はこの日本酒を飲みきれないと思うから、<u>ボトルキープ</u>して、今週中にまた来て飲み切ろう。

I don't think we will drink this whole bottle of sake tonight. Let's do <u>*bottle keep*</u> and come back and finish it later this week.

Translated to English:

I don't think we will drink this whole bottle of sake tonight. Let's ask the bar to <u>*save it for us*</u>, and we can come finish it later this week.

Cleaning

ku-rī-nin-gu 

クリーニング

Meaning in Japan:

Only dry cleaning

Example Japanglish Sentence:

服を<u>クリーニング</u>に
出さないといけない。

I need to take my clothes
for <u>*cleaning*</u>.

Translated to English:

I need to take my clothes for <u>*dry cleaning*</u>.

Culture Center

ka-ru-chā-sen-tā 

カルチャーセンター

Meaning in Japan:

Usually a *culture center* is a type of learning center for adults but is most typically focused on hobbies and art skills one may want to pursue like sewing, knitting, flower arrangement, music, poetry, etc. Depending on the context it could be similar to a community center, adult education center, or community arts center.

Example Japanglish Sentence:

私のおばは、最近<u>カルチャーセンター</u>に行って、
編み物とフラワーアレンジメントを習っている。

My aunt has been going to a <u>*culture center*</u> recently and started learning how to knit and do flower arrangement.

Translated to English:

My aunt has been going to a <u>*community center*</u> recently and started learning how to knit and do flower arrangement.

EPISODE

e-pi-sō-do

エピソード

Meaning in Japan:

A real story or experience that's interesting or worth retelling, something interesting that happened

Example Japanglish Sentence:

昨日あったエピソードを話しておかないといけない。

I have to tell you an *episode* that happened yesterday!

Translated to English:

I have to tell you a *story* about what happened yesterday!
I have to tell you *what happened* yesterday!

GORGEOUS

gō-ja-su

ゴージャス

Meaning in Japan:

Luxurious

Example Japanglish Sentence:

ホテルのシーツは、触り心地がとてもゴージャスだった！

The sheets at the hotel felt so *gorgeous*.

Translated to English:

The sheets at the hotel felt so *luxurious*.

Missa

ミサ

mi-sa

Meaning in Japan:

Catholic mass

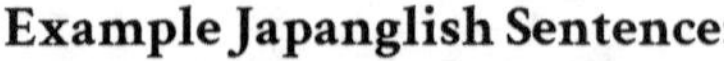

Example Japanglish Sentence:

彼らはカトリックではないけれど、
クリスマスの<u>ミサ</u>に参加した。

They joined the Christmas *<u>missa</u>* even though they aren't Catholic.

Translated to English:

They went to the Christmas *<u>mass</u>* even though they aren't Catholic.

Mood

ムード

mū-do 

Meaning in Japan:

Ambiance or atmosphere in a restaurant or place

Example Japanglish Sentence:

新しいレストランの<u>ムード</u>(雰囲気)はきっと気に入るよ!
上品だけど、気取ってなくてリラックスできる感じなんだ。

You'll love the *<u>mood</u>* at the new restaurant! It's classy but chill.

Translated to English:

You'll love the *<u>ambiance</u>* at the new restaurant! It's classy but chill.

My Boom

mai-bū-mu

マイブーム

Meaning in Japan:

Whatever interest or hobby a person is really into at any given moment

Example Japanglish Sentence:

今、J-popがマイブームなんだ。

Now, J-pop is *my boom*.

Translated to English:

I'm *really into* J-pop right now.
I've been *really into* J-pop recently.

Outside

au-to-sai-do

アウトサイド

Meaning in Japan:

This can mean out of one's house or office or current place. "Let's go *outside* for dinner," is a suggestion to go to a restaurant. "I didn't go *outside* for one week," might mean you went outdoors, but you didn't leave your house. It's very similar to how we use "go out" in English.

Example Japanglish Sentence:

今週ずっと雨で家にこもりっぱなしで、もううんざりだ。
今夜は外で食べようよ!

I'm so tired of sitting at home with all the rain this week.
Let's eat *outside* tonight!

Translated to English:

I'm so tired of sitting at home with all the rain this week.
Let's eat *out* tonight!

Sister

shi-su-tā

シスター

Meaning in Japan:

Only a Catholic nun

Example Japanglish Sentence:

彼女は敬虔な信者になり、今ではシスターだ。

She became very religious, and now she is a *sister*.

Translated to English:

She became very religious, and now she is a (Catholic) nun.

Terrace

te-ra-su

テラス

Meaning in Japan:

Terrace usually describes a large, luxurious balcony at a restaurant or upscale hotel. It could also be used to describe a large patio of outside seating at a restaurant.

Example Japanglish Sentence:

レストランではテラス席に座ろうよ。
地上階よりも高いところの方が好きなんだ。

Let's sit on the *terrace* at the restaurant;
I prefer to be up high rather than on the ground level.

Translated to English:

Let's sit on the *balcony* at the restaurant;
I prefer to be up high rather than on the ground level.

Sports & Exercise

19

スポーツ・運動

Aerobike

ear-o-bai-ku

エアロバイク

Meaning in Japan:

Exercise bike, Stationary bike

Example Japanglish Sentence:

最近<u>エアロバイク</u>を購入したので、
ジムに行く必要がなくなった。

We recently got an *<u>aerobike</u>*, so we don't have to go to the gym as often.

Translated to English:

We recently got an *<u>exercise bike</u>*,
so we don't have to go to the gym as often.

Ame Foot

a-me-fu-to

アメフト

Meaning in Japan:

American football

Example Japanglish Sentence:

<u>アメフト</u>はとても危なそう!
子どもにさせるのは、ちょっと迷う。

<u>Ame foot</u> seems so dangerous!
I'm not sure I'd let my kids play that sport!

Translated to English:

<u>American football</u> seems so dangerous!
I'm not sure I'd let my kids play that sport!

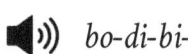

BACK NET

バックネット

bak-ku net-to

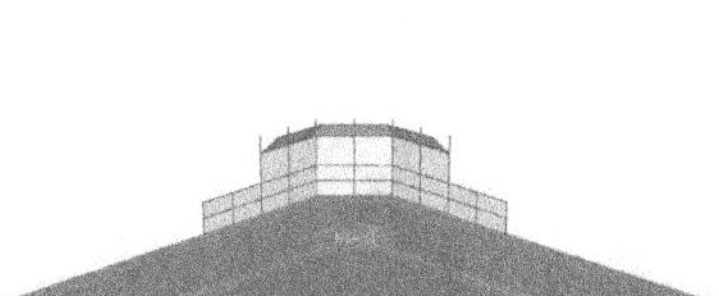

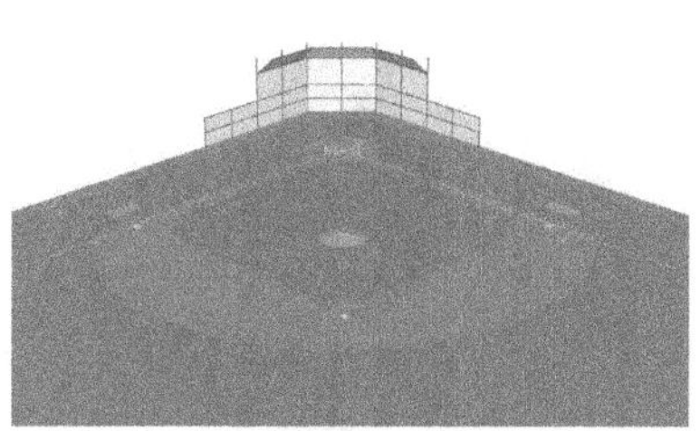

Meaning in Japan:

Backstop in baseball

Example Japanglish Sentence:

バックネットのおかげでファウル
ボールが観客に当たらずに済んだ。

The *back net* protected the fans from the foul ball.

Translated to English:

The *backstop* protected the fans from the foul ball.

BODY BUIL

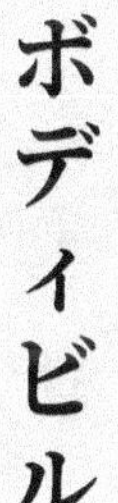

bo-di-bi-ru

Meaning in Japan:

Body building

Example Japanglish Sentence:

高校卒業後、彼女はボディビルに
興味を持つようになった。

After high school,
she got interested in *body buil*.

Translated to English:

After high school, she got interested in *body building*.

Bound

ba-un-do 

バウンド

Meaning in Japan:

To bounce a ball

Example Japanglish Sentence:

子どもたち、家の中でボールをつかない!

Kids, don't *bound* the ball inside the house.

Translated to English:

Kids, don't *bounce* the ball inside the house.

Catch Ball

kyat-chi-bō-ru

キャッチボール

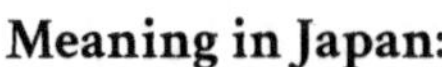

Meaning in Japan:

Playing catch; Throwing the ball back and forth

Example Japanglish Sentence:

うちの子たちは、週末になるとお父さんとキャッチボールをするのが好きなのよ。

My kids like to play *catch ball* outside with their dad on the weekends.

Translated to English:

My kids like to play *catch* outside with their dad on the weekends.

chi-a-dan-su

Cheer Dance

チアダンス

Meaning in Japan:

Cheerleading

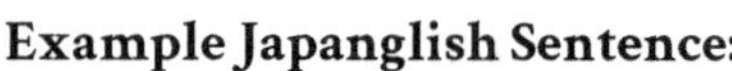

Example Japanglish Sentence:

チアガールたちは、
アメフトの試合でチアダンスをした。

The *cheer girls* did *cheer dance* at the *ame foot* game.

Translated to English:

The cheerleaders *cheered* / did *cheerleading* at the American football game.

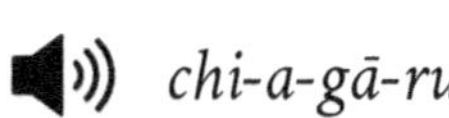

chi-a-gā-ru

Cheer Girl

チアガール

Meaning in Japan:

Female cheerleader

Example Japanglish Sentence:

チアガールたちは、
アメフトの試合でチアダンスをした。

The *cheer girls* did *cheer dance* at the *ame foot* game.

Translated to English:

The *cheerleaders* did cheerleading at the American football game.

Course

kō-su

コース

Meaning in Japan:

Hiking trail

Example Japanglish Sentence:

その国立公園には、素晴らしいコースがたくさんある。

The national park has a lot of really great *courses*.

Translated to English:

The national park has a lot of really great *hiking trails*.

Crawl

ku-rō-ru

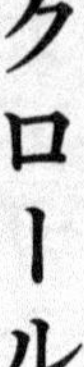

Meaning in Japan:

Freestyle or front crawl (UK) stroke in swimming

Example Japanglish Sentence:

彼女の息子は、本当にクロールが上手い。
去年いくつも賞を受賞したんだ！

Her son is really good at *crawling*.
He won several awards last year!

Translated to English:

Her son is really good at *freestyle*.
He won several swimming awards last year!

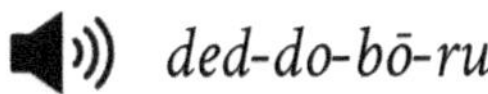

ded-do-bō-ru

Dead Ball

デッドボール

Meaning in Japan:

Hit-by-pitch in baseball (when the pitcher hits the batter with the ball)

Example Japanglish Sentence:

試合は、めちゃくちゃだったよ。デッドボールが3回もあったんだ。

The game was crazy! There were three *dead balls*!

Translated to English:

The game was crazy! There were three *hit-by-pitches*!

dō-mu

Dome

ドーム

Meaning in Japan:

Typically used as part of a sports stadium's name (e.g., Osaka Dome, Tokyo Dome)

Example Japanglish Sentence:

私たちの学校の文化祭は、ドームで行われる。

Our school festival will be held at the *dome*.

Translated to English:

Our school festival will be held at the *stadium*.

Fitness

fit-to-ne-su

フィットネス

Meaning in Japan:

Gym

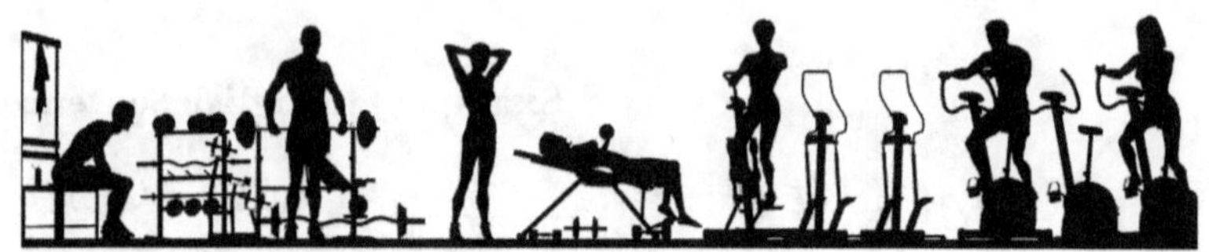

Example Japanglish Sentence:

私は、毎日フィットネスに行っている。

I go to the *fitness* every day.

Translated to English:

I go to the *gym* every day.

Flying (start)

fu-ra-in-gu su-tā-to 

フライング（スタート）

Meaning in Japan:

False start in a race

Example Japanglish Sentence:

彼女はフライングスタートで失格になった。

She was disqualified from the race for a *flying start*!

Translated to English:

She was disqualified from the race for a *false start*!

fo-a-bō-ru FOUR BALL

フォアボール

Meaning in Japan:

A walk in baseball or base on balls (when the pitcher throws four *balls* to the same batter during his chance at batting)

Example Japanglish Sentence:

フォアボールが多くて、試合の流れがゆっくりでちょっと退屈だった。

The baseball game was kind of boring and slow; there were a lot of *four balls*.

Translated to English:

The baseball game was kind of boring and slow; there were a lot of walks.

fu-ru-bē-su FULL BASE

フルベース

Meaning in Japan:

In baseball, full base means the bases are loaded (there is currently a runner on each base)

Example Japanglish Sentence:

満塁だ！彼はグランドスラムを打てるのか？！

It's *full base*! Can he hit a grand slam?!

Translated to English:

The bases are loaded! Can he hit a grand slam?

Game Set

gē-mu-set-to

ゲームセット

Meaning in Japan:

An abbreviation of "game, set, match" and used to indicate the end of a game or sporting event, especially baseball

Example Japanglish Sentence:

ゲームセット!今のが最終回だったね。家に帰ろう。

Game set! That was the last inning! Let's go home!

Translated to English:

Game, set, match! *Game over*! That was the last inning! Let's go home!

Gerende

ge-ren-de

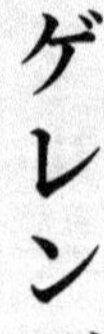

Meaning in Japan:

Ski slopes

Example Japanglish Sentence:

夜のゲレンデはライトアップされていて、とても幻想的だ。

The *gerende* is illuminated at night, creating a truly magical atmosphere!

Translated to English:

The *ski slopes* are illuminated at night, creating a truly magical atmosphere!

Goal

gō-rū

ゴール

Meaning in Japan:

The finish line in a race or any other type of sports goal

Example Japanglish Sentence:

彼がゴールラインを越えたとき、観客は歓声を上げた。彼にとってレースで初めての優勝だった。

When he ran across the *goal*, the crowd cheered. It was the first time he had ever gotten first place in a race.

Translated to English:

When he ran across the *finish line*, the crowd cheered. It was the first time he had ever gotten first place in a race.

Goal Net

gō-ru-net-to

ゴールネット

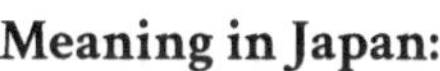

Meaning in Japan:

The net of any goal

Example Japanglish Sentence:

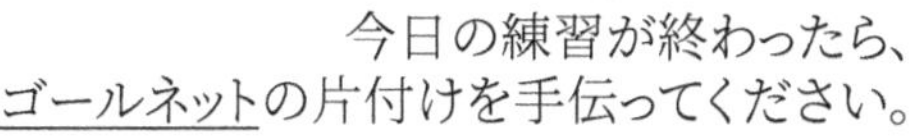

今日の練習が終わったら、ゴールネットの片付けを手伝ってください。

Please help remove the *goal nets* after practice today.

Translated to English:

Please help remove the *nets* from the soccer goals after practice today.

Ground

グラウンド

gu-ra-un-do 

Meaning in Japan:

1. Field or space for sports or athletics, pitch (UK)
2. Playground

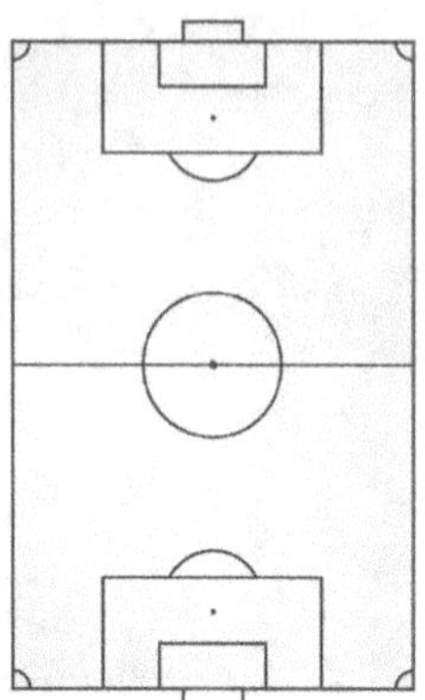

Example Japanglish Sentence:

生徒は全員、今日の放課後にグラウンドへ集合すること。

All students should go to the *ground* after school today.

Translated to English:

All students should go to the *field* after school today.

Gym

ジム

ji-mu 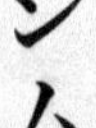

Meaning in Japan:

Gym only describes a place to work out, like a fitness center. It is not used to describe a school gymnasium

Example Japanglish Sentence:

日本の学校には、トレーニング用のマシンがあるジムはなく、バスケットボールや体育の授業に使う体育館しかない。

Schools in Japan don't have a *gym ジム (jimu)* with machines to work out, only a *gymnasium* 体育館 *(taiikukan)* for basketball games and PE.

Translated to English:

Schools in Japan don't have a *gym* with machines to work out, only a *gym* for basketball games and PE.

han-di

Handi / Handy

ハンディ・ハンディー

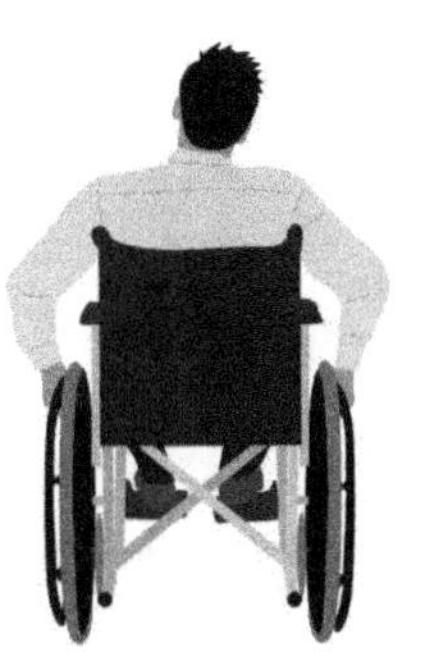

Meaning in Japan:

1. (ハンディ) Handicap, disability, or disadvantage, usually with a negative connotation
2. Hand-held, portable, compact, with a positive connotation
3. Handicap in golf

Example Japanglish Sentence:

彼女にはハンディがある。

She has a *handy.*

私は、ハンディーサイズの辞書が欲しい。

I want a *handy-size* dictionary.

彼のゴルフのハンディは、7だ。

He has a golf *handy* of 7.

Translated to English:

She has a *disability*.

I want a *compact*/*portable* dictionary.

His golf *handicap* is 7.

Left Over

re-fu-to-ō-ba

レフトオーバー

Meaning in Japan:

A hit in baseball that goes over the left-fielder's head

Example Japanglish Sentence:

彼は試合の終盤で大きなレフトオーバーの打球を決めて、
三塁まで到達した。スリーベースヒットだった！

He did a *left over* at the end of the game and made it all the way to third base. It was a triple!

Translated to English:

He had a huge *hit to left field* at the end of the game. It went over the left-fielder's head, and he made it all the way to third base. It was a triple!

Loss Time

ro-su-tai-mu 

ロスタイム

Meaning in Japan:

Stoppage time, Added/additional time, Injury time, Extra time

Example Japanglish Sentence:

審判は試合終了時に3分の
ロスタイムを追加した。

The referee added three minutes of *loss time* at the end of the game.

Translated to English:

The ref added five minutes of *injury time* / *stoppage time* at the end of the game.

nai-tā

Nighter

ナイター

Meaning in Japan:

A baseball game that takes place at night or at least in part after sunset

Example Japanglish Sentence:

今日は、チームのナイター試合があるから、夕食を一緒にできない。

I can't meet you for dinner today because our team has a *nighter*.

Translated to English:

I can't meet you for dinner today because our baseball team has a *night game*.

nō-ka-un-to

No Count

ノーカウント

Meaning in Japan:

A goal that doesn't count, a "no goal"

Example Japanglish Sentence:

そのサッカー選手がきれいなゴールを決めたけど、
審判はオフサイドでノーカウントにした。

The soccer player scored a beautiful goal,
but the referee said it was *no count* since she was slightly offside.

Translated to English:

The soccer player scored a beautiful goal,
but the referee said it was a *no goal* since she was slightly offside.

ONE TEAM

wan-chī-mu

ワンチーム

Meaning in Japan:

To work together as a team

Example Japanglish Sentence:

試合の前半はあまり良くなかったけれど、
後半はワンチームになって逆転し、勝つことができた。

The game started off poorly in the first half, but in the second half, we did *one team* and were able to come back and win the game.

Translated to English:

The game started off poorly in the first half, but in the second half, we *started working together as a team* and were able to come back and win the game.

REVENGE

ri-ben-ji

リベンジ

Meaning in Japan:

1. To get a rematch against a team that previously beat you/your team
2. To try again after failing

Example Japanglish Sentence:

今回うまくいかなくても大丈夫。また立ち上がって、リベンジすればいいんだ。

It's okay that you didn't succeed this time; just get back up and *revenge*.

野球の試合は、全部負けたけど、最後の試合でリベンジした。

We lost all of our baseball games, but at the last game, we *revenged*!

Translated to English:

It's okay that you didn't succeed this time; just get back up and *try again*.

We lost all of our baseball games, but at the last game, *we finally won a game*!

Rugger

ra-gā

ラガー

Meaning in Japan:

1. A rugby player
2. Lager beer

Example Japanglish Sentence:

試合のあと、有名なラガーマンたちは、私がよく行くバーでラガー（ビール）を飲む。

Famous *ruggers* always drink *ruggers* after the game at the bar I go to.

Translated to English:

Famous *rugby players* always drink *lager* after the game at the bar I go to.

Running Home Run

ran-nin-gu-hō-mu-ran

ランニングホームラン

Meaning in Japan:

An inside-the-park home run in baseball

Example Japanglish Sentence:

最終回、彼がランニングホームランを打って同点に追いついた。

In the last inning, he hit a *running home run* and tied the game.

Translated to English:

In the last inning, he hit an *inside-the-park home run* and tied the game.

SAND BAG

san-do bag-gu

サンドバッグ

Meaning in Japan:

Punching bag, boxing bag

Example Japanglish Sentence:

ジムにはサンドバッグがある。

They have *sand bags* at my gym.

Translated to English:

They have *punching/boxing bags* at my gym.

SAYONARA HIT

sa-yo-na-ra hit-to

さよならヒット

Meaning in Japan:

A winning and game-ending hit in baseball, a walk-off

Example Japanglish Sentence:

負けていたが、最終回にスター選手がサヨナラヒットを打って、
逆転勝利した!

They were behind, but the star player had a *sayonara hit* in the last inning!

Translated to English:

They were behind, but the star player had *a walk-off* in the last inning!

They were behind, but the star player had *a great hit in the last inning that won the game*!

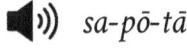

shī-zun-o-fu

Season Off

シーズンオフ

Meaning in Japan:

Off-season

Example Japanglish Sentence:

今は<u>シーズンオフ</u>なので、放課後のバスケ練習はない。

It's <u>*season off*</u>, so I don't have basketball practice after school.

Translated to English:

It's the <u>*off-season*</u>, so I don't have basketball practice after school.

sa-pō-tā

Supporter

サポーター

Meaning in Japan:

1. Fans of a sports team or celebrity
2. A brace used for a joint, like a knee or elbow, after an injury

Example Japanglish Sentence:

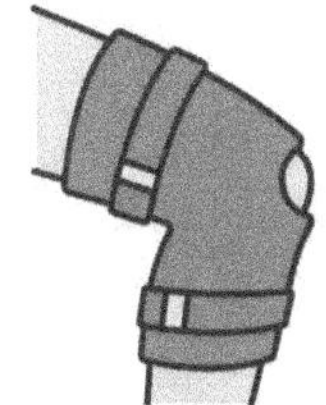

その<u>サッカーチーム</u>にはとても熱心なサポーターがいる。

The soccer team has some really enthusiastic <u>*supporters*</u>!

彼女は、肘をケガしてから、4週間<u>サポーター</u>をつけないといけなかった。

She had to wear a <u>*supporter*</u> for four weeks after she injured her elbow.

Translated to English:

The soccer team has some really enthusiastic <u>*fans*</u>!

She had to wear a <u>*brace*</u> for four weeks after she injured her elbow.

Touch Out

tat-chi-au-to

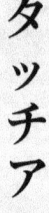

タッチアウト

Meaning in Japan:

A force out in baseball

Example Japanglish Sentence:

外野手はセカンドベースにボールを投げて、<u>タッチアウト</u>になった。

The outfielder threw the ball to second base for the *<u>touch out</u>*.

Translated to English:

The outfielder threw the ball to second base for the *<u>force out</u>*.

Touch Up

tat-chi-ap-pu 

タッチアップ

Meaning in Japan:

To tag up on a base before running in baseball after a fly ball is caught by a fielder

Example Japanglish Sentence:

選手はフライを取ったあと、ファーストベースに<u>タッチアップ</u>するのを忘れて、外野手がファーストに投げてアウトになった。

The player forgot to *<u>touch up</u>* first base after the fly ball. So the outfielder threw the ball to the first baseman and got an out.

Translated to English:

The player forgot to *<u>tag up</u>* on first base after the fly ball. So the outfielder threw the ball to the first baseman and got an out.

ba-rē

VOLLEY

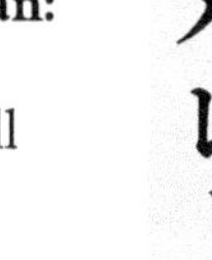

バレー

Meaning in Japan:

Volleyball

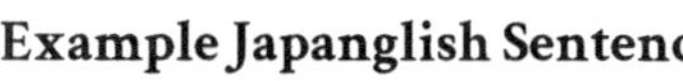

Example Japanglish Sentence:

<u>バレー</u>できる所、どこか知ってる?

Do you know where we can play *<u>volley</u>*?

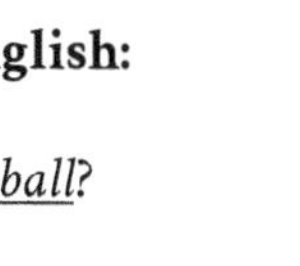

Translated to English:

Do you know where we can play *<u>volleyball</u>*?

yot-to

YACHT

ヨット

Meaning in Japan:

Any kind of sailboat, both big and small, including everything from a windsurfing board to a luxury super yacht

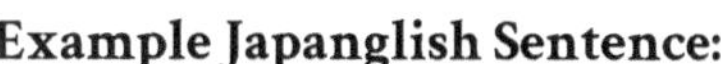

Example Japanglish Sentence:

今週末は湖で<u>ヨット</u>のレッスンを受けてきた。すごく楽しかった!

We took a *<u>yacht</u>* lesson at the lake this weekend. It was so fun!

Translated to English:

We took a *<u>windsurfing</u>* lesson at the lake this weekend. It was so fun!

TECHNOLOGY

テクノロジー

20

APPLI

a-pu-ri

アプリ

Meaning in Japan:

App, Application

Example Japanglish Sentence:

新しいアプリは、ひどい。

Their new *appli* is terrible.

Translated to English:

Their new *app* is terrible.

BS

bī-e-su

ビーエス

Meaning in Japan:

Satellite TV

Example Japanglish Sentence:

BS持ってる？私は、持ってる。

Do you have *BS*? I do!

Translated to English:

Do you have *satellite TV*? I do!

de-ji-ka-me

DIJI CAME

デジカメ

Meaning in Japan:

An abbreviation for digital camera

Example Japanglish Sentence:

ほとんどの人が、スマホで写真を撮っているけれど、私は、まだ、デジカメが好きだ。

I still like using my *diji came* even though most people just use their phones now.

Translated to English:

I still like using my *digital camera* even though most people just use their phones now.

fu-rī-dai-ya-ru

FREE DIAL

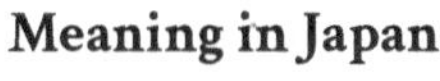

Meaning in Japan:

Toll-free phone number

Example Japanglish Sentence:

詳しい情報については、フリーダイヤルで問い合わせできるはずだ。

They should have a *free dial* you can call to get more information.

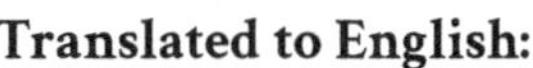

Translated to English:

They should have a *toll-free number* you can call to get more information.

HANDLE NAME

han-do-ru-nē-mu 

ハンドルネーム

Meaning in Japan:

Screenname, username, handle

Example Japanglish Sentence:

SNSのハンドルネームは何？

What's your *handle name* for your social media?

Translated to English:

What's your *username* / *handle* for your social media?

HIGH VISION TELEBI

hai-bi-jon te-re-bi 

ハイビジョンテレビ

Meaning in Japan:

HDTV

Example Japanglish Sentence:

うちで一緒に試合観戦しない？ハイビジョンテレビがあるよ。

Do you want to watch the game at our house? We have *high vision TV*.

Translated to English:

Do you want to watch the game at our house? We have HDTV.

Mail

mē-ru

ル

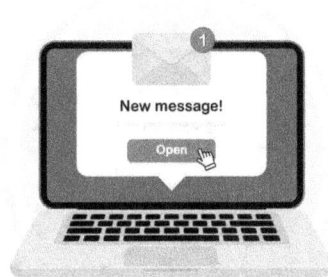

Meaning in Japan:

Only e-mail

Example Japanglish Sentence:

2週間の休暇からオフィスに戻ったら、多量の<u>メール</u>が届いていた。

When I came back to my office after a two-week vacation, I had so much <u>*mail*</u> to sort through!

Translated to English:

When I came back to my office after a two-week vacation, I had so many <u>*emails*</u> to sort through!

Mail Ad

me-ru-a-do

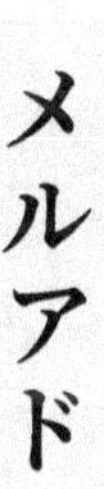

Meaning in Japan:

E-mail address

Example Japanglish Sentence:

私は、中学の時に使っていた<u>メルアド</u>を今でも使っている。

I still use the <u>*mail ad*</u> that I used when I was in middle school.

Translated to English:

I still use the same <u>*e-mail address*</u> that I used when I was in middle school.

Mail Address

mē-ru-a-do-re-su 

メールアドレス

Meaning in Japan:

E-mail address

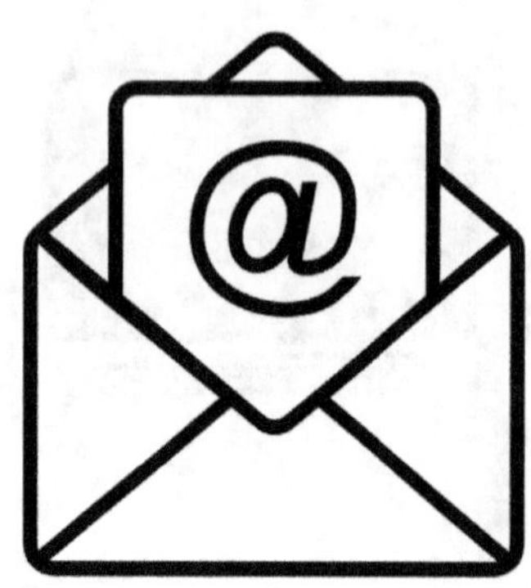

Example Japanglish Sentence:

私は、中学の時に使っていた
メールアドレスを今でも使っている。

I still use the *mail address* that I used when I was in middle school.

Translated to English:

I still use the *e-mail address* that I used when I was in middle school.

Mail Magazine

mē-ru-ma-ga-jin 

メールマガジン

Meaning in Japan:

E-mail newsletter

Subscribe
to our
newsletter

Example Japanglish Sentence:

私は、毎週メールマガジン（メルマガ）
を受け取っている。

I receive their *mail magazine* every week.

Translated to English:

I receive their *e-mail newsletter* every week.

MANNER MODE

マナーモード

ma-nā-mō-do

Meaning in Japan:

Silent or vibrate mode on a phone

Example Japanglish Sentence:

プレゼンが始まる前に、携帯電話をマナーモードにしてください。

Please put your phones on *manner mode* before the presentation begins!

Translated to English:

Please put your phones on *silent* before the presentation begins!

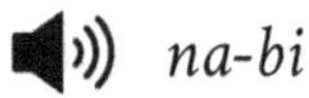

na-bi

NAVI

ナビ

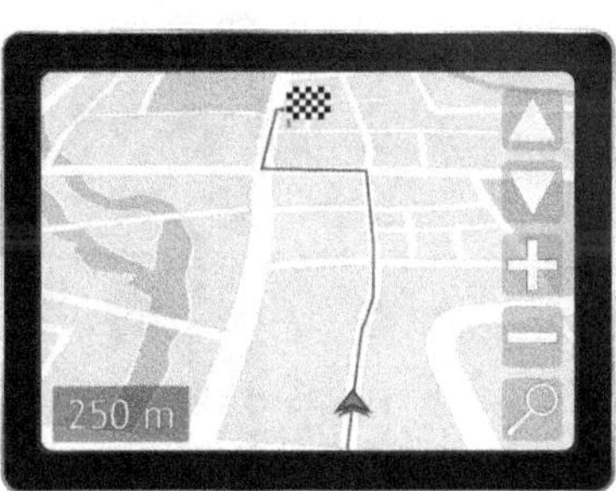

Meaning in Japan:

Car navigational system, GPS

Example Japanglish Sentence:

君の車、ナビついてる？最近はだいたいの車についてるよね。

Does your car have *navi*?
I heard a lot of cars have it now.

Translated to English:

Does your car have a *navigational system*?
I heard a lot of cars have it now.

Note Perso Com

nō-to-pa-so-kon 

ノートパソコン

Meaning in Japan:

Laptop computer

Example Japanglish Sentence:

最新の<u>ノートパソコン</u>の中には、10年前のものと比べて非常に軽量なものもある。

Some of the newest *<u>note perso coms</u>* are so lightweight compared to the ones from 10 years ago.

Translated to English:

Some of the newest *<u>laptops</u>* are so lightweight compared to the ones from 10 years ago.

Remo Con

ri-mo-kon

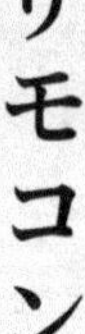

Meaning in Japan:

Remote control

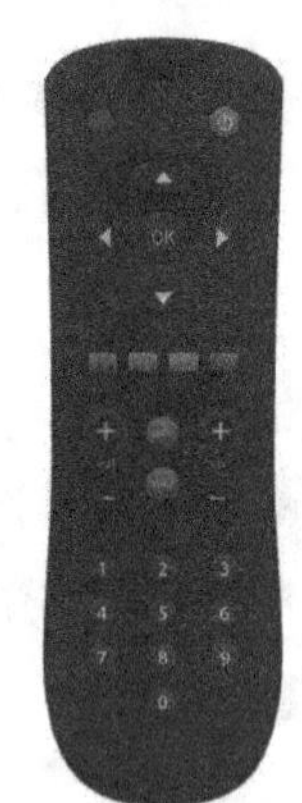

Example Japanglish Sentence:

<u>リモコン</u>をとってくれる。

Can you pass me the *<u>remo con</u>*?

Translated to English:

Can you pass me the *<u>remote control</u>*?

e-su-e-nu-e-su

SNS

エスエヌエス

Meaning in Japan:

An acronym for "Social Networking Services," meaning social media

Example Japanglish Sentence:

お互いにSNSでフォローしようよ。

Let's follow each other on *SNS*.

Translated to English:

Let's follow each other on *social media*.

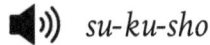

su-ku-sho

Suksho

スクショ

Meaning in Japan:

Screenshot

This is an abbreviation of **sc**reen**sho**t that became *sc sho* but when given Japanese katakana symbols and pronunciation, it sounds more like *suk sho*

Example Japanglish Sentence:

私が送ったものをスクショに撮っておいて。

Please take a *suksho* of what I sent you.

Translated to English:

Please take a *screenshot* of what I sent you.

Telop

te-rop-pu

テロップ

Meaning in Japan:

Text, captions, or graphics superimposed onto a TV or video image

Example Japanglish Sentence:

SNSでバズってる人たちは、動画の中で面白いコメントを<u>テロップ</u>で出してるよね。

Many social media personalities use <u>*telop*</u> to show funny comments during their videos.

Translated to English:

Many social media personalities use <u>*graphics and text over their videos*</u> to show funny comments during their posts.

Version Up

bā-jon-ap-pu

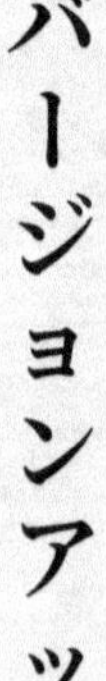

Meaning in Japan:

To upgrade to a new version of software, to update software to the latest operating system

Example Japanglish Sentence:

コンピューターのOSを<u>バージョンアップ</u>する必要がある。

I need to <u>*version up*</u> my computer operating system.

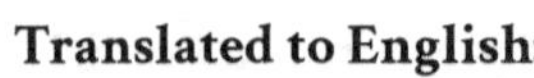

Translated to English:

I need to <u>*update*</u> my computer operating system.

Tools & Useful Items

道具・便利グッズ

21

ALUMI (FOIL)

a-ru-mi (ho-i-ru)

アルミ（ホイル）

Meaning in Japan:

Alumi is an abbreviation of "aluminum", and alumi foil is an abbreviation of "aluminum foil"

Example Japanglish Sentence:

私たちの研究は、アルミをより効率的にリサイクルする方法を探ることを目的としている。

Our research will look for more efficient ways to recycle *alumi*.

テイクアウト用の箱はないけれど、アルミホイルならつかえるよ。

I don't have a to-go box, but you can use *alumi foil*.

Translated to English:

Our research will look for more efficient ways to recycle *aluminum*.

I don't have a to-go box, but you can use *alumium foil*.

CUTTER

kat-tā

カッター

Meaning in Japan:

Utility knife, X-acto knife

Example Japanglish Sentence:

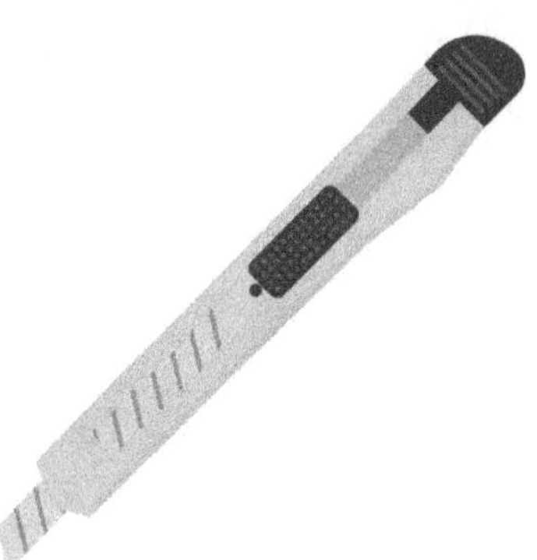

学校のプロジェクトでカッターがいる。

I need a *cutter* for my school project.

Translated to English:

I need a *utility knife* for my school project.

do-rai-bā

Driver

ドライバー

Meaning in Japan:

Screwdriver

Example Japanglish Sentence:

彼はL's Hardwareで<u>ドライバー</u>を買った。

He bought a <u>*driver*</u> at L's Hardware..

Translated to English:

He bought a <u>*screwdriver*</u> at L's Hardware.

Where Can I Buy a Driver?

I once had this confusing conversation with a student.

Student - I need a *driver*. Do you know where I can buy one?
Me - What do you mean? Do you need a taxi?
Student - No.
Me - Do you need to rent a car?
Student - No, the car is fine. I don't need a ride anywhere.
Me - But you said you need a *driver*. What do you need? A golf club?

She then acted out the motion of using a screwdriver and explained that he needed to fix something.

"Ohhhhhh," I said, "A screwdriver!"

Kitchen Paper

kit-chin-pē-pā

キッチンペーパー

Meaning in Japan:

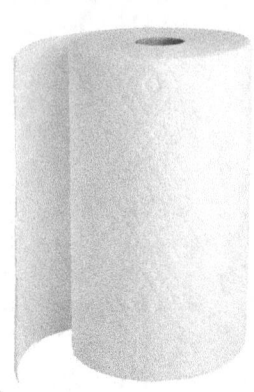

Paper towels, Kitchen roll (UK)

Example Japanglish Sentence:

アメリカ人は<u>キッチンペーパー</u>をたくさん使うことに気づいたよ。掃除にまで使うんだね！

I noticed that Americans use a lot of *<u>kitchen paper</u>* - even for cleaning!

Translated to English:

I noticed that Americans use a lot of *<u>paper towels</u>* - even for cleaning!

Knife

nai-fu 

ナイフ

Meaning in Japan:

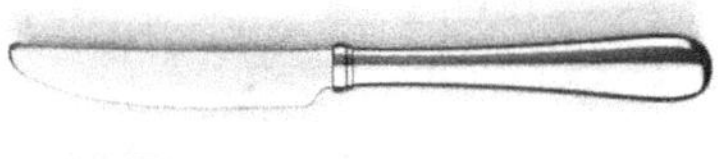

Dinner knife or pocketknife, but not a chopping knife

Example Japanglish Sentence:

シェフは普通の<u>ナイフ</u>だけではなく、シェフナイフ(<u>包丁</u>)が必要だ。

A chef can't just use a *<u>knife ナイフ (naifu)</u>*; he needs a chef's *<u>knife 包丁 (hōchō)</u>* for chopping.

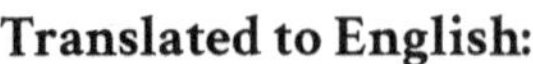

Translated to English:

A chef can't just use a steak *<u>knife</u>*; he needs a chef's *<u>knife</u>* for chopping.

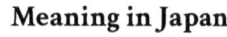

🔊 *mai-na-su-do-rai-bā* **MINUS DRIVER**

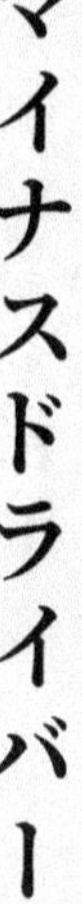

Meaning in Japan:

Flathead screwdriver

Example Japanglish Sentence:

シンクは、修理できると思うけれど、まずは<u>マイナスドライバー</u>を手に入れないといけない。

I think I know how to fix the problem with the sink, but first I need to get a *<u>minus driver</u>*.

Translated to English:

I think I know how to fix the problem with the sink, but first I need to get a *<u>flathead screwdriver</u>*.

🔊 *pen-chi* **PENCHI**

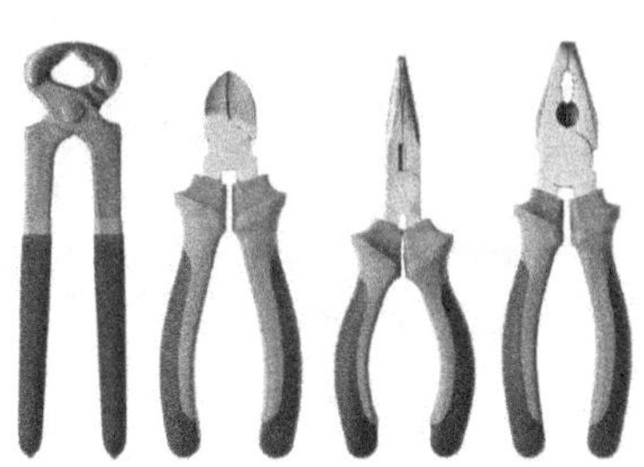

Meaning in Japan:

Pliers

Example Japanglish Sentence:

このパイプを直すのに、ハンマーと<u>ペンチ</u>が要るよ。

I need a hammer and some *<u>penchi</u>* to fix this pipe.

Translated to English:

I need a hammer and some *<u>pliers</u>* to fix this pipe.

PET Bottle

pet-to-bo-to-ru

ペットボトル

Meaning in Japan:

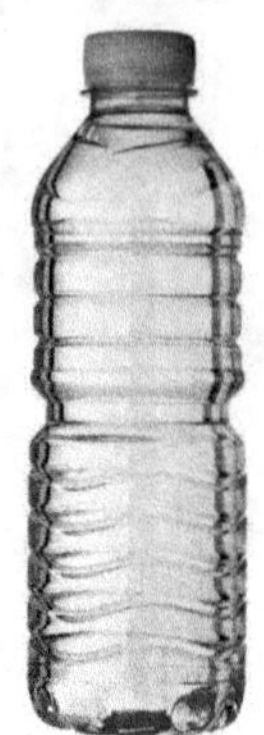

Plastic, disposable, single-use water bottle

Example Japanglish Sentence:

その日本企業は、<u>ペットボトル</u>の新しいエコデザインを提案している。

This Japanese company has proposed some new *eco* designs for their <u>*PET bottles*</u>.

Translated to English:

This Japanese company has proposed some new eco-friendly designs for their <u>*disposable plastic bottles*</u>!

Plus Driver

pu-ra-su-do-rai-bā 

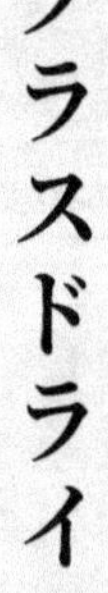

Meaning in Japan:

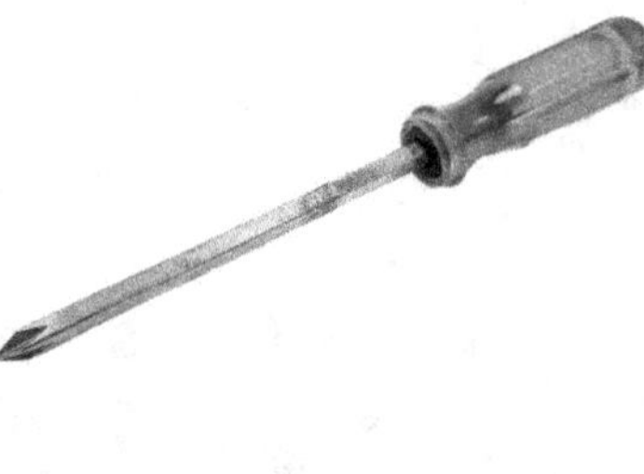

Phillips-head screwdriver

Example Japanglish Sentence:

シンクは修理できると思うけれど、まずは<u>プラスドライバー</u>を手に入れないといけない。

I think I know how to fix the problem with the sink, but first I need to get a <u>*plus driver*</u>.

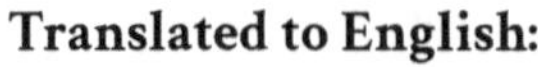

Translated to English:

I think I know how to fix the problem with the sink, but first I need to get a <u>*Phillips screwdriver*</u>.

🔊 *pot-to* — Pot

ポット

Meaning in Japan:

Electric kettle

Example Japanglish Sentence:

大学に入るときに両親が<u>ポット</u>をくれて、
それが本当に最高のプレゼントだった！

My parents gave me a <u>*pot*</u> when I went to college, and it was the best gift ever!

Translated to English:

My parents gave me an <u>*electric kettle*</u> when I went to college, and it was the best gift ever!

🔊 *tap-pā* — Tuppa

タッパー

Meaning in Japan:

Tupperware

Example Japanglish Sentence:

私は<u>タッパー</u>製の水筒が好きだ。

I like the water bottles made from <u>*tuppa*</u>.

Translated to English:

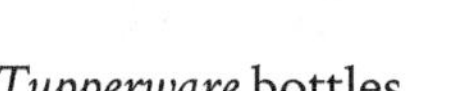

I like the <u>*Tupperware*</u> bottles.

Vinyl

bi-nī-ru

ビニール

Meaning in Japan:

Plastic bag

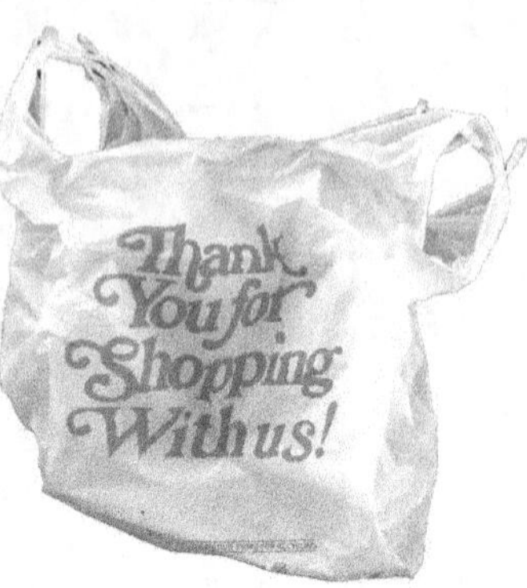

Example Japanglish Sentence:

私たちは、環境を守るために、ビニール袋の使用をやめる必要がある。

We need to stop using *vinyl bags* to save the environment.

Translated to English:

We need to stop using *plastic bags* in order to save the environment.

Wrap

rap-pu

Meaning in Japan:

Saran wrap, plastic wrap
cling wrap

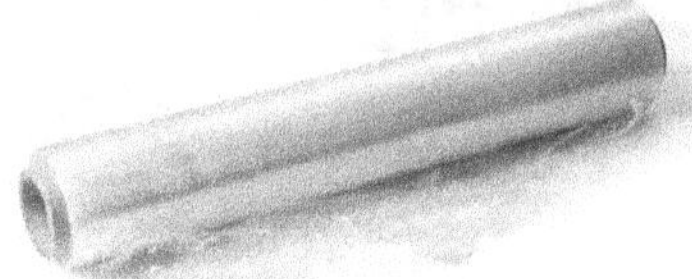

Example Japanglish Sentence:

ラップは、プラスティック製だ。

The *wrap* is made of plastic.

Translated to English:

The *cling wrap* is made of plastic.

TRAVEL & TOURISM

旅行・観光

22

Body Check

bo-dī-chek-ku

ボディーチェック

Meaning in Japan:

Frisk, Search, Pat-down

Example Japanglish Sentence:

ボディーチェックが必要だったせいで、危うく飛行機に乗り遅れるところだった。

We almost missed our flight because we had to do *body check*.

Translated to English:

We almost missed our flight because we got *searched/frisked/randomly selected for a pat-down*.

Boy

bō-i

ボーイ

Meaning in Japan:

Bellboy, bellhop, hotel porter

Example Japanglish Sentence:

泊まったホテルはとても素敵だったよ。なんとボーイまでいたんだ。

Our hotel was so nice;
it even had a *boy*!

Translated to English:

Our hotel was so nice; it even had a *bellhop*!

bi-ji-ne-su ho-te-ru — BUSINESS HOTEL

ビジネスホテル

Meaning in Japan:

Budget hotel, no-frills hotel. In the West, traveling for business typically means you will be staying at a comfortable hotel. It won't be a luxury experience, but the hotel will likely have a comfortable room, decent amenities, and an on-site breakfast. In Japan, traveling for work means you'll be staying at a *business hotel* with very small rooms.[52]

Example Japanglish Sentence:

私は出張での旅行があまり好きじゃない。というのも、たいていビジネスホテルに泊まることになり、部屋がとても狭いからだ。

I don't like traveling for work because we stay at *business hotels* with small rooms.

Translated to English:

I don't like traveling for work because we usually stay at *budget hotels* with small rooms.

kya-bin a-ten-dan-to — CA

キャビンアテンダント

Meaning in Japan:

CA stands for "cabin attendant" which means a flight attendant

Example Japanglish Sentence:

彼女は4か国語を話し、旅行が好きなので、CAの仕事を簡単に見つけた。

She easily found a job as a *CA* because she speaks four languages and likes to travel.

Translated to English:

She easily found a job as a *flight attendant* because she speaks four languages and likes to travel.

Form (Home)

hō-mu

フォーム・ホーム

Meaning in Japan:

This is an abbreviation of "platform," meaning a train platform. When pronounced, it sounds closer to "home." To many non-Japanese-speakers, the katakana F and H often sound the same, and to further complicate it, some foreign words starting with an F are even written with a katakana H (like this one - ホーム *hōmu*).

Example Japanglish Sentence:

<u>ホーム</u>で電車を待っていたら、ボブが新しい彼女といるのを見た。

I was waiting at <u>*home*</u> for the train, and I saw Bob from work.

Translated to English:

I was waiting on the <u>*platform*</u> for the train, and I saw Bob from work.

Front

fu-ron-to 

フロント

Meaning in Japan:

The front desk at a hotel or Japanese inn (ryokan). *Front* does not refer to a front desk at a business or other location.

Example Japanglish Sentence:

<u>フロント</u>に頼めば、タオルもらえるよ。

You can ask for towels at <u>*front*</u>!

Translated to English:

You can ask for towels at the <u>*front desk*</u> / <u>*at reception*</u>!

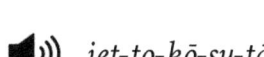

gon-do-ra

Gondola

ゴンドラ

Meaning in Japan:

The ride capsules on a Ferris wheel

Example Japanglish Sentence:

私たちは、シンガポールで<u>ゴンドラ</u>に乗った。

We rode in the *<u>gondola</u>* in Singapore.

Translated to English:

We rode the *<u>Ferris wheel</u>* in Singapore.

jet-to-kō-su-tā

Jet Coaster

Meaning in Japan:

Roller coaster

Example Japanglish Sentence:

「<u>ジェットコースター</u>は好き？」

Do you like *<u>jet coasters</u>*?

Translated to English:

Do you like *<u>roller coasters</u>*?

Los

ロス

ro-su

Meaning in Japan:

Los Angeles, California

Example Japanglish Sentence:

今週末は<u>ロス</u>へ行こう!

Let's go to *<u>Los</u>* this weekend!

Translated to English:

Let's go to *<u>Los Angeles</u>* this weekend!

Morning Call

モーニングコール

mō-nin-gu-kō-ru 

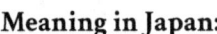

Meaning in Japan:

Wake-up call at a hotel

Example Japanglish Sentence:

午前7時に<u>モーニングコール</u>をしてもらえますか。

Can I get a *<u>morning call</u>* at 7 a.m.?

Translated to English:

Can I get a *<u>wake-up call</u>* at 7 a.m.?

mō-nin-gu-sā-bi-su **MORNING SERVICE**

モーニングサービス

Meaning in Japan:

Room service breakfast at a hotel

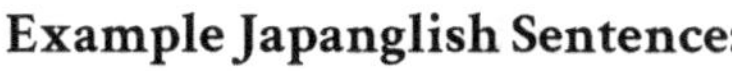

Example Japanglish Sentence:

ホテルは、素敵な<u>モーニングサービス</u>を提供している。

The hotel offers nice *<u>morning service</u>*!

Translated to English:

The hotels offers a nice *<u>room service breakfast</u>*!

pen-shon **PENSION**

ペンション

Meaning in Japan:

Similar to a Western-style Bed & Breakfast and more simple than a traditional Japanese ryokan[53]

Example Japanglish Sentence:

日本を訪れるときは、<u>ペンション</u>に泊まるのがおすすめだ。

I recommend staying at a *<u>pension</u>* when you visit Japan.

Translated to English:

I recommend staying at a *<u>local Bed and Breakfast</u>* when you visit Japan.

Ropeway

rō-pu-wē

ロープウェー

Meaning in Japan:

Cable car, gondola, aerial tram

Example Japanglish Sentence:

富士山には景色のいいロープウェイがあって、眺めが本当にすばらしいよ！

Mt. Fuji has a really scenic *ropeway* with fantastic views!

Translated to English:

Mt. Fuji has a really scenic *gondola/ cable car/ tram* with fantastic views.

Silver Seat

shi-ru-bā-shī-to 

シルバーシート

Meaning in Japan:

A priority seat on public transportation, especially trains, reserved for elderly people. This seat should be left open and available for those who may need it.

Example Japanglish Sentence:

「優先席（シルバーシート）は、必要とする方のために空けておいてください。」とバスの運転手は言った。

The bus driver said, "Please save the *silver seat* for any passengers who may need it."

Translated to English:

The bus driver said, "Please save the *priority seat for any elderly passengers* who may need it."

chi-ket-to — TICKET

チケット

Meaning in Japan:

Ticket is only used to describe something positive, like an entrance ticket for a play, museum, or other exciting event. It is not used for public transportation, such as bus or airplane tickets, or for fines.

Example Japanglish Sentence:

バスの運転手は、スピード違反の切符を切られないためにも、安全運転を心がけている。

Our bus drivers will drive safely to avoid *speeding tickets* 切符 *(kippu)*!

Translated to English:

Our bus drivers will drive safely to avoid speeding *tickets*!

tsū-rin-gu — TOURING

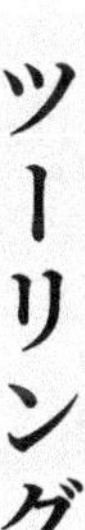

Meaning in Japan:

Riding around on a motorcycle with friends, usually through scenic areas

Example Japanglish Sentence:

週末は友達と一緒に国立公園をツーリングするのが好きなんだ。

My friends and I love to go *touring* on the weekends through the national park!

Translated to English:

My friends and I love to *ride motorcycles together* on the weekends through the national park!

Twin

tsu-in 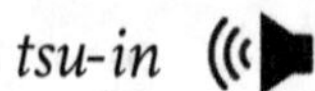

ツイン

Meaning in Japan:

Twin is only used to describe a hotel room that offers a twin-size bed.

Example Japanglish Sentence:

ホテルにツインルームがあるか見てみよう。
Let's see if the hotel has *twins*.

Translated to English:

Let's see if the hotel has any *twin rooms* / *rooms with twin beds*.

TV, Music, Movies, Entertainment

23

テレビ・音楽
映画・エンタメ

AF RECO (AFREKO)

a-fu-re-ko

アフレコ

Meaning in Japan:

This is an abbreviation of "after recording" and means dubbing or voice-over when the original audio of a movie or film is replaced with different audio (often in an alternative language).

Example Japanglish Sentence:

声優たちは吹き替え版のアフレコをした。

The voice actors did the *af reco* for the film.

Translated to English:

The voice actors did the voices for the *dubbed* version of the film.

ANIME

a-ni-me 

アニメ

Meaning in Japan:

Any kind of animation or animated film, movie, cartoon, and not limited to Japanese-style anime.

Example Japanglish Sentence:

私の子どもは、アメリカのアニメが好きだ。

My kids love American *anime*.

Translated to English:

My kids love American *animated movies* / *cartoons*.

bak-ku-dan-sā

Back Dancer

バックダンサー

Meaning in Japan:

Backup dancer

Example Japanglish Sentence:

その歌手には、良いバックダンサーがついている。

That singer has excellent *back dancers*!

Translated to English:

That singer has excellent *backup dancers*!

bak-ku-myū-jik-ku

Back Music (BGM)

バックミュージック

Meaning in Japan:

Background music

Example Japanglish Sentence:

そのCMはBGM（バックミュージック）で有名だ。

That *CM* is famous for its *BGM*/*back music*.

Translated to English:

That commercial is famous for its *background music*.

Back Number

bak-ku-nan-bā

バックナンバー

Meaning in Japan:

1. An old magazine issue that's not the latest edition; a back issue
2. A famous singer's old famous hits
3. License plate number on a car; registration number (UK)

Example Japanglish Sentence:

Lマガジンの昨年12月号のバックナンバーは本当に良い内容だ。
あの映画の舞台裏が詳しく紹介されていて素晴らしかった。

There's a really good *back number* of L Magazine from last December. It had a really amazing inside look on the making of that movie!

あの歌手のバックナンバーが大好き！
今夜カラオケで歌おう！

I love that singer's *back numbers* so much!
Let's sing them tonight at karaoke!

「私たちの車のバックナンバーって何だったっけ？
ちょうどここから、ナンバープレートが見えない」。

What's our *back number*?
I can't see our number plate from right here.

Translated to English:

There's a really good *back issue* / *old issue* of L Magazine from last December. It had a really amazing inside look on the making of that movie!

I love that singer's *old famous hits* so much!
Let's sing them tonight at karaoke!

What's our *license plate number*?
I can't see our license plate from right here.

bak-ku-shin-gā

Back Singer

バックシンガー

Meaning in Japan:

Backup singer

Example Japanglish Sentence:

バックシンガーで音楽がさらに良くなるね。

That *back singers* make the music better!

Translated to English:

The *backup singers* make the music better!

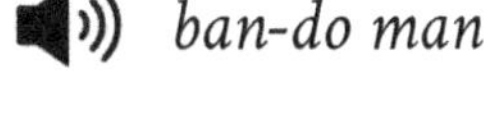

ban-do man

Band Man

バンドマン

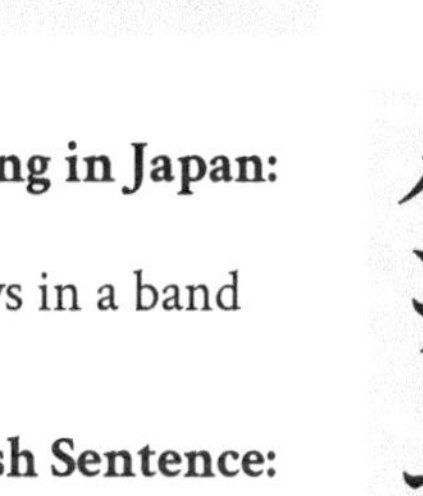

Meaning in Japan:

A person who plays in a band

Example Japanglish Sentence:

私の彼は、バンドマンだ。

My boyfriend is a *band man*.

Translated to English:

My boyfriend is *in a band*.

Bra Pi / Bla Pi

bu-ra-pi

ブラピ

Meaning in Japan:

Brad Pitt; BLACKPINK

Example Japanglish Sentence:

あの映画にブラピが出てると思う。
I think *Bra Pi* is in that movie.

ブラックピンクは、素敵だけど、ちょっと最近年をとってきたね。
Bla Pi is cool but getting kind of old now.

Translated to English:

I think *Brad Pitt* is in that movie.

BLACKPINK is cool but getting kind of old now!

Bri Chan

bu-ri-chan 

ブリちゃん

Meaning in Japan:

Britney Spears

Example Japanglish Sentence:

ブリちゃんがまだ人気なのはすごいね。
It's amazing that *Bri Chan* is still popular!

Translated to English:

It's amazing that *Britney Spears* is still popular!

ka-me-ra-man

Cameraman

カメラマン

Meaning in Japan:

Photographer, Cameraman, Videographer

Example Japanglish Sentence:

彼は、結婚式の<u>カメラマン</u>だ。

He's a <u>*cameraman*</u> for weddings.

Translated to English:

He's a <u>*photographer*</u>/<u>*videographer*</u> for weddings.

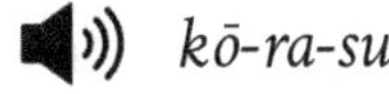 *kō-ra-su*

Chorus

コーラス

Meaning in Japan:

Chorus only refers to a choir and does not refer to the chorus of a song, a choral music performance, a chorus line, or ensemble.

Example Japanglish Sentence:

高校では<u>コーラス</u>部に所属していた。

In high school, I was a member of the <u>*chorus*</u> club.

Translated to English:

In high school, I was in the <u>*choir*</u>.

CM

シーエム

shī-e-mu

Meaning in Japan:

Commercial or ad on TV or radio

Example Japanglish Sentence:

あのCM 見た？すごく変だったね。

Did you see that *CM*? It was so weird!

Translated to English:

Did you see that *commercial*? It was so weird!

CM Song

シーエムソング

shī-e-mu-son-gu 

Meaning in Japan:

Jingle in an ad or commercial associated with a specific brand, company, or product

Example Japanglish Sentence:

あのブランドは、CMソングで有名だ。
今日はずっとその曲が頭から離れないよ。

That brand is famous for its *CM song*!
I've had it stuck in my head all day!

Translated to English:

That brand is famous for its *jingle*!
I've had it stuck in my head all day!

kon-bi

Combi

コンビ

Meaning in Japan:

A pair of two people who perform together or act as partners (e.g., a comedy duo)

Example Japanglish Sentence:

彼らは、とても良いお笑いコンビだ。

They're a really good comedy *combi*.

Translated to English:

They're a really good comedy *duo*.

kon-to

Conto

コント

Meaning in Japan:

Skit

Example Japanglish Sentence:

コントは、日本のお笑いでとても人気がある。

Conto is really popular in Japanese comedy.

Translated to English:

Skits are really popular in Japanese comedy.

Crank In

クランクイン

ku-ran-ku-in 

Meaning in Japan:

The start of shooting a film

Example Japanglish Sentence:

製作が決まってクランクインまで丸1年かかった。

It took a full year from the decision to produce to the *crank in*!

Translated to English:

It took a full year from the greenlighting of the film to the *start of filming*!

Drama

ドラマ

do-ra-ma 

Meaning in Japan:

TV show/series, especially Asian dramas. *Drama* doesn't necessarily mean the genre is drama. It can include most genres of shows that run as a series and aren't sitcoms.

Example Japanglish Sentence:

どんなドラマを見るの。私は、コメディーがすき。

What kind of *dramas* do you watch? I enjoy comedies.

Translated to English:

What kind of *shows* do you watch? I enjoy comedies.

da-bin-gu

Dubbing

ダビング

Meaning in Japan:

Copying a video/movie/DVD/etc., onto your own personal device; burning or ripping a CD/DVD/etc.

Example Japanglish Sentence:

著作権者の許可がない場合、ダビングは違法な著作権侵害となる可能性がある。

Dubbing could be illegal copyright infringement if you don't have the permission of the copyright holder.

Translated to English:

Ripping DVDs or CDs could be illegal copyright infringement if you don't have the permission of the copyright holder.

fi-ru-mu

Film

フィルム

Meaning in Japan:

Film only refers to the photographic film in a camera. It does not mean a movie, nor does it mean the film reel used in making movies.

Example Japanglish Sentence:

新しいMovieTown博物館はとても魅力的だ！ここでは、昔ながらの写真用フィルムの現像方法や、映画のフィルムをリールにする仕組み、そして無声映画から音声付き映画への移り変わりを学ぶことができるんだ。

The new MovieTown museum is really cool! You can see how they process *film フィルム (firumu)* for photos, how they use *film 映画フィルム (eiga filumu)* to make a movie reel, and how they eventually moved from silent *films 映画 (eiga)* to modern *films 映画 (eiga)* with sound.

Translated to English:

The new MovieTown museum is really cool! You can see how they process *film* for photos, how they use *film* to make a movie reel, and how they eventually moved from silent *films* to modern *films* with sound.

Gag

gya-gu

Meaning in Japan:

A play on words joke like a pun or dad joke

THIS IS HOW I ROLL

Example Japanglish Sentence:

父は、いつも<u>ギャグ</u>を言うのが好きだ。

My dad always likes to tell <u>*gags*</u>.

Translated to English:

My dad always likes to tell <u>*dad jokes/puns*</u>.

Golden Time/Hour

gō-ru-den tai-mu/ a-wā 

ゴールデンタイム

Meaning in Japan:

Prime time TV between 5-9 p.m.

Example Japanglish Sentence:

私のインタビューは、<u>ゴールデンタイム</u>に放送される予定だ。

My interview is supposed to show tomorrow during <u>*golden time*</u>!

Translated to English:

My interview is supposed to air tomorrow during <u>*prime time TV*</u>!

gya-ra — GUARA

ギャラ

Meaning in Japan:

This is an abbreviation of "guarantee" and refers to the performance fee, appearance fee, or honorarium that a performer, singer, actor, or speaker is entitled from a performance or other gig.

Example Japanglish Sentence:

「その歌手のギャラは1,500ドルなんだよ。私たちに払えると思う?」と学園祭実行委員長は、私に言った。

The school festival chairman said, "The singer's *guara* is $1,500. Do you think we can afford it?"

Translated to English:

The school festival chairman said, "The singer's *performance fee* is $1,500. Do you think we can afford it?"

hō-mu-do-ra-ma — HOME DRAMA

ホームドラマ

Meaning in Japan:

A family-friendly TV show or soap opera that is made for a wide range of viewers and often focused around family life. *Home dramas* can be made in different genres including drama, comedy, and sitcoms.

Example Japanglish Sentence:

妻と私は毎週金曜日の夜にお気に入りのホームドラマを見る。

My wife and I watch our favorite *home drama* every Friday evening.

Translated to English:

My wife and I watch our favorite *TV show* every Friday evenings.

Idol

ai-do-ru

アイドル

Meaning in Japan:

A young famous pop star, typically under 30, who sings, dances, and performs on TV shows; A star

Example Japanglish Sentence:

この動物園ではトラがアイドルだ。

The tiger is the *idol* at this zoo!

彼は、私の好きなアイドルだ。

He is my favorite *idol*!

Translated to English:

The tiger is the *star* / *most popular animal* of this zoo!

He is my favorite *celebrity/singer*!

Live

rai-bu

ライブ

Meaning in Japan:

A concert

Example Japanglish Sentence:

私たちはお気に入りのJ-POP
バンドのライブに行く。

We're going to a *live* of our favorite J-pop band.

Translated to English:

We're going to a *concert* of our favorite J-pop band.

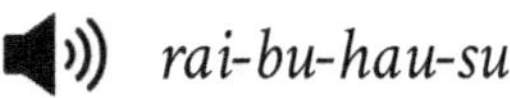

rai-bu-hau-su

Live House

ライブハウス

Meaning in Japan:

Live music venue

Example Japanglish Sentence:

私たちの家の近くにライブハウスがあるので、
毎週末無料でライブを聞けるんだ。

There's a *live house* next to where we live,
so we can hear a free *live* every weekend.

Translated to English:

There's a *live music venue* next to where we live,
so we can hear a free concert every weekend.

ro-ke

Loke

ロケ

Meaning in Japan:

Filming location or setting of a movie

Example Japanglish Sentence:

新しい映画のロケ地は、私の故郷のすぐ近くなんだ！

The *loke* of the new movie is really close to my hometown!

ハワイでは、多くの有名映画のロケ地を訪れることができる。

In Hawaii, you can visit the *loke* of many famous movies.

Translated to English:

The *filming location* of the new movie is really close to my hometown!

In Hawaii, you can visit the *filming locations* of many famous movies!

Love Comedy

ra-bu-ko-me-dī 

ラブコメディー

Meaning in Japan:

Romantic comedy

Example Japanglish Sentence:

彼は、私がラブコメ(ラブコメディー)を一緒に見ようとするとすごく嫌がるの。展開が読めすぎるって言うのよ。

My boyfriend hates when I make him watch *love comedies*. He says they're so predictable.

Translated to English:

My boyfriend hates when I make him watch *romantic comedies*. He says they're so predictable.

Melodrama

me-ro-do-ra-ma 

メロドラマ

Meaning in Japan:

Romantic drama

Example Japanglish Sentence:

彼女は、本当にメロドラマを見るのが好きだ。

She really likes to watch *melodramas*.

Translated to English:

She really likes to watch *romantic dramas*.

MULTI TALENT

ma-ru-chi-ta-ren-to

マルチタレント

Meaning in Japan:

A TV celebrity who does multiple acts or types of work (e.g., someone who is both a TV actress and singer)

Example Japanglish Sentence:

彼女は、女優であり歌手だ。彼女は、マルチタレントだ。

She's an actress and a singer; she's a *multi talent*!

Translated to English:

She's an actress and a singer!

MV

e-mu-vu~ī

エムヴィー

Meaning in Japan:

Music video

Example Japanglish Sentence:

私の高校生の生徒たちは、好きなアイドルのMV（ミュージックビデオ）を見るのが大好きだ。

My high school students love to watch *MV* of their favorite idols.

Translated to English:

My high school students love to watch *music videos* from their favorite idols.

No Cut

nō-kat-to

ノーカット

Meaning in Japan:

Uncut version of a movie

Example Japanglish Sentence:

これは、ノーカット版の映画だ。

This is a *no cut* movie.

Translated to English:

This is the *uncut version* of the movie.

Off Reco

o-fu-re-ko

Meaning in Japan:

An abbreviation for "off the record" that is used to express that something should be kept a secret

Example Japanglish Sentence:

これは、内緒だよ。言わないで。オフレコだよ。

It's a secret. Don't tell. This is *off reco*.

Translated to English:

It's a secret. Don't tell. This is *confidential* / *off the record*.

ō-pun-su-tē-ji

Open Stage

オープンステージ

Meaning in Japan:

An outdoor stage

Example Japanglish Sentence:

その劇は公園の<u>オープンステージ</u>で上演される予定だ。

They're going to perform the play at the park on the *<u>open stage</u>*.

Translated to English:

They're going to perform the play at the park on the *<u>outdoor stage</u>*.

pi-e-ro

Pierrot

ピエロ

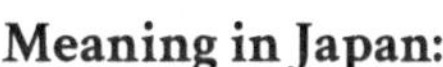

Meaning in Japan:

Clown

Example Japanglish Sentence:

私は、<u>ピエロ</u>の衣装を着て、パートをしていた。

I worked part-time wearing a *<u>pierrot</u>* costume.

Translated to English:

I worked part-time wearing a *<u>clown</u>* costume.

Pops

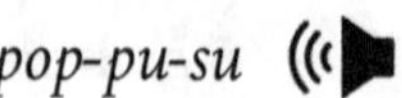

ポップス

Meaning in Japan:

Pop music, especially J-pop

Example Japanglish Sentence:

ラジオでポップスが流れると、気分が上がる。

I love it when *pops* comes on the radio!

Translated to English:

I love it when *J-pop* comes on the radio!

Talent

ta-ren-to

Meaning in Japan:

A comedian who has also become a famous actor or actress, TV personality, or TV celebrity

Example Japanglish Sentence:

私の好きなタレントが新しいドラマに出てるのよ!

My favorite *talent* is in the new drama!

Translated to English:

My favorite *comedian* is in the new TV show!

te-re-bi ta-ren-to

TELEBI TALENT

Meaning in Japan:

A comedian who has also become a famous actor or actress, TV personality, or TV celebrity

Example Japanglish Sentence:

この番組には私の好きなタレントが出てるんだ！

This show has my favorite *TV talent*!

Translated to English:

This show has my favorite *comedian as an actor*!

te-re-bi

TELEBI

テレビ

Meaning in Japan:

TV

Example Japanglish Sentence:

趣味はテレビを見ることだ。

My hobby is watching *telebi*.

Translated to English:

My hobby is watching *TV*.

Voice Drama

boi-su do-ra-ma 

ボイスドラマ

Meaning in Japan:

Audio drama, audio play, or audio theater

Example Japanglish Sentence:

さっき電話に出られなくてごめんね。新しいボイスドラマを聴いてたんだ。

Sorry I missed your phone call earlier. I was listening to an *voice drama*!

Translated to English:

Sorry I missed your phone call earlier. I was listening to an *audio play*!

Wide Show

wai-do-shō 

ワイドショー

Meaning in Japan:

A type of TV variety show, similar to late night entertainment, a late night talk show, or a celebrity gossip show.

Example Japanglish Sentence:

同僚は毎晩ワイドショーを見るのが好きだ。

My coworker loves watching *wide shows* every night.

Translated to English:

My coworker loves watching *late night entertainment shows*.

Work, Office, Jobs

24

仕事・オフィス・職業

Scan for Audio

Arbeit(o) / Beit(o)

a-ru-bai-to 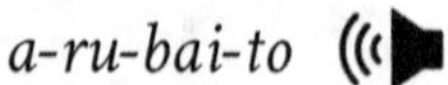

アルバイト・バイト

Meaning in Japan:

Part-time job, usually for young people or students

Example Japanglish Sentence:

日本の一部の高校では、学生が放課後にアルバイトをすることを禁止している。

Some high schools in Japan prohibit students from getting *arbeito* after school.

Translated to English:

Some high schools in Japan prohibit students from getting a *part-time job* after school.

Baton Touch

ba-ton-tat-chi 

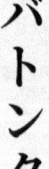

バトンタッチ

Meaning in Japan:

Hand over responsibilities or tasks to someone else, often at work

Example Japanglish Sentence:

休暇前に終わらせないといけない重要な仕事があるんだけど、チームで進めている案件だから、必要なら他のメンバーにバトンタッチできると思う。

I have an important task to finish at work before my vacation, but I think I can *do baton touch* if I need to since it's a team project.

Translated to English:

I have an important task to finish at work before my vacation, but I think I can *hand it over/off* to someone else if I need to since it's a team project.

bu-ran-ku **BLANK**

ブランク

Meaning in Japan:

Gap in your resume; A break or absence from an activity

Example Japanglish Sentence:

履歴書にブランクがあると、仕事探しが難しくなる場合がある。

It can be difficult to find a job with a *blank*.

まずは、サックスに挑戦したかったので、ピアノには数年間のブランクがある。

I have a few years *blank* for piano because I wanted to try the saxophone.

Translated to English:

It can be difficult to find a job with *a gap in your resume*.

I *took a break* from piano for a few years because I wanted to try saxophone.

bi-ru **BUIL**

ビル

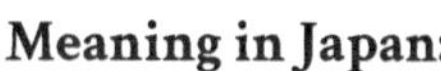

Meaning in Japan:

Office building

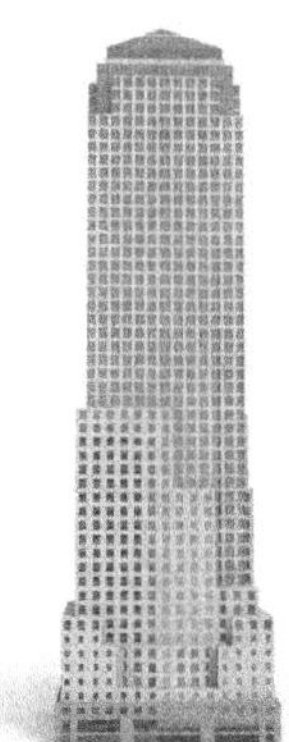

Example Japanglish Sentence:

私の新しいビルは、本当に大きい。

My new *buil* is really big.

Translated to English:

My new *office building* is really big.

Career Up

kya-ri-a ap-pu

キャリアアップ

Meaning in Japan:

Improving your career or career-related skills and achievements

Example Japanglish Sentence:

この認定コースは、あなたのキャリアアップに役立つ。特に、ヨーロッパや北米での就職を目指しているなら、より大きなメリットになる。

This certification course will be good for your *career up*, especially if you plan to work in Europe or North America.

Translated to English:

This certification course will be good for *advancing your career* / *improving your resume*, especially if you plan to work in Europe or North America.

Checkpoint

chek-ku-po-in-to

チェックポイント

Meaning in Japan:

Something that needs to be checked, revisited, or reviewed

Example Japanglish Sentence:

私たちのプロジェクトはほぼ完了しているが、
重要なチェックポイントが3つある。

Our project is almost complete,
but we have three major *checkpoints*.

Translated to English:

Our project is almost complete,
but we have three major *things to review and potentially revise*.

ko-ne

Conne

コネ

Meaning in Japan:

Connections to people who can benefit you

Example Japanglish Sentence:

彼は、いいコネがあったからこそいい仕事につけた。

He only got the job because he had good *conne*.

Translated to English:

He only got the job because he had good *connections*.

kū-ru-bi-zu

Cool Biz

クールビズ

Meaning in Japan:

In 2005, the Japanese government started a campaign called *cool biz* that encouraged people to wear lighter clothing in the summer to reduce the use of air conditioning, energy costs, and emissions. This is still observed in the summer, and *cool biz* refers to the more casual dress code in most offices from about May to September with light-colored short-sleeve dress shirts, no jacket, no suit, no tie.[54, 55, 56, 57]

Example Japanglish Sentence:

昔は、日本のビジネスマンのほとんどがスーツを着てネクタイをしていた。しかし、今はクールビズが非常に普及しており、ジャケットやネクタイが必ずしも必要ではなくなっている。

In the past, most businessmen in Japan wore formal business attire; now *cool biz* is really popular, so a jacket and tie aren't always required.

Translated to English:

In the past, most businessmen in Japan wore formal business attire; now *lighter/cooler clothing* is popular, so a jacket and tie aren't always required.

Food Fighter

fū-do-fai-tā

フードファイター

Meaning in Japan:

A competitive eater

Example Japanglish Sentence:

その祭りでは、フードファイターがいた。

They had *food fighters* at the festival this year!

Translated to English:

They had *competitive food eaters* at the festival this year!

Free

fu-rī

フリー

Meaning in Japan:

Freelance

Example Japanglish Sentence:

彼は、フリージャーナリストで世界中の仕事を請け負っている。

He's a *free* journalist and takes contracts around the world.

Translated to English:

He's a *freelance* journalist and takes contracts around the world.

fu-rī-a-do-re-su FREE ADDRESS

フリーアドレス

Meaning in Japan:

Open office concept where employees don't have their own assigned personal desks and can move around and work at different places, desks, or stations

Example Japanglish Sentence:

私たちのオフィスは、今フリーアドレスだ。
それが好きな人もいるけど、嫌いな人もいる。

Our office is *free address* now. Some people love it, and others hate it.

Translated to English:

Our office is *open concept and open desk* now. Some people love it, and others hate it.

fu-rī-rai-tā FREE WRITER

フリーライター

Meaning in Japan:

Freelance writer

Example Japanglish Sentence:

彼女は、フリーライターだ。

She's a *free writer*.

Translated to English:

She's a *freelance writer*.

Freeter

fu-rī-tā

フリーター

Meaning in Japan:

This word describes a specific type of part-time worker who is otherwise employable at a full-time job but chooses to work only part-time, often at a lower income job. There are different views on whether this is a positive or negative term, and people have differing reasons for becoming *freeters*. Some people want to become full-time workers but are simply unable to find work. Others lack ambition and enjoy the freedom of being *freeters*, while still others want to avoid the demanding and stressful "conveyor belt" of Japanese career salarymen. Pros include flexible working hours, diverse experiences, free time, and less career pressure. Cons include financial instability, loss of career development opportunities, unfavorable societal position, and difficulty getting approved for mortgages and credit due to negative perceptions of freeters.[58, 59]

Example Japanglish Sentence:

あのカフェの店員と一度だけデートしたわ。彼は優しかったけれど、フリーターのようだったわ。学歴は良かったけれど、人生に対する野心がまったくなかったの。私は目標を持って、自分から努力する人のほうが好き。

I had one date with that coffee shop guy. He was nice but seemed like a *freeter*. He had a good education but zero ambition in life. I prefer someone who has some goals for the future and self-motivation.

Translated to English:

I had one date with that guy. He was nice but seemed like a *slacker with no goals*. He had a good education and zero ambition in life. I prefer someone who has some goals for the future and self-motivation.

🔊 *gā-do-man*

Guard Man

ガードマン

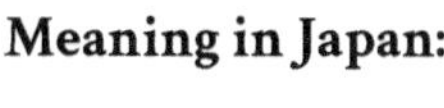

Meaning in Japan:

Security guard, Crossing guard

Example Japanglish Sentence:

私の友人は、アメリカに引っ越したばかりの頃、<u>ガードマン</u>として働いていた。

My friend worked as a *guard man* when he first moved to the UK.

Translated to English:

My friend worked as a *security guard* when he first moved to the UK.

🔊 *ma-su-tā*

Master

マスター

Meaning in Japan:

The manager or owner of a small shop, bar, store, facility, etc.

Example Japanglish Sentence:

私の兄は、新しいコーヒーショップの<u>マスター</u>だ。

My brother is the *master* of the new coffee shop.

Translated to English:

My brother is the *owner* / *manager* of the new coffee shop.

Neat / NEET

nī-to 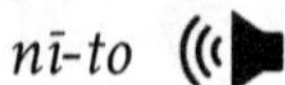

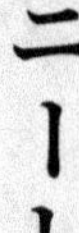

Meaning in Japan:

This is an acronym for Not in Education, Employment, or Training, but sounds like neat when pronounced. It refers to people who are unemployed by choice and are not actively seeking employment or any type of training or education to help improve their career options.

Example Japanglish Sentence:

彼は、ニートだ。

He is *NEET*!

Translated to English:

He *doesn't work or go to school and is not actively seeking employment*.

Neck

nek-ku 

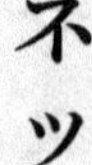

Meaning in Japan:

An abbreviation of "bottleneck," meaning an obstacle that prevents you from making progress on a project

Example Japanglish Sentence:

このプロジェクトのネックは資金。予算が少なすぎる。

The *neck* of this project is money. Our budget is too small.

Translated to English:

The *biggest obstacle* to this project is money. Our budget is too small.

OL

ō-e-ru

オーエル

Meaning in Japan:

An abbreviation of "office lady," meaning a woman who works in an office, or the female equivalent of *salaryman*

Example Japanglish Sentence:

母はOLで、父は同じ会社のサラリーマンだ。

My mom is an *OL*, and my dad is a *salaryman* for the same company.

Translated to English:

My mom and dad work for the same company as *general business employees*.

Part

pā-to

パート

Meaning in Japan:

A part-time worker

Example Japanglish Sentence:

彼女はパートだ。

She is *part*.

Translated to English:

She *works a part-time job*.
She is a *part-time worker*.

PRESEN

pu-re-zen

プレゼン

Meaning in Japan:

Presentation

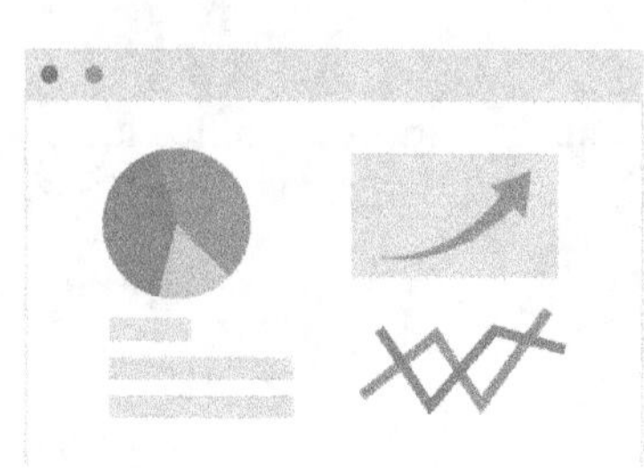

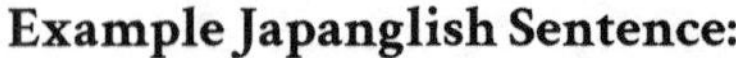

Example Japanglish Sentence:

明日、大きなプレゼンをしなければ
ならないので、少し緊張している。

I'm feeling a little nervous because
I have to give a big *presen* tomorrow.

Translated to English:

I'm feeling a little nervous because I have to give a big *presentation* tomorrow.

PRESENTATOR

pu-re-zen-tei-tā 

プレゼンテイター

Meaning in Japan:

A presenter or anyone giving a formal presentation

Example Japanglish Sentence:

明日、私はプレゼンテイターなので、ちょっと緊張している。

I'm feeling a little nervous because I'm the *presentator* tomorrow.

Translated to English:

I'm feeling a little nervous because I'm the *presenter/speaker* tomorrow.

pu-re-zen-tā

Presenter

プレゼンター

Meaning in Japan:

Only a TV presenter, TV anchor, Newscaster, Host, Commentator

Example Japanglish Sentence:

彼は本当に優れたプレゼンターだ。スポーツ番組の司会を務めていて、時々スポーツの表彰式で司会者として招かれることもある。

He's a really good *presenter* プレゼンター *(purezentā)*. He works as a *sports presenter* 番組の司会 *(bangumi no shikai)* and sometimes gets invited to be the *presenter* 司会者 *(shikai-sha)* at certain sports award ceremonies.

Translated to English:

He's a really good *presenter*. He works as a sports *commentator* and sometimes gets invited to be the *host* at certain sports award ceremonies.

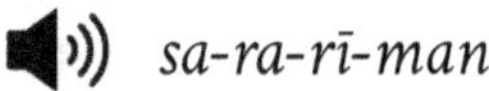

Salaryman

サラリーマン

Meaning in Japan:

A *salaryman* includes any male who works as an employee under a boss at a general business as a full-time, salaried worker of a non-exec position at a large company. A *salaryman* is a type of general businessman, who is often rotated between positions in his company and does not hold a specific job title like "lawyer" or "engineer."

Example Japanglish Sentence:

僕のお父さんは、サラリーマンだ。

My dad is a *salaryman*.

Translated to English:

My dad *works for XYZ company*.

Salary Up

sa-ra-rī-ap-pu

サラリーアップ

Meaning in Japan:

To get a raise in pay or increase in salary

Example Japanglish Sentence:

ずっと<u>サラリーアップ</u>を待ってるんだ。今年こそアップするといいな。

I've been waiting a long time for my *<u>salary up</u>*, hopefully this year!

Translated to English:

I've been waiting a long time for *<u>a raise</u>*, hopefully this year!

Side Business

sai-do bi-ji-ne-su 

サイドビジネス

Meaning in Japan:

A side job or second job

Example Japanglish Sentence:

彼は<u>サイドビジネス</u>として、地元の家庭教師センターで高校生のエッセイを編集している。

He has a *<u>side business</u>* editing essays for high school students for a local tutoring center.

Translated to English:

He has a *<u>side job</u>* / *<u>second job</u>* editing essays for high school students for a local tutoring center.

Sign

サイン

sa-in

Meaning in Japan:

Your signature or written name or an autograph from a celebrity

Example Japanglish Sentence:

私は、その歌手に「ここにサインをもらえますか?」とお願いした。

I asked the singer, "Can I have your *sign* here?"

Translated to English:

I asked the singer, "Can I have your *autograph* here?"

Silver Center

shi-ru-bā-sen-tā

Meaning in Japan:

A center where seniors, often retired, can go to find a simple, often short-term job in their local community[60, 61]

Example Japanglish Sentence:

祖父はシルバーセンターを通じて面白い仕事を見つけた。今は地元の園芸家を手伝いながら、花の世話や販売をしている。

My grandpa found an interesting job through a *silver center*. Now he's helping a local gardener prepare and sell some of his flowers.

Translated to English:

My grandpa found an interesting job through a *local job center for seniors*. Now he's helping a local gardener prepare and sell some of his flowers.

Step Up

su-tep-pu ap-pu

ステップアップ

Meaning in Japan:

To advance your career, to improve your career opportunities, or to be promoted

Example Japanglish Sentence:

この講座は、<u>ステップアップ</u>に役立ちそうだ。

This course will be helpful for your *<u>step up</u>*!

Translated to English:

This course will help you *<u>improve your career-related skills</u>*!

ACKNOWLEDGMENTS

To Tamaki Tiballi, thank you for all your hard work and the hours you put into discussing, consulting, and translating in order to help make this book and its counterpart a reality. Your insights have been invaluable, and this book would not have been possible without your help! Thank you also for your years of hard work at Lauren's Language Lessons as a wonderful Japanese teacher.

To my husband, Kurt Imai, thank you for supporting me throughout this process (again), for believing in me, and reminding me to trust my gut when I doubted myself. Thank you for your extensive help in developing the audio resources for this book, for once again humoring me the many times I leaned over and asked, "Hey, what does this word mean to you?" and for looking through unending piles of variations of layouts, fonts, and photos to give me your thoughtful opinion. I love you and am grateful beyond words to have you on this journey with me.

To my brother, Daniel Green, thank you for your valuable help as audio engineer, for taking the time and effort to clean up all the recorded audio for the audio resources to make it all sound pristine. Thank you also for your and Larissa's valuable input along the way regarding style and design.

To Dr. Steven Turley, thank you for your sharing your special expertise in baseball in relation to some of the terminology included in this book and for your general friendship, guidance, and support over the years.

To all my Japanese students, past and present, thank you for allowing me to be part of your English-learning experience. Thank you for letting me enter your world, sometimes even your homes and offices, for sharing fresh brewed tea and delicious snacks, and for sharing your culture with me as you learned mine. I am proud of you all for being brave enough to continue learning a new language as adults (or young adults)! It is never easy to learn an additional language, especially English, but don't give up! Remember to never let yourself feel ashamed of your English mistakes. They are essential for your learning and will help you grow if you let them!

To all my friends and students who shared ideas and recommendations of Japanglish words to include in this book, thank you! Your suggestions have made this book better!

Image Credits

The authors and publishers acknowledge the following sources of copyright material and are grateful for the permissions granted. While every effort has been made, it has not always been possible to identify the sources of all the material used, or to trace all copyright holders. If any omissions are brought to our notice, we will be happy to include the appropriate acknowledgments on reprinting and in the next update, as applicable.

Photographs, Images, & Graphis

The following images are from **AC Illustr**:

P. 66 (long hair girl): Houjicha @Okan; p. 95 (hooligan): イラストあつぼん; p. 106 (tap card): YOSHIM; p. 128 (morning and lunch sign): りん; p. 131 (pineapple juice): ぶー; p. 138 (candies): ACworks; p. 155 (rehab): ちょこバナナ; p. 166 (semi double bed): amippi; p. 189 (wedding): クニコ925; p. 195 (no good): koga; p. 197 (postal box): TAKAPON; p. 213 (calendar): プリプラ; p. 219 (convenient store): mazedesign; p. 227 (sale): imacvery; p. 257 (windsurf): ACworks; p. 267 (SNS): イチタ; p. 267 (screenshot): よっと; p. 268 (tv graphics): Toki; p. 268 (update device): おばちゃあこ; p. 284 (gondola): 君の瞳にバンザイ; p. 284 (priority seat): 楠　英浩; p. 320 (presentation): とりこや; p. 323 (job center): ACworks

The following images are from **AC Photo**:

p. 25 (clip-ons): hanenone; p. 119 (ham and egg): ちび助; p. 147 (patch): 津呂さんちのどてちん; p. 165 (convection microwave): RG8; p. 169 (bidet): 風龍; p. 217 (street scene): Fujimama; p. 222 (kiosk store): kanomao

The following images are from **Adobe Stock Photos**:

cover (flags): Aroastock; p. 24 (earrings): Tarzhanova; p. 24 (purse): aneduard; p. 25 (zipper): Maxim_Kazmin; p. 26 (zipper): Maxim_Kazmin; p. 26 (rubber ball): Giorgio Castellanza; p. 27 (hair band): Hanna Syvak; p. 27 (hair ties): sasimoto; p. (hair clip): pixarno; p. 32 (sale): rou_; p. 38 (best seller): Suppachok N; p 44 (vacant): butterflyeffect; p. 46 (gas pedal): Ceyhun; p. 47 (motorcycle): artproba; p. 48 (rearview mirror): Tabthipwatthana; p. 49 (motorcycle): artproba; p. 49 (RV and camper): studioworkstock; p. 50 (horn): sirikornt; p. 50 (road): Pixmarket; p. 51 (windshield): Dumitru; p. 52 (gas station): Shanvood; p. 52 (steering wheel): Photobeps; p. 54 (scooter): pioneer111; p. 58 (rush hour): rob z; p. 62 (lady): hesti12; p. 62 (dress): Kathleen; p. 67 (dress): vectorikart; p. 67 (turtleneck): vitaly tiagunov; p. 68 (jacket): fashion2factory; p. 69 (vest): BSD; p. 69 (safety vest): moonrise; p. 69 (jumper): viktorijareut; p. 70 (scarf): oleh11; p. 71 (dress): Hein Nouwens; p. 72 (matching couple): Nathan Hutchcraft; p. 73 (pants suit): Creative Juice; p. 75 (sleeveless shirt): chapinasu; p. 80 (letter jacket): Nattanopdesign; p. 82 (dress shirt): runrun2; p. 84 (hair): kiko; p. 85 (combover): chapinasu; p. 89 (beauty contest): M-SUR; p. 90 (beauty contest): M-SUR; p. 93 (short hair): LuckyStep; p. 95 (short hair): kisasage; p. 109 (corn dog): Handies Peak; p. 110 (drink): DenisMArt; p. 111 (creamer): Roxy; p. 112 (pasta): Farzaneh; p. 113 (drink): akaomayo; p. 113 (noodles): matsukiyo; p. 114 (curry): Nishihama; p. 115 (pilaf curry): promolink; p. 115 (extract): shironagasukujira; p. 116 (sausage): torsakarin; p. 119 (hamburger steak): kazoka303030; p. 121 (pancake): ayaka; p. 123 (kfc): Bon_man; p. 124 (kfc): LT; p. 126 (McDonald's): Bon_man; p. 132 (microwave meal): Sittirak Jadlit; p. 133 (retorte pasta): Tsuki; p. 133 (retorte curry): Kento, O; p. 134 (sandwich): Natalie; p. 136 (pasta): tatsushi; p. 136 (Starbucks): Bon_man; p. 137 (sweet potato dessert): Kurumi cafe; p. 140 (costumes): Jemastock; p. 141 (video game console): Konstantinos Moraiti; p. 142 (video game): Oleg and Polly; p. 145 (photo booth): Kiku; p. 146 (stickers): infzero; p. 150 (body shapes): natbasil; p. 153 (birth control): Jacob Kearns; p. 154 (body shapes): natbasil; p. 158 (apartment): phocks eye; p. 160 (outlets): oxinoxi; p. 162 (induction cooktop): YummyBuum; p. 162 (intercom): 正人 竹内; p. 163 (building): 3103jp; p. 167 (space heater): rjuniormb; p. 171 (floor plans): studio marble; p. 172 (floor plans): studio marble; p. 172 (floor plans): studio marble; p. 174 (hair dryer): Maksim; p. 175 (body wash): Rawpixel.com; p. 175 (makeup remover): Zalina; p. 176 (hair dryer): Maksim; p. 177 (hair dye): ann131313.a; p. 181 (face mask): DruZhi Art; p. 181 (sandwich): ヨシノカイ; p. 182 (conditioner): castecodesign; p. 184 (crib): zdyma4; p. 184 (stroller): moonrise; p. 185 (playpen): bsd studio; p. 195 (highlighting): 3dwithlove; p. 202 (magic marker): Aliaksandr Ivanou; p. 203 (note): sean824; p. 203 (notebook): nata777_7; p. 204 (hole punch): pixelrobot; p. 205 (pens): Dmitri Stalnuhhin; p. 205 (mechanical pencil): Olga Kovalenko; p. 206 (postmark): savanno; p. 206 (white out): SATRJA; p. 224 (second hand shop): chapinasu; p. 225 (self-checkout): Icons8; p. 227 (supermarket): ayano; p. 230 (bartender): drawlab19; p. 238 (football): Hanna Syvak; p. 239 (backstop): WINDERFULL STUDIO; p. 240 (playing catch): Vector Juice; p. 243 (dome): kumao; p. 244 (gym): Adrian Hillman; p. 249 (fan): neena; p. 249 (handicap): Creative_Juice_Art; p. 253 (rugby): Redwater Vectors; p. 260 (apps): Scanrail; p. 265 (navigation system): savanno; p. 270 (foil): Lumos sp; p. 270 (knife): あんころもち(ankomando); p. 271 (screwdriver): skyrakot; p. 272 (paper towel): artiom. photo; p. 273 (flathead screwdriver): spyrakot; pg. 273 (pliers): donatas1205; p. 274 (screwdriver): waltericsy; p. 275 (tupperware): SlayStorm; p. 275 (plastic bag): Celeste; p. 276 (cling wrap): AlenKadr; p. 278 (frisk): bsd studio; p. 278 (bellhop): Kipaworks; p. 280 (train platform): absent84; p. 280 (front desk): tere; p. 281 (ferris wheel): k_tatsiana; p. 281 (roller coaster): blueringmedia; p. 282 (los angeles): lunamarina; p. 283 (room service): rostyslav84; p. 285 (scene): Paylessimages; p. 295 (comedy duo): uniuni; p. 298 (pun): OliverShort; p. 300 (idol): mayucolor; p. 300 (concert): bsd studio; p. 305 (stage): bsd studio; p. 305 (clown): Alexander Raths; p. 314 (shirt): sumsun graphic; p. 317 (guard): shintako; p. 323 (signature): prezent

The following images are from **Pexels**:

p. 112 (corn): mail maeder; p. 117 (fries): Polina Tankilevitch; p. 132 (fries): Polina Tankilevitch

The following images are from **Pixabay**:

p. 17 (ruler): ArtsyBeeKids; p. 34 (shipping boxes): AbsolutVision; p. 35 (protest): Mohamed_hassan; p. 51 (dump truck): SebastianCB; p. 74 (suit): Mohamed_hassan; p. 109 (chocolate): OpenClipart-Vectors; p. 112 (ice cream cone): VetVisst; p. 135 (ice cream): VetVisst; p. 159

(comforter): Jazella; p. 174 (shaver): TonyZhu; p. 198 (San Francisco): Alexey_Hulsov; p. 200 (pen): Clker-Free-Vector-Images; p. 220 (dozen): dgazdik; p. 220 (bag): unknown; p. 223 (bag); unknown; p. 260 (satellite dish): PublicDomainPictures; p. 261 (camera): Clker-Free-Vector-Images; p. 307 (TV): Jazella

The following images are from **Shutterstock**:

(sound symbol): CB studio; p. 21 (alumni): Media Guru; p. 28 (hair pins, barrettes, clips): ONYXprrj, p. 28 (jewelry): catary; p. 29 (velcro): Josep Curto; p. 30 (earrings): Elnur; p. 30 (wallet): Elnur; p. 43 (solar panels): aslysun; p. 53 (helicopter): YG Studio; p. 55 (license plate): M.KOS; p. 56 (convertible): Dimitris Leonidas; p. 57 (police car): YG Studio; p. 57 (flat tire): KsanderDN; p. 58 (SUV): autovector; p. 59 (emergency brake): brand1st; p. 59 (train): Harry Kasyanov; p. 60 (blinker): bsd studio; p. 64 (jean jacket): hifashion; p. 64 (jeans): hifashion; p. 66 (short hair girl): ayelet-keshet; p. 69 (sewing machine): T.Vyc; p. 72 (sleeveless shirt): ga-ko; p. 73 (underwear): VikiVector; p. 74 (hoodie): Stefanphotozemun; p. 79 (panties): Evgeniy yes; p. 79 (yoga pants): OlgaDykun; p. 81 (sweats): mongione; p. 81 (measurements): Albert Stephen Julius; p. 82 (sweats): Oleg Romanko; p. 93 (man): Kurt Achatz; p. 100 (man): mapo_japan; p. 102 (high five): Vector_escape; p. 104 (cat): Photology1971; p. 104 (clover): Zelijko Radojko; p. 104 (votive): tukinoto; p. 108 (coffee machine): unknown; p. 118 (fruit salad): baibaz; p. 118 (tea): grafvision; p. 120 (hash browns): MERCURY studio; p. 121 (ice cream bar): Inna Kharlamova; p. 122 (popsicle): Ricky Aditya Perdana; p. 122 (gummies): Bibadash; p. 122 (jello): WinWin artlab; p. 123 (beer mug): Uncle Leo; p. 125 (bay leaves): Nattika; p. 125 (tea): evgeeenius; p. 126 (liver): Ermak Oksana; p. 127 (pasta): etorres; p. 128 (ground meat): Mironov Vladimir; p. 129 (mug): chelovector; p. 129 (mushrooms): Yeti studio; p. 131 (tomatoes): Valentyn Volkov; p. 134 (shoe cream): MaraZe; p. 137 (tea): Anna_Pustynnikova; p. 138 (buffet): Net Vector; p. 141 (arcade games): klyaksun; p. 142 (arcade games): klyaksun; p. 144 (railroad): Sergiy Kuzmin; p. 146 (puzzle): AtlasStudio; p. 155 (vomit): Blueastro; p. 165 (microwave): ABB photo; p. 168 (balcony): BOOCYS; p. 178 (hair straightener): bsd studio; p. 178 (chapstick): Alina.Alina; p. 179 (makeup): Inna Kharlamova; p. 179 (put on makeup): charless; p. 180 (nail polish): Vector Tradition; p. 193 (guinea pig): Happy Monkey; p. 200 (glue): Anton Starikov; p. 202 (stapler): udaix; p. 224 (cash register): Net Vector; p. 232 (dry cleaning): Kilroy79; p. 234 (mass): Artisticco; p. 236 (nun): Kumeko; p. 240 (bounce): Tenstudio; p. 242 (hiking): GreenSkyStudio; p. 246 (ski slopes): YuliiaDU; p. 247 (net): Aesthetic Studio); p. 248 (field): sabri deniz kizil; p. 250 (stoppage time): momoforsale; p. 253 (lager): Valentyn Volkov; p. 254 (boxing bag): ARTYuSTUDIO; p. 255 (fans): inspiring team; p. 255 (knee brace): bsd studio; p. 257 (volleyball): FANDESIGN; p. 261 (toll free): Blaka suta; p. 263 (e-mail): Robbiya; p. 264 (e-mail): Robbiya; p. 264 (newsletter): Oleg and Polly; p. 265 (vibrate): sultana akther; p. 272 (knife): Inna Kharlamova; p. 272 (pocketknife): Sashkin; p. 274 (bottle): pics five; p. 275 (kettle): Elnur; p. 279 (flight attendant): Zubada; p. 291 (band): redrangerstudio; p. 296 (filming): VectorPlotnikoff; p. 311 (building): Maxx-Studio

The following images are from **Vecteezy**:

p. 29 (tie clip): Ivanova Nataliia; p. 78 (shorts): Anton Rysak; p. 130 (open face sandwich): Vladimir Mironov; p. 130 (bread): Matt Cole; p. 143 (sudoku): rightmeow2; p. 147 (video games): Evgenii Naumov; p. 182 (tweezers): Silvi Yuhanah; p. 210 (green light): Aglonema Design; p. 214 (daylight savings time): rini astiyah; p. 238 (exercise bike): Andres Ramos; p. 241 (cheerleaders): rini astiyah; p. 242 (swimming): Parinya Panyana; p. 247 (finish line): rini astiyah; p. 290 (record hits): Alexandra Pavlova; p. 293 (photographer): Lio putra

Other Image Credits:

p. 339 (author photo): Nate Messarra Photography
p. 340 (logo): design by Renee Blodgett

Audio Credits: Ko Takehiro

Notes

1. 本田手株 [Honda Toshinobu], "ネームバリューとは?意味とその効果・高める方法 [What is name value? It's meaning, effects, and ways to increase it]," Kenjans, April 9, 2025. https://kenjins.jp/magazine/company-interview/51955/

2. 弓削桃代 [Momoyo Yuge], "コンサバとは？　意味とコーディネートのコツ(イラスト付き解説) [What is conservative? Its meaning and tips for coording it (with illustrations)]," Mynavi Woman, September 15, 2022. https://woman.mynavi.jp/article/200730-5/

3. ぽんたまん[Pontaman], "【ギャル】を英語で言うと？ギャル文化や語源を紹介！ [How do you say "gal" in English? Learn about gal culture and its origins!]," *Native Camp English Conversation Blog*, July 3, 2019. https://nativecamp.net/blog/20190703_gal

4. "ギャルとは？-由来や特徴- [What is a gal? -Origins and characteristics-]," Galture, Accessed May 29, 2025. https://galture.com/about/about.html

5. "新しいギャル時代の幕開け！「令和ギャル」の定義や特徴とは？ [The dawn of a new era of gals! What are the definitions and characteristics of "Reiwa gals"?]," Galture, Accessed May 29, 2025. https://galture.com/history/reiwa-gal.html

6. いとうみほ[Miho Ito], "年代別 ギャルの歴史｜「ギャル」とは何なのか [History of Gyaru by Era | What is a "Gyaru"?]," *KLD (Blog)*, September 8, 2023. https://kld-c.jp/blog/what-is-gal

7. "ロリータとゴスロリの違いが知りたい [I want to know the difference between Lolita and Gothic Lolita]," Seasonz, June 24, 2023. https://seasonz.thebase.in/blog/2023/06/04/141656

8. "リクルートスーツ(就活スーツ)とは？ビジネススーツとの違い、選び方や着こなし方を解説！ [What is a recruit suit (job hunting suit)? We explain the difference between a recruitment suit and a business suit, and how to choose and wear it!]," GINZA Global Style, Last updated June 2, 2025. https://www.global-style.jp/enjoy-order/?p=13237

9. "ヒーリングとは？効果やその意味、リラックスに最適な音楽も紹介 [What is healing? Introducing its effects, meaning, and the best music for relaxation]," Mynavi, Last updated January 11, 2024. https://co-medical.mynavi.jp/contents/therapistplus/lifestyle/beauty/130/

10. 渡邊　真也(わたなべ　しんや) [Shinya Watanabe], "ヒステリー(転換性障害・解離性障害) [Hysteria (conversion disorder/dissociative disorder)]," 品川メンタルクリニック [Shinagawa Mental Clinic], Accessed May 30, 2025. https://www.shinagawa-mental.com/column/psychosomatic/hysteria/

11. 降矢英成 [Hidenari Furuya], "ヒステリー(解離性障害) [Hysteria (dissociative disorder)]," みんなのお悩み医学, Last updated March 9, 2022. https://kateinoigaku.jp/disease/200

12. "「ヒステリー」とは何なのか、なぜ女性ばかりヒステリーを起こすと思われているのか？ [What is "hysteria" and why is it thought that only women suffer from it?]," Gigazine, October 3, 2024. https://gigazine.net/news/20241003-hysteria-women/

13. 渡邊　真也(わたなべ　しんや) [Shinya Watanabe], "ノイローゼ(神経症)とは？うつ病との違いと治療方法 [What is neurosis? How it differes from depression and how to treat it]," 品川メンタルクリニック [Shinagawa Mental Clinic], https://www.shingawa-mental.com/column/psychosomatic/neurose/#:~:text=ノイローゼとは、神経症,説明していきます。

14. 櫻井 良平 [Ryohei Sakurai], "ノイローゼになる原因とは？代表的な症状や治し方について解説 [What causes neurosis? Explaining typical symptoms and how to cure them], "こころケア[Kokoro Care], November 15, 2024. https://www.dr-bridge.co.jp/kokorocare/column/neurosis/

15. "神経症 [Neurosis]," 医療法人 桂川 洛西口 くれたにクリニック [Kuretani Clinic], Accessed on May 30, 2025. https://www.kuretani-clinic-kyoto.com/neurosis/

16. 金井育子(かない　いくこ) [Kanai Ikuko], "アメリカンコーヒーとは？おいしい作り方・おすすめのコーヒー豆を解説 [What is American coffee? How to make it delicious and recommended coffee beans]," Key Coffee, February 17, 2025. https://www.keycoffee.co.jp/experience/knowledge/detail/american-coffee/#:~:text=アメリカンコーヒーとは、「浅,軽くゴクゴクと飲めます。

17. "Chilled Coffee Milk Originated in Japan?" J-Simple Recipes, August 23, 2024. https://j-simplerecipes.com/plaza/japanesefoodtips/drink/chilled-coffee-milk-originated-in-japan/#google_vignette

18. "Japan," The World Factbook. CIA. Last updated June 4, 2025. https://www.cia.gov/the-world-factbook/countries/japan/#people-and-society

19. Erin Barton, "Why Japan celebrates Christmas with KFC," BBC, December 19, 2016. https://www.bbc.com/worklife/article/20161216-why-japan-celebrates-christmas-with-kfc

20. "Tokyo Q&A: How does Japan celebrate Christmas?" TimeOut, December 2, 2024. https://www.

timeout.com/tokyo/things-to-do/tokyo-q-a-how-does-japan-celebrate-christmas

21. Charmaine Mok, "Why KFC at Christmas is 'really big' in Japan, as a Michelin-star Tokyo restaurant chef and a cookbook author explain what makes fried chicken great," South China Morning Post, December 22, 2023. https://www.scmp.com/lifestyle/food-drink/article/3245964/why-kfc-christmas-really-big-japan-michelin-star-tokyo-restaurant-chef-and-cookbook-author-explain

22. Namiko Hirasawa Chen, "Royal Milk Tea ロイヤルミルクティー," Just One Cookbook, Updated February 9, 2025. https://www.justonecookbook.com/royal-milk-tea/

23. "夜の社交場「スナック」を英語でなんて説明する？ポイントに分けて説明します!! [How do you explain the nighttime social venue "snack bar" in English? We'll explain it in key points!]," スナック横丁 [Snack Yokocho], Last updated March 10, 2025. https://www.snackyokocho.com/article/8596/

24. "下着で作る、プロポーションバランス [Creating a balanced proportion]," WACOAL, Accessed May 28, 2025. https://www.wacoal.jp/advice/contents/post-45.html

25. "プロポーションづくり [Creating Proportions]," Diana Salon, Accessed May 28, 2025. https://www.diana.co.jp/concept/

26. "Which body type are you? We introduce recommended Lolita coordination based on bone structure," Ron Ron, July 6, 2023. https://ronron-lolita.myshopify.com/en/blogs/ronron-column/body-frame-outfit

27. 山田 ハナ [Yamada Hana], "あなたはどのタイプ？ ぽっちゃりさん向け骨格診断・似合うファッションスタイリング・髪型（ヘアスタイル）[Which type are you? Bone structure analysis for chubby people, fashion styling, and hairstyles that suit them]," Nissen, Accessed May 28, 2025. https://www.nissen.co.jp/s/smileland/colorear/article/fashion/18122501/

28. "ナチュラル・ウェーブ・ストレートからあなたの似合うが見つかる骨格診断によるアクセサリーの選び方 [How to Choose Accessories based on your Bone Structure and find the Hairstyle that suits you best: Natural, Wavy, or Straight]," Novice, March 25, 2022. https://novicetokyo.com/blogs/blog/frametype_accessory#:~:text=What%20is%20skeletal%20diagnosis?,"

29. "Frame Type あなたに「似合う」を見つける 骨格スタイル診断 [Find out what suit you with a body style diagnosis]," Pierrot, Accessed May 28, 2025. https://pierrotshop.jp/f/frametype

30. "「スタイルいい」人の特徴や性格的傾向は？ スタイル維持の方法も併せて紹介 [What are the characteristics and personality traits of people with godo style? We also introduce ways to maintain style]," Oggi.jp, May 3, 2024. https://oggi.jp/6786676

31. GaijinPot Blog, "Japanese Apartment Layouts: Terms and Meanings," GaijinPot Blog, July 3, 2024. https://blog.gaijinpot.com/what-do-japanese-apartment-layout-terms-mean/

32. GaijinPot Blog, "Japanese Apartment Layouts: Terms and Meanings."

33. 工藤 智也 [Tomoya Kudo], "セミダブルとダブルの違いを比較！ベッドの選び方・サイズ別のおすすめ商品も紹介 [Comparing the differences between semi-double and double beds! How to choose a bed and recommended products by size]," RASIK, Last updated June 7, 2025. https://rasik.style/blogs/bed/47?srsltid=AfmBOookBAyrczZb6Z40jAFK68i1HluO68i58JQZ19DGcJlJoaNr7bxv

34. "Towel Blanket (Towelket)," Futon Tokyo, Accessed June 1, 2025. https://futontokyo.com/product-category/comforter/towel-blanket/?srsltid=AfmBOoqBFAJn-eqgeqCZwVp1-9RoLRGqHlT54t2WEpIA-k5TRPNU9pK5

35. GaijinPot Blog, "Japanese Apartment Layouts: Terms and Meanings."

36. Tammy Dang, "The Japanese Apartment Layout Guide: Finding a Perfect Place," Mailmate, Last updated April 12, 2025. https://mailmate.jp/blog/japanese-apartment-layout

37. "1R, 3LDK, 2DK: Apartment Floor Plan in Japan," Ehousing Blog, August 7, 2024. https://e-housing.jp/post/1k-1ldk-2dk-apartment-floorplan-in-japan

38. "1R, 1K, 1DK, 1LDK Apartment: What's the Difference and Which Should I Rent?" Real Estate Japan Blog, February 21, 2018. https://resources.realestate.co.jp/living/1r-1k-1dk-1ldk-apartment-whats-the-difference-and-which-should-i-rent/

39. GaijinPot Blog, "Japanese Apartment Layouts: Terms and Meanings."

40. Tammy Dang, "The Japanese Apartment Layout Guide: Finding a Perfect Place."

41. "1R, 3LDK, 2DK: Apartment Floor Plan in Japan."

42. "1R, 1K, 1DK, 1LDK Apartment: What's the Difference and Which Should I Rent?"

43. GaijinPot Blog, "Japanese Apartment Layouts: Terms and Meanings."

44. Tammy Dang, "The Japanese Apartment Layout Guide: Finding a Perfect Place."

45. "1R, 3LDK, 2DK: Apartment Floor Plan in Japan."

46. "1R, 1K, 1DK, 1LDK Apartment: What's the Difference and Which Should I Rent?"

47. JCB, "Cashing," Accessed June 1, 2025. https://www.jcb.co.jp/cashing/index.html

48. Orico, "Cashing service," Accessed June 1, 2025. https://www.orico.co.jp/costco/en/contractor/caching.html

49. JP BANK, "キャッシング[Cashing]," Accessed June 1, 2025. https://wwws.jp-bank.japanpost.jp/credit1/cashing/cashing.html

50. "キャッシングとは？クレジットカードで現金を借りる方法や注意点などを詳しく解説 [What is cash advance? A detailed explanation of how to borrow cash with a credit card and things to be careful about]," 三井住友カード株式会社 [SMBC], December 11, 2024. https://www.smbc-card.com/nyukai/magazine/knowledge/caching.jsp

51. Elliot Hale, "Japan's unique tradition of bottle keep, where your drink literally has your name on it," Sora News 24, February 2, 2025. https://soranews24.com/2025/02/02/japans-unique-tradition-of-bottle-keep-where-your-drink-literally-has-your-name-on-it/

52. "Types of Accommodation," Happy Jappy, Accessed June 2, 2025. https://www.happyjappy.com/travel_tips/types-of-accommodation.html

53. "Types of Accommodation."

54. "クールビズはいつからいつまで？期間中の服装やマナーを解説【2025年最新】[When does Cool Biz start and end? Explaining clothing and etiquette during this period [Updated for 2025]]," Suit Ya, April 27, 2025. https://www.suit-ya.com/column/how-to-dress/when-did-cool-biz-start/?srsltid=AfmBOopxWQijl_-jYo6RePmjheCmO4C_GZPdY2I6TZ-G6xe1seLxelz9

55. "クールビズとは？実施期間や服装など社会人が知っておくべき基礎知識 [What is Cool Biz? Basic information that working adults should know, including implementation period and dress code]," Mycard, MUFG, Updated June 3, 2025. https://www.cr.mufg.jp/mycard/beginner/23062/index.html

56. "CoolBiz オフィス篇 [Office Edition]," 環境省 [Ministry of the Environment], Accessed June 3, 2025. https://ondankataisaku.env.go.jp/decokatsu/coolbiz/office/

57. "クールビズにおける服装の選び方！メンズのおしゃれな着こなしからクールビズに関するマナーを解説 [How to choose your clothes for Cool Biz! We explain the etiquette for Cool Biz from stylish men's fashion]," Orihica, Last updated June 9, 2025. https://www.orihica.com/column/business-casual/cool-biz-male.php?srsltid=AfmBOopQzitnKLMEi7nEsYQV2_Pm_LWUG64fd5syVWuT_BHr6wUVZ-ue

58. 熊野 公俊 [Kimitoshi Kumano], "フリーターとは？正社員とのリアルな違いや将来性を徹底解剖 [What is a part-time worker? A thorough analysis of the real differences between part-time workers and full-time employees and their future prospects," The Port, March 19, 2025. https://www.theport.jp/portcareer/article/27505/#:~:text=フリーターは、フリーアルバイター,があるのでしょうか。

59. 新田 圭 (ニッタ ケイ) [Kei Nitta], "フリーターとして働くことのメリット・デメリットとその注意点 [The advantages and disadvantages of working as a part-timer and points to note," Career Research Lab, Mynavi, December 17, 2024. https://career-research.mynavi.jp/column/20241217_89862/

60. 公益社団法人全国シルバー人材センター事業協会 [National Silver Human Resources Center Association], "シルバー人材センターとは [What is the Silver Human Resources Center?]" Accessed June 4, 2025. https://www.zsjc.or.jp/about/about_02.html#:~:text= 全国シルバー人材センター事業協会&text=シルバー人材センター（センター）と,運営をしています。

61. Kaonavi HR Glossary Editorial Department, "シルバー人材センターとは？ 仕事内容、料金、依頼の流れ [What is the Silver Human Resources Center? Job content, fees, and request process]," Kaonavi, Updated June 3, 2025. https://www.kaonavi.jp/dictionary/silver-jinzai-center/#:~:text= 指定は不可-,1. シルバー人材センターとは？,に設置されています。

Bibliography

"1R, 1K, 1DK, 1LDK Apartment: What's the Difference and Which Should I Rent?" Real Estate Japan Blog, February 21, 2018. https://resources.realestate.co.jp/living/1r-1k-1dk-1ldk-apartment-whats-the-difference-and-which-should-i-rent/

"1R, 3LDK, 2DK: Apartment Floor Plan in Japan," Ehousing Blog, August 7, 2024. https://e-housing.jp/post/1k-1ldk-2dk-apartment-floorplan-in-japan

Barton, Erin. "Why Japan celebrates Christmas with KFC," BBC, December 19, 2016. https://www.bbc.com/worklife/article/20161216-why-japan-celebrates-christmas-with-kfc.

"Chilled Coffee Milk Originated in Japan?" J-Simple Recipes, August 23, 2024. https://j-simplerecipes.com/plaza/japanesefoodtips/drink/chilled-coffee-milk-originated-in-japan/#google_vignette.

"CoolBiz オフィス篇 [Office Edition]," 環境省 [Ministry of the Environment], Accessed June 3, 2025. https://ondankataisaku.env.go.jp/decokatsu/coolbiz/office/.

Dang, Tammy. "The Japanese Apartment Layout Guide: Finding a Perfect Place," Mailmate, Last updated April 12, 2025. https://mailmate.jp/blog/japanese-apartment-layout

"Frame Type あなたに「似合う」を見つける 骨格スタイル診断 [Find out what suit you with a body style diagnosis]," Pierrot, Accessed May 28, 2025. https://pierrotshop.jp/f/frametype

降矢英成 [Furuya, Hidenari], "ヒステリー(解離性障害) [Hysteria (dissociative disorder)]," みんなのお悩み医学, Last updated March 9, 2022. https://kateinoigaku.jp/disease/200

GaijinPot Blog, "Japanese Apartment Layouts: Terms and Meanings," GaijinPot Blog, July 3, 2024. https://blog.gaijinpot.com/what-do-japanese-apartment-layout-terms-mean/

"キャッシングとは?クレジットカードで現金を借りる方法や注意点などを詳しく解説 [What is cash advance? A detailed explanation of how to borrow cash with a credit card and things to be careful about]," 三井住友カード株式会社 [SMBC], December 11, 2024. https://www.smbc-card.com/nyukai/magazine/knowledge/caching.jsp

"ロリータとゴスロリの違いが知りたい [I want to know the difference between Lolita and Gothic Lolita]," Seasonz, June 24, 2023. https://seasonz.thebase.in/blog/2023/06/04/141656

"リクルートスーツ(就活スーツ)とは?ビジネススーツとの違い、選び方や着こなし方を解説! [What is a recruit suit (job hunting suit)? We explain the difference between a recruitment suit and a business suit, and how to choose and wear it!]," GINZA Global Style, Last updated June 2, 2025. https://www.global-style.jp/enjoy-order/?p=13237

Hale, Elliot. "Japan's unique tradition of bottle keep, where your drink literally has your name on it," Sora News 24, February 2, 2025. https://soranews24.com/2025/02/02/japans-unique-tradition-of-bottle-keep-where-your-drink-literally-has-your-name-on-it/

山田 ハナ [Hana, Yamada], "あなたはどのタイプ? ぽっちゃりさん向け骨格診断・似合うファッションスタイリング・髪型(ヘアスタイル) [Which type are you? Bone structure analysis for chubby people, fashion styling, and hairstyles that suit them]," Nissen, Accessed May 28, 2025. https://www.nissen.co.jp/s/smileland/colorear/article/fashion/18122501/

Hirasawa Chen, Namiko. "Royal Milk Tea ロイヤルミルクティー," Just One Cookbook, Updated February 9, 2025. https://www.justonecookbook.com/royal-milk-tea/

金井育子(かない いくこ) [Ikuko, Kanai], "アメリカンコーヒーとは?おいしい作り方・おすすめのコーヒー豆を解説 [What is American coffee? How to make it delicious and recommended coffee beans]," Key Coffee, February 17, 2025. https://www.keycoffee.co.jp/experience/knowledge/detail/american-coffee/#:~:text=アメリカンコーヒーとは、「浅,軽くゴクゴクと飲めます。

いとうみほ[Ito, Miho], "年代別 ギャルの歴史 | 「ギャル」とは何なのか [History of Gyaru by Era | What is a "Gyaru"?]," *KLD (Blog),* September 8, 2023. https://kld-c.jp/blog/what-is-gal

"クールビズとは?実施期間や服装など社会人が知っておくべき基礎知識 [What is Cool Biz? Basic information that working adults should know, including implementation period and dress code]," Mycard, MUFG, Updated June 3, 2025. https://www.cr.mufg.jp/mycard/beginner/23062/index.html

"クールビズにおける服装の選び方!メンズのおしゃれな着こなしからクールビズに関するマナーを解説 [How to choose your clothes for Cool Biz! We explain the etiquette for Cool Biz from stylish men's fashion]," Orihica, Last updated June 9, 2025. https://www.orihica.com/column/business-casual/cool-biz-male.php?srsltid=AfmBOopQzitnKLMEi7nEsYQV2_Pm_LWUG64fd5syVWuT_BHr6wUVZ-ue

"クールビズはいつからいつまで?期間中の服装やマナーを解説【2025年最新】 [When does Cool Biz start and end? Explaining clothing and etiquette during this period [Updated for 2025]]," Suit Ya, April 27, 2025.

https://www.suit-ya.com/column/how-to-dress/when-did-cool-biz-start/?srsltid=AfmBOopxWQijl_-jYo6RePmjheCmO4C_GZPdY2I6TZ-G6xe1seLxelz9

"Japan," The World Factbook. CIA. Last updated June 4, 2025. https://www.cia.gov/the-world-factbook/countries/japan/#people-and-society

JCB, "Cashing," Accessed June 1, 2025. https://www.jcb.co.jp/cashing/index.html

JP BANK, "キャッシング[Cashing]," Accessed June 1, 2025. https://wwws.jp-bank.japanpost.jp/credit1/cashing/cashing.html

Kaonavi HR Glossary Editorial Department, "シルバー人材センターとは？ 仕事内容、料金、依頼の流れ [What is the Silver Human Resources Center? Job content, fees, and request process]," Kaonavi, Updated June 3, 2025. https://www.kaonavi.jp/dictionary/silver-jinzai-center/#:~:text= 指定は不可-,1. シルバー人材センターとは?,に設置されています。

"ナチュラル・ウェーブ・ストレートからあなたの似合うが見つかる骨格診断によるアクセサリーの選び方 [How to Choose Accessories based on your Bone Structure and find the Hairstyle that suits you best: Natural, Wavy, or Straight]," Novice, March 25, 2022. https://novicetokyo.com/blogs/blog/frametype_accessory#:~:text=What%20is%20skeletal%20diagnosis?,"

工藤 智也 [Kudo, Tomoya], "セミダブルとダブルの違いを比較！ベッドの選び方・サイズ別のおすすめ商品も紹介 [Comparing the differences between semi-double and double beds! How to choose a bed and recommended products by size]," RASIK, Last updated June 7, 2025. https://rasik.style/blogs/bed/47?srsltid=AfmBOookBAyrczZb6Z40jAFK68i1HluO68i58JQZ19DGcJlJoaNr7bxv

熊野 公俊 [Kumano, Kimitoshi], "フリーターとは？ 正社員とのリアルな違いや将来性を徹底解剖 [What is a part-time worker? A thorough analysis of the real differences between part-time workers and full-time employees and their future prospects," The Port, March 19, 2025. https://www.theport.jp/portcareer/article/27505/#:~:text=フリーターは、フリーアルバイター,があるのでしょうか。

"ヒーリングとは？効果やその意味、リラックスに最適な音楽も紹介 [What is healing? Introducing its effects, meaning, and the best music for relaxation]," Mynavi, Last updated January 11, 2024. https://co-medical.mynavi.jp/contents/therapistplus/lifestyle/beauty/130/

"ギャルとは?-由来や特徴- [What is a gal? -Origins and characteristics-]," Galture, Accessed May 29, 2025. https://galture.com/about/about.html

"「スタイルいい」人の特徴や性格的傾向は？　スタイル維持の方法も併せて紹介 [What are the characteristics and personality traits of people with godo style? We also introduce ways to maintain style]," Oggi.jp, May 3, 2024. https://oggi.jp/6786676

"「ヒステリー」とは何なのか、なぜ女性ばかりヒステリーを起こすと思われているのか？ [What is "hysteria" and why is it thought that only women suffer from it?]," Gigazine, October 3, 2024. https://gigazine.net/news/20241003-hysteria-women/

Mok, Charmaine. "Why KFC at Christmas is 'really big' in Japan, as a Michelin-star Tokyo restaurant chef and a cookbook author explain what makes fried chicken great," South China Morning Post, December 22, 2023. https://www.scmp.com/lifestyle/food-drink/article/3245964/why-kfc-christmas-really-big-japan-michelin-star-tokyo-restaurant-chef-and-cookbook-author-explain

"神経症 [Neurosis]," 医療法人 桂川 洛西口 くれたにクリニック [Kuretani Clinic], Accessed on May 30, 2025. https://www.kuretani-clinic-kyoto.com/neurosis/

新田 圭 (ニッタ ケイ) [Nitta, Kei], "フリーターとして働くことのメリット・デメリットとその注意点 [The advantages and disadvantages of working as a part-timer and points to note," Career Research Lab, Mynavi, December 17, 2024. https://career-research.mynavi.jp/column/20241217_89862/

公益社団法人全国シルバー人材センター事業協会 [National Silver Human Resources Center Association], "シルバー人材センターとは [What is the Silver Human Resources Center?]" Accessed June 4, 2025. https://www.zsjc.or.jp/about/about_02.html#:~:text= 全国シルバー人材センター事業協会&text=シルバー人材センター（センター）と,運営をしています。

Orico, "Cashing service," Accessed June 1, 2025. https://www.orico.co.jp/costco/en/contractor/caching.html

ぽんたまん[Pontaman], "【ギャル】を英語で言うと？ギャル文化や語源を紹介！ [How do you say "gal" in English? Learn about gal culture and its origins!]," *Native Camp English Conversation Blog*, July 3, 2019. https://nativecamp.net/blog/20190703_gal

櫻井 良平 [Sakurai, Ryohei], "ノイローゼになる原因とは？代表的な症状や治し方について解説 [What causes neurosis? Explaining typical symptoms and how to cure them], "こころケア[Kokoro Care], November 15, 2024. https://www.dr-bridge.co.jp/kokorocare/column/neurosis/

"新しいギャル時代の幕開け！「令和ギャル」の定義や特徴とは？ [The dawn of a new era of gals! What are the definitions and characteristics of "Reiwa gals"?]," Galture, Accessed May 29, 2025. https://galture.com/history/reiwa-gal.html

"下着で作る、プロポーションバランス [Creating a balanced proportion]," WACOAL, Accessed May 28, 2025. https://www.wacoal.jp/advice/contents/post-45.html

"Tokyo Q&A: How does Japan celebrate Christmas?" TimeOut, December 2, 2024. https://www.timeout.com/tokyo/things-to-do/tokyo-q-a-how-does-japan-celebrate-christmas

本田手株 [Toshinobu, Honda], "ネームバリューとは?意味とその効果・高める方法 [What is name value? It's meaning, effects, and ways to increase it]," Kenjans, April 9, 2025. https://kenjins.jp/magazine/company-interview/51955/

"Towel Blanket (Towelket)," Futon Tokyo, Accessed June 1, 2025. https://futontokyo.com/product-category/comforter/towel-blanket/?srsltid=AfmBOoqBFAJn-eqgeqCZwVp1-9RoLRGqHlT54t2WEpIA-k5TRPNU9pK5

"Types of Accommodation," Happy Jappy, Accessed June 2, 2025. https://www.happyjappy.com/travel_tips/types-of-accommodation.html

渡邊　真也(わたなべ　しんや) [Watanabe, Shinya], "ヒステリー(転換性障害・解離性障害)[Hysteria (conversion disorder/dissociative disorder)]," 品川メンタルクリニック [Shinagawa Mental Clinic], Accessed May 30, 2025. https://www.shinagawa-mental.com/column/psychosomatic/hysteria/

渡邊　真也(わたなべ　しんや) [Watanabe, Shinya], "ノイローゼ(神経症)とは?うつ病との違いと治療方法 [What is neurosis? How it differes from depression and how to treat it]," 品川メンタルクリニック [Shinagawa Mental Clinic], https://www.shingawa-mental.com/column/psychosomatic/neurose/#:~:text=ノイローゼとは、神経症,説明していきます。

"Which body type are you? We introduce recommended Lolita coordination based on bone structure," Ron Ron, July 6, 2023. https://ronron-lolita.myshopify.com/en/blogs/ronron-column/body-frame-outfit

"夜の社交場「スナック」を英語でなんて説明する?ポイントに分けて説明します!! [How do you explain the nighttime social venue "snack bar" in English? We'll explain it in key points!]," スナック横丁 [Snack Yokocho], Last updated March 10, 2025. https://www.snackyokocho.com/article/8596/

弓削桃代 [Yuge, Momoyo], "コンサバとは?　意味とコーディネートのコツ(イラスト付き解説) [What is conservative? Its meaning and tips for coording it (with illustrations)]," Mynavi Woman, September 15, 2022. https://woman.mynavi.jp/article/200730-5/

English Index

Japanese Index

About the Author

Lauren is the owner and founder of Lauren's Language Lessons, LLC and has been teaching English for over 15 years. She has a degree from Texas A&M University in International Studies and certifications in TEFL/TESL/TESOL for teaching English as a Second Language. She has taught numerous Japanese students of various ages and levels from a variety of fields and professions. Lauren is also the author of *Belong with Konglish: A Guide to Understanding Korean-style English and Avoiding Common Miscommunications* and *Wronglish Konglish: A Guide to Avoiding Miscommunications when Speaking English with North Americans.* Lauren is passionate about language and culture and travels every chance she gets. She lives in Houston, Texas with her husband, cat, and dog, and enjoys playing soccer and spending time with friends and family.

About Lauren's Language Lessons

Lauren's Language Lessons is an online language school offering a variety of private and small group lessons in 10 languages including English, Japanese, Korean, French, German, Italian, Portuguese, Mandarin, Arabic, and Spanish. We are passionate about language and love preparing people to succeed in a new language! With Lauren's Language Lessons, you can start a new language from scratch, pick up where you left off, or perfect where you are now. All language instructors are native speakers or speak with native level fluency and accent and hold relevant qualifications and teaching experience. Private Japanese lessons are offered year-round and are customized to the goals of each student to achieve the best results. Small group classes with maximums of four to six students are also offered periodically throughout the year.

Please visit our website at LaurensLanguageLessons.com or send us an email at LaurensLanguageLessons@gmail.com to learn more!

About the Translator

Tamaki is a native Japanese speaker originally from Japan and currently teaches Japanese as an adjunct college instructor. She holds advanced degrees in language and culture, developmental psychology, and Russian, and is also certified in teaching Japanese as a second language. She is the author of *Is It Okay That My Child Still Isn't Talking?* 「うちの子、まだおしゃべりできないのですが大丈夫でしょうか」 a book addressing concerns surrounding children's language development in an accessible and compassionate way. In addition to teaching adult learners through a college's lifelong learning program, where she offers classes in Japanese language, calligraphy, and Japanese art, she also teaches online private and small group Japanese lessons through Lauren's Language Lessons. Tamaki lives in Illinois. She enjoys a peaceful life with her husband and two bunnies, cherishing the daily discoveries and joys that come from meeting others and continuing to learn.

Other Books by Lauren Green Imai

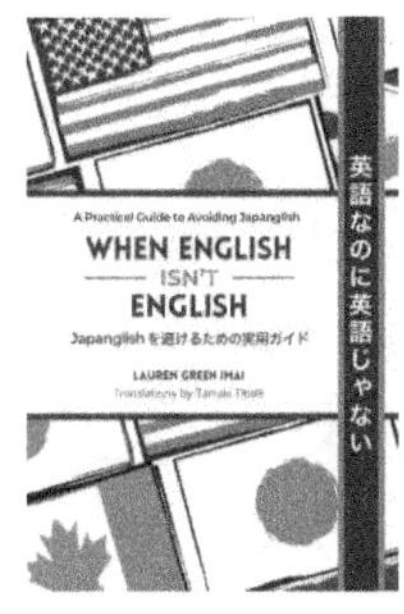

When English Isn't English:
A Practical Guide to Avoiding Japanglish

英語なのに英語じゃない:
Japanglishを避けるための実用ガイド

*(**For Japanese speakers** who want to speak English more like native speakers)*

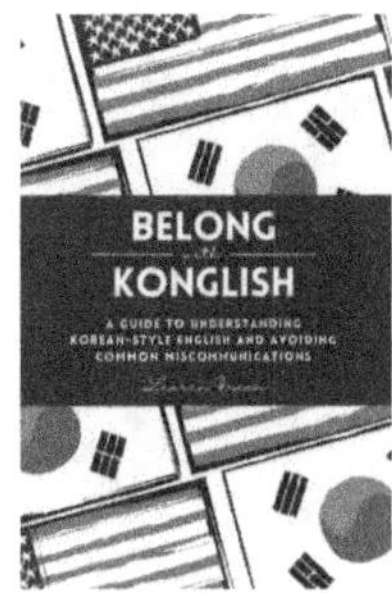

Belong with Konglish:
A Guide to Understanding Korean-style English and Avoiding Common Miscommunications

*(**For English speakers** who are interested in Korean language and culture)*

Wronglish Konglish:
A Guide to Avoiding Miscommunications when Speaking with North Americans

콩글리쉬 잘못됫쉬:
북미사람들과 대화 할 때 자주 할 수 있는 오해를 막아주는 가이드북

*(**For Korean speakers** who want to speak English more like native speakers)*

www.ingramcontent.com/pod-product-compliance
Lightning Source LLC
Chambersburg PA
CBHW070907130626
46555CB00001B/33

9798989907861